EUROPEAN HANDBOOK No. 5

# SWISS RAILWAYS

## LOCOMOTIVES, MULTIPLE UNITS & TRAMS

### THIRD EDITION

The complete guide to all Locomotives, Multiple Units and Trams of the Railways of Switzerland

David Haydock, Peter Fox & Brian Garvin

Published by Platform 5 Publishing Ltd., Wyvern House, Sark Road, Sheffield S2 4HG, En'
Printed in England by Wyndeham Gait, Grimsby, Lincolnshire
ISBN 1 872524 90-7.

**Above:** SBB's Class 521 FLIRT EMUs are not normally used in the Ticino canton but, prior to delivery of TILO Class 524, 521 002 visited the area for demonstration runs and is seen near Bellinzona on 13 August 2005. SBB Class 521, 522, 523, 524 and 526.6 FLIRT EMUS all look very similar.
**Maurizio Tolini**

**Front Cover:** Rhätische Bahn Re 4/4 II no. 619 "Samedan" is seen between Klosters Dorf and Klosters with train RE 1037 Landquart–Davos on 4 July 2009. **Matthias Müller**

**Back Cover Top:** A very lucky photo of all three of SBB's classic electric classes at Ostermundingen on 19 March 2009. Ae 6/6 610 420 "APPENZELL A. RH" waits to take out a tank train while Re 4/4 11330, one of the last in green livery, and Re 6/6 11636 "VERNIER-MEYRIN" pass through with a container train bound for Italy. **David Haydock**

**Back Cover Bottom:** 141, one of the Wengernalpbahn's most modern Stadler EMUs, stands in Grindelwald with a train for Kleine Scheidegg on 18 June 2009. **David Haydock**

# CONTENTS

# INTRODUCTION TO THIRD EDITION

Welcome to the third edition of Swiss Railways, which contains details of all locomotives and multiple units of Swiss Federal Railways (SBB), around 50 independent railways, varying from 381 km down to 294 metres, which are mainly owned by the Swiss cantons, open access freight operators and track maintenance contractors.

Since the second edition of this book was published, Swiss railways have continued to modernise their fleets, there have been many mergers and open access freight operation has started. At the same time, SBB and BLS now operate into neighbouring countries. SBB has gained many new locomotives and EMUs since the 1997 edition. The computer renumbering scheme continues to be applied patchily but vehicles will probably all receive the new European Vehicle Numbers in the near future.

# A BRIEF HISTORY OF SWITZERLAND

Switzerland is a very beautiful mountainous country which makes up for being landlocked with its many lakes. The spectacular scenery, ease of travel, welcoming people and well-run towns attract around 10 million tourists a year.

The position of Switzerland on the major trade routes, particularly north–south between today's Germany and Italy, led to early settlement. Among the early settlers were a Celtic people known as the Helvetes – today's country is known as the Helvetic Confederation which reversed explains the CH letters used for the country. The area was fought over by German people from the north, Burgundians from the area now in France and the Lombards from the south, now Italy. This explains Switzerland's multilingual status. It was early as 1 August 1291 that the first part of the federation was formed by the cantons of Schwyz, Uri and Unterwald. The name Switzerland, plus Schweiz, Suisse and Svizzera in German, French and Italian all come from founder member Schwyz. Between 1332 and 1353, five more cantons joined and by 1513 the total reached 13, all German-speaking. In 1815, the treaty of Wien took the total to 22 and the modern federal state was created in 1848. It was not until 1979 that the Jura canton joined. Other changes have taken the total to 26 cantons today.

Swiss has a long history of neutrality – the country has not been at war since 1815 – and therefore has attracted many humanitarian agencies. The Red Cross was created by Henry Dunant here. The country also has a long history of direct democracy through referenda.

Switzerland is not part of the EU but its crucial position between Member States and the need for free trade has led Switzerland to adopt certain EU rules – including those on open access to neighbouring rail networks. Switzerland joined the Schengen area in 2005.

# LANGUAGES

Switzerland has four official languages. The most widely spoken is German, with a large French-speaking area in the west of the country and Italian spoken in the areas south of the Gotthard and Bernina passes. The fourth language, Romantsch, is spoken in parts of Graubünden canton in the south-east. The national timetable uses all languages as appropriate to each table; this system has been adopted in this publication for place names. It should be noted that some towns are bilingual, Biel/Bienne (German/French) being the best-known example.

The official use of three languages in the areas where the Federal Railways operate requires it to display an official name in each of the three languages:

German: Schweizerische Bundesbahnen    SBB
French:  Chemins de Fer Fédéraux       CFF
Italian: Ferrovie Federali Svizzere    FFS

The Romantsch name – Viafers Federalas Svizras (VFF) – appears only in the timetable, which also has an introduction in English.

Swiss Federal locomotives and coaches are either lettered "SBB CFF FFS" on both sides or "SBB CFF" on one side and "SBB FFS" on the other. Their controls are labelled in German, French and Italian.

In this publication, the initials "SBB" are used throughout.

▲ SBB electric tractor Te III 157, allocated to the Passenger division, pauses between shunting movements at Locarno station on 7 June 2006.                                    **Brian Denton**

▼ SBB electro-diesel tractor Tem 337 is seen at Martigny on 15 April 2009.          **David Haydock**

# SBB TRACTORS

▶ SBB mini tractor Tm 915 is seen at Erstfeld depot on 27 March 2009. **Brian Leighton**

▼ SBB track trolley 234 111-3 is seen at Rapperswil on 7 April 2009. **Keith Fender**

◀ Tm IV 8777 is seen shunting a train of oil tanks at Ostermundingen on 19 March 2009. Locos 9651 to 9685 are identical. **David Haydock**

# THE RAILWAYS OF SWITZERLAND

The first train in Switzerland arrived in 1845 – at Basel from France. It was not until 1847 that the first railway opened within Switzerland from Zürich to Baden (30 km). Known as the Spanisch-Brötli Bahn, as it carried fresh rolls from Baden to Zürich. A plan for a national from Britain's Stephenson family was rejected in favour of the cantons granting concessions to private railways. Development was quite slow but by 1870 the first rack railway had started to allow access for tourists to the mountains and in 1882 the monumental 15 km Gotthard tunnel opened. Many private lines were a limited success and power over planning the railways was transferred to the confederation in 1872. A plan to create a national network was accepted by referendum in 1898 and in 1902 Swiss Federal Railways was born from the merger of eight railways of which the Schweizerische Nordostbahn and Schweizerische Centralbahn were the biggest. In the following years the whole of the Swiss standard gauge network was electrified at 15 kV AC 16.7 Hz, the same system as in Germany and Austria.

Despite the creation of a national network, Switzerland has retained many local railways, mainly owned by the cantons. The biggest is BLS which owns one of the main north–south lines through the Alps, although this is managed as part of the national network. BLS also owns many suburban lines serving Bern. Other local standard gauge lines are also electrified at 15 kV AC and through working on the SBB network often occurs.

Despite closures over the years there are also many narrow gauge lines in Switzerland, metre gauge being the most common, with a variety of electrification systems. Some rack lines are 800 mm gauge.

# RACK OPERATION

Many Swiss mountain lines are fitted with rack equipment to allow trains to climb very steep gradients, and brake the train on its way back down. These are known as cog-wheel railways in the USA as rack systems work by pinions (cogs) fixed on the train's axles engaging in teeth on a rail between the running rails. Four different systems were devised by Swiss engineers Abt, Locher, Riggenbach and Strub and all are still in use today. As a general rule all coaches of multiple units used on rack lines are fitted with rack equipment but if a rack locomotive or power car is used, the coaches are not equipped and, as a general rule, the locomotive is positioned at the lower end of the train so it pushing up a mountain and braking from underneath on the way down so that unpowered coaches cannot run away if they become uncoupled. In a small number of cases in this book, a power unit is used at the front of a train on the way up a mountain section. This is the case of Class HGe 4/4 locos on the Glacier Express from Visp to Zermatt and on the Zentralbahn over the Brünig Pass. In these cases, the hauled coaching stock is also fitted with rack equipment for braking purposes. In the technical details of rack/adhesion trains in this book, two speeds are given – for rack and adhesion operation. However, space is not availabe to include all speed limits for rolling stock. In general, the limit uphill on a rack railway is higher than that on the way downhill and even these limits may vary according to the gradient.

# TICKETS & PASSES

Despite the Swiss railway network being operated by many different companies, the national rail timetable is planned so that all trains connect as far as possible and almost all tickets are valid on all companies.

Apart from the ordinary single and return tickets (the cost of a return being less than twice the single fare for journeys of about 40 km), numerous concessions are available, usually through the purchase of "passes" or "cards".

The **Swiss Pass** gives unlimited travel on almost all railways, boats, the transport systems of 24 cities and many post buses together with a reduction on many privately-owned funiculars and mountain railways. The current prices are : 4 days – £153 second class, £229 first class, 8 days – £221 second, £332, 15 days – £268 second, £402 first, 22 days – £309 second, £464 first and 1 month – £340 second, £510 first. There is also a **Swiss Flexi Pass** for three to six days in one month plus 50% discount on other days.

The **Swiss Card** provides a transfer from the point of entry into Switzerland to the holder's destination and back and a 50% reduction on other tickets purchased. It is valid for one month and costs £107 second class and £150 first. In fact, the first and last days are effectively rover tickets, giving opportunities limited only by the timetable, ingenuity and stamina. The **Swiss Transfer Ticket** is similar but omits the 50% reduction, costing £75 second class and £113 first.

**Regional Passes** can be obtained covering six different areas. The length of validity (two to five days out of seven to 15) and class of travel available varies according to the area. Day, family and half-fare cards are also available and the latter two can be used to obtain a reduction on the cost of regional passes.

The prices quoted are correct at August 2009. Full details of all these tickets and other facilities are available from Switzerland Travel Centre, 30 Bedford Street, London, WC2E 9ED, England. URL: www.stc.co.uk

Prices and conditions are updated each spring in the magazine **Today's Railways Europe**.

# HOW TO GET THERE

## By Rail

TGVs run direct from Paris to Basel, Zürich, Lausanne, Bern and Genève. ICEs from Germany run to Basel, Zürich, Bern and Interlaken. Trains from Milano, Italy run to Montreux, Lausanne, Genève, Bern, Basel and Zürich. Zürich can be reached from Austria. A dwindling IC service runs from Brussels and Luxembourg to Basel and Zürich.

## By Air

There are flights from all over Europe to Genève and Zürich which have very good onward rail service. In addition, Basel-Mulhouse is situated in France but has a bus shuttle to Basel.

# LAYOUT OF DATA

For each class of vehicles technical and historical information is given followed by a list of individual vehicles arranged as follows:

(1) Number.
(2) Previous number in parentheses (if any).
(3) Livery code (if applicable) – in bold condensed type.
(4) Sector code (if applicable) – in italic type.
(4) Column notes (if applicable).
(5) Code for depot allocation.
(6) Name (if any).

# ABBREVIATIONS

Standard abbreviations used in this book are:

| | |
|---|---|
| km/h | kilometres per hour |
| kN | kiloNewtons |
| kW | kilowatts |
| m | metres |
| DB | Deutsche Bahn (German Railways) |
| ÖBB | Österreichische Bundesbahn (Austrian Railways) |
| Power | One hour rating. |
| de | diesel-electric |
| dh | diesel-hydraulic |
| dm | diesel-mechanical |
| e | electric |
| HP | high pressure |
| LP | low pressure |
| | (cylinders for steam locos) |

▲ ICN tilting set 500 040 "Graf Zeppelin" stands at Yverdon on 18 March 2009 with a St. Gallen-Zürich-Genève Aéroport service. **David Haydock**

▼ 514 049, one of SBB's newest Siemens double-deck EMUs, stands at Rapperswil on 14 May 2009 with an S7 service to Winterthur. **David Haydock**

# CLASSIFICATION OF SWISS MOTIVE POWER

All Swiss railways use a standard classification system for their motive power. It should be noted that separate systems are used for locos and railcars; hence it is possible for a loco and a railcar to have the same classification.

## PREFIX LETTERS (Locomotives)

R   Max. speed more than 110 km/h
A   Max speed 85 to 110 km/h
B   Max speed 70 to 80 km/h
C   Max speed 60 to 65 km/h
D   Max speed 45 to 55 km/h
E   Shunting loco
G   Narrow gauge loco

H   Rack fitted loco (combined with above if rack & adhesion)
O   Open wagon body
T   Tractor
X   Departmental vehicle (some of these are ex-railcars)

## PREFIX LETTERS (Railcars/Multiple Units)

Note: Further prefixed by R if max speed is more than 110 km/h.

A   First class accommodation
B   Second class accommodation
D   Baggage compartment

S   Saloon vehicle
Z   Postal compartment

## SUFFIX LETTERS (All Motive Power)

a       Battery powered.
e       Electric powered.
em      Electric & diesel powered (i.e. an electro-diesel).
h       Rack fitted (only used with railcars & tractors); if this precedes the a, e or m then the unit is pure rack; if it follows, the unit is rack & adhesion.
m       Diesel or petrol powered.
r       Restaurant vehicle.
rot     Rotary snowplough.
t       (only used with X in the form of Xt) Self propelled departmental vehicle, but not a loco (e.g. a self propelled crane or snowplough).

## NUMBERS

These indicate the number of powered and total number of axles, e.g.
4/4 = all six axles powered (e.g. Bo-Bo)
3/6 = six axles of which three are powered (e.g. 2-Co-I)

## SUB-CLASS INDICES

To differentiate between classes with otherwise similar classifications, small Roman numeals are used, e.g. Re 4/4$^I$, Re 4/4$^{II}$ etc.

All the above are combined as required to give full classifications, e.g.

Ae 6/6       Co-Co electric loco, maximum speed 85–110 km/h
Be 4/6       1B-B1 electric loco, maximum speed 70–80 km/h
ABDe 4/4     Bo-Bo electric railcar, first, second & baggage accommodation

The above system is now being replaced by new computer numbers. The classification letters are retained, but the "fraction" numbers are replaced by a three digit class number. The system originally only included SBB but has since been expanded to incorporate most of the standard gauge private railways. This has caused some new computer numbers to be changed! See the section on SBB numbering system for further details.

# ACKNOWLEDGMENTS

We would like to thank all who have helped with the preparation of this book, especially Christian Ammann, Sylvain Meillasson, Mike Taplin, Mario Stefani, Theo Stolz, various officials and staff of the numerous railways and all who submitted photographs.

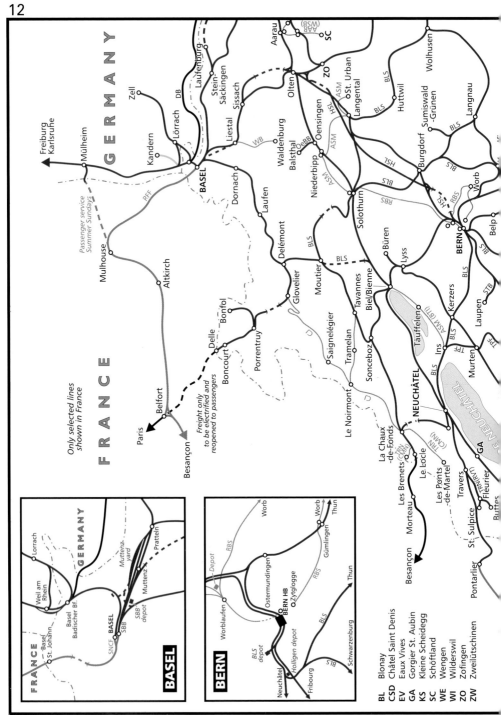

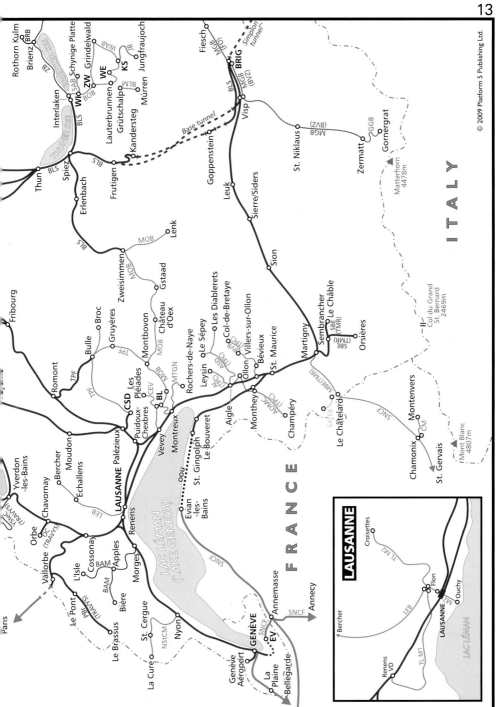

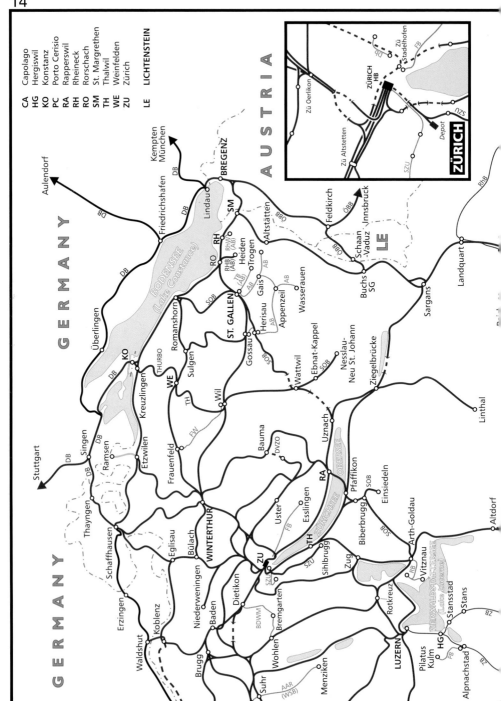

CA  Capolago
HG  Hergiswil
KO  Konstanz
PC  Porto Cerisio
RA  Rapperswil
RH  Rheineck
RO  Rorschach
SM  St. Margrethen
TH  Thalwil
WE  Weinfelden
ZU  Zürich

LE  LICHTENSTEIN

© 2009 Platform 5 Publishing Ltd.

**KEY:**

Non-electrified
Electrified 600–2200 V DC
Electrified 11 kV AC
Electrified 15 kV AC
Electrified 3000 V DC
Electrified 25 kV AC
Electrified 3 Phase
Tourist services
Line in tunnel
Line under construction
Freight only

Thick lines are standard gauge (1435 mm)
Thin lines are narrow gauge

SWITZERLAND

ITALY

LAGO DI COMO

LAGO MAGGIORE

Sagliains
Susch
Zernez
Arosa
Davos Platz
Filisur
Bever
Samedan
St. Moritz
Pontresina
Poschiavo
Tirano
Campocologno
RhB
Bernina Bahn

Ilanz
Disentis/ Muster
Sedrun
MGB (FO)
Andermatt
Engelberg
Göschenen
Realp
Gletsch
Oberwald
Meiringen
Innertkirchen
MIB
To open 2010
MGB (FO)
DFB

Gotthard Base tunnel
Gotthard Tunnel 15003m
Airolo
Biasca
Cama
Bellinzona
Locarno
Camedo
SSIF
Simplon tunnel
Domodossola
Domo 2 yard
FART

Chiavenna
Colico
Lecco
Asso
FNM
Merone
Como
Mendrisio
Chiasso
Monte Ceneri base tunnel
Lugano
Luino
Ponte Tresa
FLP
Generoso Vetta
MGB
Stabio
PC
CA
Laveno-Mombello
Varese
FNM
Stresa
Arona
Novara
RFI
Bergamo
Milano

© 2009 Platform 5 Publishing Ltd.

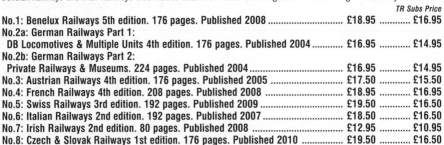

# 1. SWISS FEDERAL RAILWAYS

The SBB was formed in 1902 when most of the major private companies were nationalised, and a few other railways have been absorbed since.

The SBB network is electrified at 15 kV AC 16.7 Hz overhead, the only exceptions being a few lines in border areas where the systems of neighbouring countries are used. All SBB electric stock can only operate on the above system unless stated otherwise. The SBB network is standard gauge (1435 mm). SBB's former metre gauge Brünig line, is now part of Zentralbahn.

## ORGANISATION

Since the last edition of this book, SBB has gone through massive changes. SBB itself has been divided into Passenger, Cargo and Infrastructure divisions, each with its own dedicated fleet. This led to some depots and works in general being allocated by activity.

In response to market liberalisation in the EU (of which Switzerland is not a member) it was decided to allow open access to the Swiss rail network in exchange for allowing Swiss operators into the rest of the EU. SBB Cargo decided on a strategy of operating its own trains over the whole of the north–south corridor from Germany via Switzerland to Italy then founded a subsidiary in Germany (SBB Cargo Deutschland) and in another in Italy (SBB Cargo Italia). The companies now operate extensively in these two countries, SBB Cargo Deutschland is now the second biggest freight operator in Germany, behind incumbent DB Schenker.

One of the unfortunate consequences of the division of the SBB fleet has been increasing difficulty in obtaining data on allocations, and this is compounded by a policy of not giving specific allocations to many traction units.

There have also been massive changes in the Swiss train building industry. The historic works of SLM and Schindler have closed or been broken up and ADtranz also closed the former BBC works. However, Stadler has gone from a tiny family business to one of Europe's leading multiple unit builders in the space of a decade!

## PASSENGER SERVICES

International passenger services serving Switzerland are now mainly tributaries of high speed services in neighbouring countries. SNCF operates TGVs from Zürich, Basel, Bern, Lausanne and Genève to Paris and Genève to the south of France. DB operates ICEs from Basel to Berlin via Frankfurt and to Köln, with some trains starting back from Zürich or Interlaken plus from Zürich to Stuttgart. Cisalpino (this company was disbanded in late 2009) services using tilting train sets run from Genève, Basel and Zürich to Milano. Less frequent EuroCity services run to Luxembourg and Brussels, Milano and München.

Within Switzerland, a very frequent network of regular interval passenger trains operate from long distance IC services down to suburban level. SBB's IC and IR services are operated by a limited number of loco and stock types – mainly double-deck IC2000 stock or single-deck IC IV stock in push-pull or conventional mode, mainly with Class 460 electric locos. A small number of routes are operated by Class 500 ICN tilting EMUs. IR services are often formed of more lowly stock with Class 460 or older Re 4/4I electrics. Suburban trains are increasingly operated by Class 521–524 FLIRT EMUs or double-deck EMUs in Zürich. All of the conurbations are developing networks known as S-Bahn in German-speaking areas and RER where French is spoken.

## FREIGHT SERVICES

Traffic in Switzerland is dominated by north–south international flows over the Gotthard and Lötschberg routes although there is still a great deal of traffic elsewhere. Intermodal traffic, be it containers or complete lorries on trains, is heavy on the north–south routes. Switzerland retains, however, a thriving wagonload network based on yards at Muttenz (Basel), Denges (Lausanne) and Limmattal (Zürich). There is also still a busy network of postal trains.

# NUMBERING SYSTEM

Steam locomotives were numbered below 10000, and consequently when main line electric locomotives first appeared, they were numbered 10001 upwards. However, when railcars, shunting tractors and later diesel locomotives were purchased, they each had their own separate numbering systems, railcars in fact being initially numbered in the carriage series. This resulted in many duplicated numbers, and to eliminate these much renumbering occurred during the 1950s and 1960s. Although this eliminated duplicated numbers, the result was a non too logical system, particularly in the case of the 8xxx and 9xxx series tractors which were numbered in these blocks when vacant numbers in the earlier series were exhausted. The number series is as follows:

| | |
|---|---|
| 1– 250 | Electric tractors (traffic stock) |
| 251– 399 | Electro-diesel tractors (traffic stock) |
| 401– 599 | Diesel tractors (traffic stock) |
| 601– 950 | Diesel tractors (departmental stock) |
| 951– 963 | Electric tractors (departmental stock; all now withdrawn) |
| 964– 979 | Battery tractors (all are departmental) |
| 1001– 1899 | Electric railcars |
| 2001– 2999 | Electric railcars |
| 8001– 8399 | Electric tractors (traffic stock) |
| 8401– 8999 | Diesel tractors (traffic stock) |
| 9401– 9999 | Diesel tractors (departmental stock) |
| 10001–11999 | Electric locomotives, max speed more than 80 km/h |
| 12001–13999 | Electric locomotives, max speed 70 to 80 km/h |
| 14001–14999 | Electric locomotives, max speed 60 to 65 km/h |
| 15001–15999 | Electric locomotives, max speed 45 to 55 km/h (all now withdrawn) |
| 16001–16999 | Electric shunting locomotives |
| 17001–17999 | Electro-diesel locomotives (being converted to diesels) |
| 18001–18999 | Diesel locomotives |

Since 1989, a new numbering system has been introduced for new classes. However, to date it has only been applied to new classes and existing classes where renumbering has been carried out, even though all have been allotted new class numbers. There is no indication of any intention to renumber existing stock except where major refurbishment has been carried out. The new scheme consists of seven digits, comprising a three digit class number, a three digit running number and a computer check digit. On the other hand, it is apparently no longer the intention to renumber pre-war main line locos, now all classed as museum stock. The system has also been expanded to include the standard gauge private railways which have adopted the system rather more enthusiastically than the SBB. The system operates as follows:

| | | |
|---|---|---|
| First Digit: | 0 | Steam loco or historic railcar |
| | 1 | Metre gauge loco (Brünig Line) |
| | 2 | Tractor |
| | 3 | Electric loco (three powered axles) |
| | 4 | Electric loco (four powered axles) |
| | 5 | Electric railcar |
| | 6 | Electric loco (six powered axles) |
| | 7 | Departmental stock (self-propelled, but not a loco e.g. crane or tamper) |
| | 8 | Diesel loco |
| | 9 | Electric shunting loco |
| Second Digit: | 0 | Express stock (railcars only) |
| | 1–6 | Sub class index (bogie electric locos) |
| | | Type of electric railcar |
| | | No. of powered axles (diesel locos) |
| | 7–8 | Not used |
| | 9 | Used in lieu of / on rigid frame electric locos (but in practice, not used) |

Third Digit: Used to differentiate between classes with identical first and second digits. However, in some cases indicates the following:

| | |
|---|---|
| 2–4 | two, three, or four voltage loco or railcar |
| 5–8 | stock owned by private railways. |

Fourth to Sixth Digits: Generally the last three digits of the old number, but with many exceptions. After the running number there is a computer check digit which double checks that all the preceding digits are correct. It is arrived at by multiplying the class and running number digits alternately by 1 and 2. The resulting digits are added together and the sum deducted from the next whole ten gives the check number.

Example 460 033-4

$$\begin{array}{ccccccc} & 4 & 6 & 0 & 0 & 3 & 3 \\ x & 1 & 2 & 1 & 2 & 1 & 2 \\ = & \multicolumn{6}{l}{4+1+2+0+0+3+6 = 16.} \\ & \multicolumn{6}{l}{20-16 = 4.} \end{array}$$

# LAYOUT OF DATA

For each class of vehicles technical and historical information is given in metric units as shown below followed by a list of individual vehicles arranged as follows:

(1) Number.
(2) Previous number in parentheses (if any).
(3) Livery code (if applicable) – in bold condensed type.
(4) Sector code (if applicable) – in italic type.
(5) Column notes (if applicable).
(6) Code for depot allocation.
(7) Name (if any).

# SECTOR ALLOCATIONS

SBB locomotives are now all allocated to one of three activities, each with subdivisions, which we give a code in this book:

| | |
|---|---|
| C | Cargo |
| C-I* | Cargo Instandhaltung (maintenance). |
| C-O* | Cargo Ost (east) division. |
| C-S* | Cargo Süd (south) division. |
| C-W* | Cargo West division. |
| I | Infrastructure |
| I-B* | Infrastructure Betriebsführung, Lösch- und Rettungszüge: fire-fighting and rescue trains. |
| I-R* | Infrastructure Rangierbahnhöfe (marshalling yards – Switzerland opens up its yards to all, so shunting is carried out by Infra.) |
| I-S* (I-U*) | Infrastructure Strategischer Einkauf-Fahrzeugmanagement (rolling stock management) |
| P | Passenger |
| P-O | Passenger Operations |

\* The second letter is shown in this book in the "depot" column.

# SBB DEPOTS

In the past decade SBB has been reorganised by activity and maintenance has also been changed so that traction is less attached to a specific geographic location. Data on "allocations" is now difficult to obtain and much of the data here comes from "inside knowledge". Infra locomotives are allocated by Cargo.

| Code | Depot | Main activity |
|---|---|---|
| BE | Bellinzona | Cargo |
| BN | Bern | rented to BLS |
| BI | Biel/Bienne | Cargo |
| BR | Brig | Cargo |
| BS | Basel Wolf | Passenger |
| CH | Chiasso | Cargo |
| ER | Erstfeld | Cargo |
| GE | Genève | Passenger |
| LS | Lausanne | Passenger |
| LZ | Luzern | Passenger |
| OL | Olten | Cargo |
| WF | Weinfelden | THURBO (formerly MThB, work carried out by SBB staff) |
| WT | Winterthur | Passenger |
| ZU | Zürich | Passenger |

In addition to the above, many stations and other locations have small sheds housing one or more shunting tractors; often these belong to the permanent way or other engineer's departments.

The following codes for stabling points are also used:

| AI | Airolo |
|----|--------|
| BU | Buchs |
| DE | Delémont |
| GI | Giabasco |
| GO | Goldau |
| HD | Hägendorf |
| LI | Limmattal yard |
| LT | Lausanne Triage (Denges yard) |
| NE | Neuchâtel |
| RE | Renens |
| RH | Romanshorn |
| RK | Rotkreuz |
| RW | Rapperswil |
| SA | Sargans |
| SG | St. Gallen |

S = stored serviceable
U = stored unserviceable

# SBB WORKSHOPS

Four workshops are responsible for the repair and overhaul of SBB motive power. These have now been dedicated by activity. Meiringen is now part of Zentralbahn and Zürich has closed.

| Code | Works | Activity |
|------|-------|----------|
| | Bellinzona | Locomotives and wagons. |
| | Biel/Bienne | Freight locomotives and wagons. |
| OW | Olten | Passenger trains – mainly coaches. |
| YW | Yverdon | Passenger trains – mainly locomotives and EMUs. |

# LIVERIES

Until 1984, most line electric locomotives and railcars were painted dark green, while diesels and shunters were reddish-brown. In 1984, a red livery was adopted for locomotives (except for Class 450), while new railcars are blue and cream. A number of nonstandard liveries also exist, but several of these will disappear in the near future. The various liveries are shown in the lists using the following letter codes:

**A**   Overall advertising livery. Several Re 460 class have been so treated.
**B**   Brown. The original electric loco livery, a few "museum" locos have been restored to this livery.
**C**   SBB Cargo livery. Red front ends, blue sides with Cargo in large letters on side.
**D**   Domino livery. White with red front ends, window band and doors.
**E**   Recent EMU livery. White with black window band plus red front end, doors and roof. ICN sets do not have red doors. Class 514 has dark blue sole bar below sole bar level.
**G**   Dark green. The standard livery for most electric locomotives and railcars prior to 1984.
**N**   NPZ (Neue Pendel Zug). Blue and grey with red ends. The 1990s livery for local trains.
**P**   Reddish-brown. The standard livery for shunters and tractors until 1984.
**R**   Red. The current standard Passenger and Infra locomotive livery. Many Cargo locos are still in this livery. Tractors in red livery are not shown as such due to lack of information.
**S**   S-Bahn. Dark blue with white band and red ends, applied only to Class 450.
**X**   Special blue & yellow livery for "Train des Vignes" on Puidoux-Chexbres–Vevey service.
**O**   Orange/Grey ('Swiss Express') livery, applied to Mark III coaching stock and some Re4/4$^{II}$ locos during the 1970s).
**Y**   Yellow (a few tractors used as works pilots are in this livery).

# 1.1. SHUNTING TRACTORS

SBB has a much reduced fleet of tractors for light shunting duties following the division of activities between passenger, Cargo and Infra, plus the rationalisation of wagonload freight. Those numbered between 1 and 599 and in the 8000 series traditionally belonged to the traffic department and were mainly used in station goods yards where they are driven by station staff. Those numbered between 601 and 999 and in the 9000 series are in departmental use, the greatest number being allocated to the permanent way department, with others being used by the overhead line and signals departments and as depot and works pilots. It is no longer possible to give full data on depot allocation and the location of each tractor as this information is not available and most tractors move around far more than in the past.

## CLASS Te$^{III}$                                                            Bo

Small electric shunters, now mainly with the Cargo department.

**Built:** 1965/6.
**Builder–Mechanical Parts:** SLM.                 **Builder–Electrical Parts:** MFO.
**Traction Motors:** 2 single phase axle suspended.
**One Hour Rating:** 245 kW.                        **Maximum Tractive Effort:** 67 kN.
**Wheel Diameter:** 950 mm.                         **Weight:** 28 tonnes.
**Length over Buffers:** 6.64 m.                    **Maximum Speed:** 60 km/h.

| 139 | C | ZU | 153 | C | LS | 164 | C | ZU | 175 | C | LS |
|-----|---|----|-----|---|----|-----|---|----|-----|---|----|
| 142 | C | SG | 154 | C | ZU | 166 | C | BI | 176 | P | BE |
| 143 | C | BI | 156 | C | LS | 170 | C | LS | 177 | C | ZU |
| 144 | P | GE | 157 | P | BE | 171 | C | SG | 178 | C | CH |
| 149 | C | LS | 162 | C | BI | 174 | C | CH | 179 | C | LS |
| 150 | C | BI | 163 | C | LS |     |   |    |     |   |    |

## CLASS Tem$^I$                                                                B

This class, and the following Tem$^{II}$ and Tem$^{III}$ classes are electric tractors fitted with a diesel engine to enable them to shunt non-electrified sidings.

**Built:** 1950–7.
**Builder–Mechanical Parts:** Tuchschmid.          **Builder–Electrical Parts:** BBC/MFO.
**Traction Motors:** 1 single phase axle suspended with side rod drive.
**One Hour Rating:** 90 kW (electric), 50 kW (dsl).   **Engine:** Saurer C615D of 65 kW.
**Maximum Tractive Effort:** 36 kN (electric), 31 kN (diesel)
**Wheel Diameter:** 950 mm.                         **Weight:** 15 tonnes.
**Length over Buffers:** 5.87 m.                    **Maximum Speed:** 60 km/h.

| 251 | C | LS | 262 | C | LS | 265 | C | SG | 268 | P | WT |
|-----|---|----|-----|---|----|-----|---|----|-----|---|----|
| 255 | I | BE |     |   |    |     |   |    |     |   |    |

## CLASS Tem$^{III}$                                                           B

A dual-mode tractor, all now used by Cargo.

**Built:** 1967.
**Builder–Mechanical Parts:** SLM/Tuchschmid.      **Builder–Electrical Parts:** MFO.
**Traction Motors:** 1 single phase axle suspended with side rod drive.
**One Hour Rating:** 120 kW (electric), 60 kW (diesel).
**Maximum Tractive Effort:** 33 kN.                **Wheel Diameter:** 950 mm.
**Engine:** Saurer C615D of 85 kW.                 **Length over Buffers:** 6.7 m.
**Maximum Speed:** 60 km/h.                         **Weight:** 26 tonnes.

| 277 | C | SG | 279 | C | SG | 286 | C | SG | 292 | C | ZU |
|-----|---|----|-----|---|----|-----|---|----|-----|---|----|
| 278 | C | ZU | 284 | C | S  | 291 | C | CH | 298 | C | BI |

## CLASS Tem$^{II}$                                                            Bo

Another dual-mode tractor now used only by Cargo.

**Built:** 1954–62.
**Builder–Mechanical Parts:** SLM.                 **Builder–Electrical Parts:** BBC/SAAS.
**Traction Motors:** 2 single phase axle suspended.
**One Hour Rating:** 260 kW (electric), 95 kW (diesel).

**Maximum Tractive Effort:** 59 kN (electric), 64 kN (diesel)
**Wheel Diameter:** 1040 mm.
**Length over Buffers:** 7.29 m (7.35 m†).
**Engine:** SLM 12BD11 of 145 kW.
**Weight:** 32 tonnes.
**Maximum Speed:** 60 km/h.

| | | | | | | | | | | |
|---|---|---|---|---|---|---|---|---|---|---|
| 325 | C | O | 337 | C | W | 348 | C † W | 358 | | † ZU |
| 328 | C | W | 339 | C | O | 349 | C † O | 359 | C | † O |
| 329 | C | W | 340 | C | O | 351 | † LS | 361 | C | † O |
| 332 | C | CH | 341 | C | O | 355 | C † O | 363 | | † SG |
| 334 | C | SG | 343 | C | O | 356 | C † O | 365 | C | † W |
| 336 | C | O | 347 | C † W | | | | | | |

## CLASS Tm$^I$ (Tm (401))  B

A small diesel tractor with many variations and few now left in service. Originally all fitted with SLM engines, many have been rebuilt with Deutz or VM engines since 1971.

**Built:** 1957–65.
**Builder:** RACO (CMR 463, 511/2).
**Engine:**  SLM 6VD11 of 66 kW.
SLM 4VD111 of 44 kW (a).
Deutz 87 of kW (b).
VM of 90 kW (c).
Deutz F6L413 of 90 kW (d).
**Transmission:** Mechanical.
**Driving Wheel Diameter:** 600 mm.
**Length over Buffers:** 5.190 m.
**Maximum Tractive Effort:** kN.
**Weight:** 10 tonnes (13 tonnes b, c).
**Maximum Speed:** 45 km/h (50 km/h b, c).

| | | | | | | | | | | | | | |
|---|---|---|---|---|---|---|---|---|---|---|---|---|---|
| 401 | | a | OW | 453 | C | b | CH | 474 | C | c | SG | 508 | b BE |
| 422 | P | | OW | 454 | C | c | BI | 481 | P | d | BE | 511 | C b O |
| 425 | | | OW | 456 | C | | BI | 500 | C | c | I | 512 | C b W |
| 452 | C | b | I | 463 | P | b | LZ | | | | | | |

## CLASS Tm$^{II}$  B

A small track trolley with a cabin for four personnel and a platform for carrying tools and materials. Capable of hauling a few wagons for permanent way work. Almost all are used by Infra.

**Built:** 1950–68.
**Engine:** Saurer C615D of 70 kW.
**Maximum Tractive Effort:** kN.
**Weight:** 10 tonnes.
**Maximum Speed:** 45 km/h.
**Builder:** RACO.
**Transmission:** Mechanical.
**Wheel Diameter:** 600 mm.
**Length over Buffers:** 5.240 m.

\* Fitted for snowplough use.

| | | | | | | | | | | | |
|---|---|---|---|---|---|---|---|---|---|---|---|
| 604 | I | LZ | 658 | C | I | 708 | I | ZU | 806 | I | BN |
| 608 | C | I | 680 | I | ZU | 740 | I | LZ | 807 | I | LS |
| 611 | I | RS | 685 | I | ZU | 751 | I | LZ | 810 | I | ZU |
| 635 | I | \* ZU | 687 | I | LZ | 763 | I | LS | 816 | C | I |
| 637 | I | \* RS | 696 | I | OL | 764 | I | OL | 847 | I | OL |
| 640 | I | \* LS | 700 | I | BS | 786 | I | BN | 849 | I | ZU |
| 647 | I | BS | 703 | C | I | 792 | C | ZU | | | |

## CLASS Tm$^{III}$  B

Diesel-electric tractors for use as shed and works pilots.

**Built:** 1958–66.
**Builder–Mechanical Parts:** SLM.
**Engine:** SLM 12BD11 of 145 kW.
**Maximum Tractive Effort:** 92 kN.
**Weight:** 28 tonnes.
**Maximum Speed:** 30 km/h.
**Builder–Electrical Parts:** BBC.
**Transmission:** Electric.
**Wheel Diameter:** 950 mm.
**Length over Buffers:** 6.540 m.

| | | | | | | | | | | | |
|---|---|---|---|---|---|---|---|---|---|---|---|
| 904 | C | I | 910 | P | S | 917 | P | ZW | 921 | P | S |
| 905 | C | I | 911 | C | S | 918 | P | S | 922 | C | I |
| 906 | P | YW | 912 | C | S | 919 | P | S | 923 | C | I |
| 908 | P | S | 913 | | S | 920 | P | S | 924 | C | I |
| 909 | P | S | 915 | C | I | | | | | | |

# CLASS Ta                                                                 B

This assortment of battery tractors of six widely differing designs are used as works pilots.

| No. | Date | Builder | Hourly Rating | Weight | Length | Max. Speed | Location |
|---|---|---|---|---|---|---|---|
| 966 | 1987 | Stadler | 4 kW | 7 t. | 2.85 mm | 10 km/h | Olten Works |
| 968 | 1977 | SBB Yverdon | 4 kW | 6.5 t. | 2.85 mm | 10 km/h | Yverdon Works |
| 969 | 1911 | SBB Olten | 4 kW | 7 t. | 3.30 mm | 10 km/h | Yverdon Works |
| 972 | 1914 | SBB Olten | 4 kW | 7 t. | 3.30 mm | 10 km/h | Yverdon Works |
| 974 | 1965 | SBB Zürich | 4 kW | 6.5 t. | 3.32 mm | 10 km/h | Zürich Works |
| 975 | 1971 | Stadler | 4 kW | 6.5 t. | 2.85 mm | 10 km/h | Zürich Works |
| 976 | 1971 | Stadler | 4 kW | 6.5 t. | 2.85 mm | 10 km/h | Bellinzona Works |
| 978 | 1913 | AEG | 145 kW | 24 t. | 8.40 mm | 25 km/h | Bellinzona Works |

# CLASS Te$^{IV}$                                                           Bo

This loco incorporated electrical equipment recovered from a withdrawn Class De 4/4 railcar.

**Built:** 1980.
**Builder–Mechanical Parts:** Tuchschmid.          **Builder–Electrical Parts:** BBC.
**Traction Motors:** 2 single phase axle suspended.
**Maximum Tractive Effort:** kN.                   **Wheel Diameter:** 1040 mm.
**Weight:** 34 tonnes.                             **Length over Buffers:** 7.70 m.
**Maximum Speed:** 60 km/h.                        **One Hour Rating:** 480 kW.

8203     C    O        |

# CLASS Tm$^{IV}$                                                           B

In addition to the hydraulic transmission, these tractors have a two-ratio gearbox giving a maximum shunting speed of 30 km/h. 8751–8781 were delivered as 551–581. Between batches, SLM delivered identical 9651–9685. 8761 was re-engined in 2007, repainted in Cargo livery and renumbered 232 111-5. Other companies have examples of the design such as CJ 232 181 and SOB 236 006/7.

**Built:** 1968–78.                                **Builder:** SLM.
**Engine:** MAN R8V 16/18 of 280 kW.              **Transmission:** Hydraulic.
**Maximum Tractive Effort:** kN.                   **Wheel Diameter:** 1040 mm.
**Weight:** 30 tonnes.                             **Length over Buffers:** 7.67 m.
**Maximum Speed:** 60 km/h.

* Purchased 1994 from Sulzer, Winterthur.

| 8751 | C | O | | 8764 | C | O | | 8776 | C | O | | 8787 | C | O |
|---|---|---|---|---|---|---|---|---|---|---|---|---|---|---|
| 8752 | C | O | | 8765 | C | O | | 8777 | C | W | | 8788 | C | S |
| 8753 | C | W | | 8766 | C | O | | 8778 | C | W | | 8790 | C | O |
| 8754 | C | O | | 8767 | C | W | | 8779 | C | W | | 8791 | C | O |
| 8755 | C | O | | 8769 | C | O | | 8780 | C | W | | 8792 | C | O |
| 8756 | C | O | | 8770 | P | WT | | 8782 | C | W | | 8793 | C | S |
| 8757 | C | S | | 8772 | C | O | | 8783 | C | O | | 8794 | C | O |
| 8758 | C | O | | 8773 | C | S | | 8784 | C | O | | 8795 | C | O |
| 8759 | C | O | | 8774 | C | O | | 8785 | P | ZU | | 8796 | C | O |
| 8762 | C | O | | 8775 | C | O | | 8786 | C | O | | 8797 | C * | O |
| 8763 | C | O | | | | | | | | | | | | |

**Rebuilt in 2007 with Caterpillar engine and renumbered.**

232 111-5 (8761)     C    W    |

# CLASS Tm$^{III}$                                                          B

These tractors are fitted with a hydraulic platform for overhead line maintenance work.

**Built:** 1981–6.
**Builder:** RACO.
**Engine:** Saurer D2K of 165 kW.                  **Transmission:** Hydraulic.
**Maximum Tractive Effort:** kN.                   **Wheel Diameter:** 950 mm.
**Weight:** 28 tonnes.                             **Length over Buffers:** 8.74 m.
**Maximum Speed:** 60 km/h.

| | | | | | | | |
|---|---|---|---|---|---|---|---|
| 9451 | / | 9455 | / | 9458 | / | 9461 | / |
| 9453 | / | 9456 | / | 9459 | / | 9462 | / |
| 9454 | / | 9457 | / | 9460 | / | 9463 | / |

# CLASS Tm$^{III}$    B

Similar to the previous class, but fitted with a three-tonne hydraulic crane and an open platform for use on permanent way work. Most of the missing numbers are locos converted to Class 232.

**Built:** 1976–88.
**Builder:** RACO.
**Engine:** Saurer D2K of 165 kW.
**Maximum Tractive Effort:** kN.
**Weight:** 24 tonnes.
**Maximum Speed:** 60 km/h.

**Transmission:** Hydraulic.
**Wheel Diameter:** 950 mm.
**Length over Buffers:** 8.74 m.

| | | | | | | | | | | | |
|---|---|---|---|---|---|---|---|---|---|---|---|
| 9501 | / | S | 9560 | / | | 9573 | / | S | 9590 | / | S |
| 9503 | / | | 9564 | / | S | 9574 | / | | 9592 | / | |
| 9509 | / | S | 9565 | / | S | 9576 | / | S | 9593 | / | |
| 9513 | / | S | 9568 | / | | 9578 | / | | 9594 | / | S |
| 9514 | / | S | 9569 | / | | 9580 | / | | 9595 | / | S |
| 9515 | / | S | 9570 | / | S | 9581 | / | S | 9596 | / | |
| 9529 | / | S | 9571 | / | | 9583 | / | S | 9597 | / | |

# CLASS Tm$^{IV}$    B

Identical to the 8751 series, these tractors are in departmental use. 9651–9658 were numbered 861–868 when built.

**Built:** 1974–7.
**Builder:** SLM.
**Engine:** MAN R8V 16/18 of 280 kN.
**Maximum Tractive Effort:** kN.
**Weight:** 30 tonnes.
**Maximum Speed:** 60 km/h.

**Transmission:** Hydraulic.
**Wheel Diameter:** 1040 mm.
**Length over Buffers:** 7.67 m.

\* Purchased 1987 from SLM (was their works pilot).

| | | | | | | | | | | | |
|---|---|---|---|---|---|---|---|---|---|---|---|
| 9651 | C | W | 9660 | / | U | 9669 | C | U | 9678 | / | U |
| 9652 | C | O | 9661 | / | U | 9670 | / | U | 9679 | C | O |
| 9653 | C | W | 9662 | / | U | 9671 | C | O | 9680 | / | S |
| 9654 | / | U | 9663 | / | U | 9672 | / | U | 9681 | / | U |
| 9655 | / | U | 9664 | C | O | 9673 | / | U | 9682 | / | U |
| 9656 | C | W | 9665 | C | W | 9674 | C | O | 9683 | C | O |
| 9657 | / | U | 9666 | C | O | 9675 | / | U | 9684 | C | W |
| 9658 | / | U | 9667 | / | U | 9676 | / | U | 9685 | P | * |
| 9659 | C | W | 9668 | C | W | 9677 | / | U | | | |

# CLASS Tm 230    B

A unique design of low-slung tractor for shunting the traverser at Biel/Bienne works, previously numbered Tm 900.

**Built:** 1963.
**Engine:** VW of 22 kW.
**Maximum Tractive Effort:** kN.
**Weight:** 2.3 tonnes.
**Maximum Speed:** 20 km/h.

**Builder:** SBB Biel/Bienne.
**Transmission:** Mechanical.
**Wheel Diameter:** 600 mm.
**Length over Buffers:** 2.00 m.

230 900-3    |

# CLASS Tm 231    B

This is the former Sensetalbahn Tm 2/2 number 11 (238 111). Used at Biel/Bieenne.

**Built:** 1969
**Engine:** Originally Saurer of 185 kW. Re-engined
**Weight:** 23.5 tonnes.

**Builders:** Stadler/BBC.
**Transmission:** Electric.
**Maximum Speed:** 55 km/h.

231 900-2    C    S    |

# CLASS Tm 232 (Tm<sup>III</sup>)         B

When built, these were similar to Tm <sup>III</sup> tractors 9451–9463, but fitted with a 3-tonne hydraulic crane and an open platform for use on permanent way work. Originally numbered 9501–9597, 52 of the class were modernised by Windhoff and Stadler Winterthur (formerly Winpro) from August 2003 to February 2006. The rebuild involved the installation of a more powerful engine which satisfies Euro III emissions standards, with particle filters, an increase of 80% in tractive effort and an increase to 80 km/h maximum speed. The tractors now have Signum signalling system for main line running, radio control and a new crane.

**Built:** 1976–88. Rebuilt 2003–2006.
**Builder:** RACO. Rebuilt by Winpro, Windhoff.
**Engine:** Iveco of 260 kW.

**Transmission:** Hydraulic.            **Maximum Tractive Effort:** kN.
**Wheel Diameter:** 950 mm.          **Weight:** 25 tonnes.
**Length over Buffers:** 8.74 m.         **Maximum Speed:** 80 km/h.

| | | | | | | | | | |
|---|---|---|---|---|---|---|---|---|---|
| 232 001-8 | (9566) | / | ZU | 232 019-0 | (9553) | / | SG | 232 036-4 | (9504) | / | BS |
| 232 002-6 | (9516) | / | LS | 232 020-8 | (9567) | / | LS | 232 037-2 | (9542) | / | BN |
| 232 003-4 | (9510) | / | OL | 232 021-6 | (9561) | / | ZU | 232 038-0 | (9536) | / | Sa |
| 232 004-2 | (9512) | / | SG | 232 022-4 | (9582) | / | LZ | 232 039-8 | (9543) | / | ZU |
| 232 005-9 | (9584) | / | SG | 232 023-2 | (9533) | / | De | 232 040-6 | (9537) | / | SG |
| 232 006-7 | (9588) | / | SG | 232 024-0 | (9585) | / | ZU | 232 041-4 | (9534) | / | BI |
| 232 007-5 | (9525) | / | BE | 232 025-7 | (9562) | / | BE | 232 042-2 | (9575) | / | BR |
| 232 008-3 | (9528) | / | LZ | 232 026-5 | (9521) | / | SG | 232 043-0 | (9519) | / | ZU |
| 232 009-1 | (9518) | / | ZU | 232 027-3 | (9524) | / | OL | 232 044-8 | (9539) | / | BI |
| 232 010-9 | (9586) | / | ZU | 232 028-1 | (9591) | / | Gi | 232 045-5 | (9563) | / | OL |
| 232 011-7 | (9522) | / | LZ | 232 029-9 | (9552) | / | LS | 232 046-3 | (9540) | / | SG |
| 232 012-5 | (9508) | / | OL | 232 030-7 | (9577) | / | Ai | 232 047-1 | (9556) | / | ZU |
| 232 013-3 | (9555) | / | ZU | 232 031-5 | (9507) | / | BE | 232 048-9 | (9532) | / | Ne |
| 232 014-1 | (9559) | / | SG | 232 032-3 | (9520) | / | ZU | 232 049-7 | (9557) | / | LS |
| 232 015-8 | (9579) | / | GI | 232 033-1 | (9538) | / | WT | 232 050-5 | (9535) | / | BS |
| 232 016-6 | (9523) | / | OL | 232 034-9 | (9641) | / | OL | 232 051-3 | (9506) | / | ZU |
| 232 017-4 | (9558) | / | Li | 232 035-6 | (9531) | / | LS | 232 052-1 | (9554) | / | OL |
| 232 018-2 | (9589) | / | Go | | | | | | | | |

# CLASS Tm 233.900         B

This is the former Sensetalbahn Tm 2/2 14 (238 114).

**Built:** 1994.            **Builders:** Stadler/ABB.
**Engine:** Mercedes-Benz of 360 kW.     **Transmission:** Electric.
**Weight:** 28 tonnes.         **Maximum Tractive Effort:** 83 kN.
**Length over Buffers:** 7.95 m.       **Maximum Speed:** 80 km/h.

233 900-0    *C*    S    |

# CLASS Tm 233.910         B

Former MThB shunters Tm 236 643.

**Built:** ??            **Builder:** Stadler.
**Engine:** Mercedes-Benz of kW.     **Transmission:** Electric.
**Weight:**
**Length over Buffers:**

233 911-7    /        |

# CLASS Tm 233.950         B

Former MThB shunter Em 2/2 41. Ex Em 826 641; ex Tm 933 950.

**Built:** 1972.           **Builders:** SLM/BBC.
**Engine:** Caterpillar of 315 kW.     **Transmission:** Electric.
**Weight:** 30 tonnes.         **Maximum Speed:** 60 km/h.

233 950-5    /        |

# CLASS Tm 234          "AMEISE"   *↳ 56*      B

The first batch of 50 (orders of 13 plus 37) of these track maintenance machines (Ameise means ant) was ordered in 1997 and this was followed by a further 50 in 2000 and 25 in 2005. The vehicle consists of an engine compartment and cab at one end and a platform with crane at the other. The 200-224 batch have a number of differences including a crane with basket, particle filters, GSM-R radio and redesigned roof. 232 000-012 are equipped with radio for the Zürich S-Bahn area, plus Winterur and St. Gallen districts. Six locos are equipped with ETCS Level 2. 232 090 is ex MThB 236 649.

**Built:** 2000 (000-012); 2000/1 (232 050-086); 2002/3 (100-150); 2006-8 (200-224).
**Builder:** SLM Stadler, except 234 200-224 Stadler Winterthur.
**Engine:** MTU 12V 183 TD13 of 550 kW.       **Transmission:** Hydraulic.
**Maximum Tractive Effort:** 81 kN.       **Wheel Diameter:** 800 mm.
**Weight:** 30 tonnes (234 200-224 37 tonnes).    **Length over Buffers:** 11.36 m.
**Maximum Speed:** 80 km/h.

| | | | |
|---|---|---|---|
| 234 000-8 / | 234 069-3 / | 234 113-9 / | 234 144-4 / |
| 234 001-6 / | 234 070-1 / | 234 114-7 / | 234 145-1 / |
| 234 002-4 / | 234 071-9 / | 234 115-4 / | 234 146-9 / |
| 234 003-2 / | 234 072-7 / | 234 116-2 / | 234 147-7 / |
| 234 004-0 / | 234 073-5 / | 234 117-0 / | 234 148-5 / |
| 234 005-7 / | 234 074-3 / | 234 118-8 / | 234 149-3 / |
| 234 006-5 / | 234 075-0 / | 234 119-6 / | 234 200-4 / |
| 234 007-3 / | 234 076-8 / | 234 120-4 / | 234 201-2 / |
| 234 008-1 / | 234 077-6 / | 234 121-2 / | 234 202-0 / |
| 234 009-9 / | 234 078-4 / | 234 122-0 / | 234 203-8 / |
| 234 010-7 / | 234 079-2 / | 234 123-8 / | 234 204-6 / |
| 234 011-5 / | 234 080-0 / | 234 124-6 / | 234 205-3 / |
| 234 012-3 / | 234 081-8 / | 234 125-3 / | 234 206-1 / |
| 234 050-3 / | 234 082-6 / | 234 126-1 / | 234 207-9 / |
| 234 051-1 / | 234 083-4 / | 234 127-9 / | 234 208-7 / |
| 234 052-9 / | 234 084-2 / | 234 128-7 / | 234 209-5 / |
| 234 053-7 / | 234 085-9 / | 234 129-5 / | 234 210-3 / |
| 234 054-5 / | 234 086-7 / | 234 130-3 / | 234 211-1 / |
| 234 055-2 / | 234 090-9 / | 234 131-1 / | 234 212-9 / |
| 234 056-0 / | 234 100-6 / | 234 132-9 / | 234 213-7 / |
| 234 057-8 / | 234 101-4 / | 234 133-7 / | 234 214-5 / |
| 234 058-6 / | 234 102-2 / | 234 134-5 / | 234 215-2 / |
| 234 059-4 / | 234 103-0 / | 234 135-2 / | 234 216-0 / |
| 234 060-2 / | 234 104-8 / | 234 136-0 / | 234 217-8 / |
| 234 061-0 / | 234 105-5 / | 234 137-8 / | 234 218-6 / |
| 234 062-8 / | 234 106-3 / | 234 138-6 / | 234 219-4 / |
| 234 063-6 / | 234 107-1 / | 234 139-4 / | 234 220-2 / |
| 234 064-4 / | 234 108-9 / | 234 140-2 / | 234 221-0 / |
| 234 065-1 / | 234 109-7 / | 234 141-0 / | 234 222-8 / |
| 234 066-9 / | 234 110-5 / | 234 142-8 / | 234 223-6 / |
| 234 067-7 / | 234 111-3 / | 234 143-6 / | 234 224-4 / |
| 234 068-5 / | 234 112-1 / | | |

# CLASS Tm 235          B

A tractor for permanent way work with a much lower platform than its predecessors.

**Built:** 1991/2.       **Builder:** Robel.
**Engine:** Deutz of 368 kW.       **Transmission:** Hydraulic.
**Weight:** 19 tonnes.       **Maximum Speed:** 80 km/h.
**Length over Buffers:** 10.04 m.

| No. | | Depot | Location | No. | | Depot | Location |
|---|---|---|---|---|---|---|---|
| 235 001-5 | / | LZ | Rotkreuz | 235 009-8 | / | ER | Erstfeld |
| 235 002-3 | / | BR | Brig | 235 010-6 | / | | Wallisellen |
| 235 003-1 | / | WT | Winterthur | 235 012-2 | / | LS | Lausanne |
| 235 004-9 | / | WT | Winterthur | 235 013-0 | / | WT | Schaffhausen |
| 235 005-6 | / | ZU | Zürich Altstetten | | | | |

# CLASS Ta 251        Bo

A battery tractor for use as works pilots.

**Built:** 1990.
**Builder–Mechanical Parts:** Stadler.
**Builder–Electrical Parts:** Bosch.
**Transmission:** Electric.
**Wheel Diameter:** mm.
**Length over Buffers:** 3.36 m.

**Traction Motors:**
**One Hour Rating:** 9 kW.
**Maximum Tractive Effort:** kN.
**Weight:** 7 tonnes.
**Maximum Speed:** 10 km/h.

| No. | Location | No. | Location |
|-----|----------|-----|----------|
| 251 002-2 | Olten Works | 251 004-8 | Olten Works |
| 251 003-0 | Olten Works | 251 005-5 | Olten Works |

# CLASS Tm 283        Bo

A second hand tractor purchased in 1989.
**Built:** 1973.
**Engine:** MAN 650 kW.
**Weight:** 23 tonnes.
**Maximum Speed:** 60 km/h.

**Builder:** Gmeinder.
**Transmission:** Electric.
**Length over Buffers:** 7.63 m.

| 283 000-8 | OL | Solothurn |
|-----------|----|-----------|

# 1.2. MAIN LINE ELECTRIC LOCOMOTIVES

## CLASSES Re4/4ᴵᴵ & Re4/4ᴵᴵᴵ (CLASSES 420 & 430)  Bo-Bo

This was the standard SBB electric loco for some 20 years and is still to be found throughout the system. the first six appeared in 1964 with series production beginning in 1967. The different lengths arise from variations in the body below the cabs. Those which have carried "Swiss Express" livery were fitted with automatic couplers, but have now reverted to standard. 11172, 11282, 11312 and 11323 were withdrawn following accidents. The current 11172 was originally MThB Re 4/4 21. 11102 to 11107, 11110, 11113, 11117, 11119, 11123, 11137, 11142 have been sold to BLS.

Class Re 4/4ᴵᴵᴵ is a variation with a lower gear ratio for use on mountain lines. 11351–3 were sold to the Südostbahn but returned to the SBB together with an identical locomotive built new for the SOB in exchange for the Re 4/4ᴵⱽ class.

11371–11397 (11382 was withdrawn) have been equipped for use in Germany, turned out in Cargo livery and renumbered 421 371–397 (see below).

Most of the class have received air conditioned cabs in recent years.

**Built:** 1964–85.
**Builder–Mechanical Parts:** SLM.
**Builders–Electrical. Parts:** BBC/MFO/SAAS.
**Traction Motors:** 4 single phase commutator type, fully suspended with BBC spring drive.
**One Hour Rating:** 4700 (4650*) kW.   **Length over Buffers:** 14.80–15.52 m.
**Maximum Tractive Effort:** 255 (280*) kN.   **Maximum Speed:** 140 (125*) km/h.
**Wheel Diameter:** 1260 mm.   **Weight:** 80 tonnes.

**Pantographs:**

11101–11155: One, double arm Swiss (s single arm).
11195–11198: Two, single arm, one Swiss and one DB/ÖBB-type for through working to Lindau.

There are many variations in length.

| | |
|---|---|
| 11101–11106 (Prototypes) | 14.80 m. |
| 11107–11155 (First production series) | 14.90 m (15.52 m §) |
| 11156–11219, 11236–11238 (Second production series) | 15.41 m (15.465 m†, 15.52 m§) |
| 11220–11235, 11239–11254 (Second production series, mod.) | 15.51 m. |
| 11255–11349, 11350–11397 (Final production series) | 15.52 m. |

e   ETCS fitted.
r   Equipped with radio for e.c.s. working.

**Notes:**

All are push-pull and mw fitted and can multiple work with Classes Re4/4ᴵᴵᴵ, Re4/4ᴵⱽ, Re6/6 and RBe4/4. Depot allocations are not shown, as locos of this class are common user.
11350–3 were formerly SOB 41/4/2/3 respectively. 11172 was formerly MThB Re 4/4 21.

| | | | | | | | | | | | |
|---|---|---|---|---|---|---|---|---|---|---|---|
| 11101 | **R** | *P* | r | 11131 | **R** | *P* | | 11152 | **R** | *P* | |
| 11108 | **O** | *P* | § | 11132 | **R** | *P* | | 11153 | **R** | *P* | |
| 11109 | **O** | *P* | §s | 11133 | **R** | *P* | | 11154 | **R** | *P* | |
| 11111 | **R** | *P* | | 11134 | **R** | *P* | | 11155 | **R** | *P* | |
| 11112 | **R** | *P* | § | 11135 | **R** | *P* | | 11156 | **R** | *P* | |
| 11114 | **R** | *P* | | 11136 | **R** | *P* | | 11157 | **R** | *P* | † |
| 11115 | **R** | *P* | | 11138 | **R** | *P* | | 11158 | **R** | *P* | |
| 11116 | **R** | *P* | | 11139 | **R** | *P* | | 11159 | **R** | *P* | |
| 11118 | **R** | *P* | | 11140 | **R** | *P* | s | 420 160-4 | **C** | *C* | |
| 11120 | **R** | *P* | r | 11141 | **O** | *P* | § S | 11161 | **G** | *P* | |
| 11121 | **R** | *P* | | 11143 | **R** | *P* | s | 11162 | **R** | *C* | |
| 11122 | **R** | *P* | | 11144 | **R** | *P* | | 11163 | **R** | *C* | |
| 11124 | **R** | *P* | | 11145 | **R** | *P* | s | 11164 | **R** | *P* | |
| 11125 | **R** | *P* | | 11146 | **R** | *P* | | 11165 | **R** | *C* | |
| 11126 | **R** | *P* | | 11147 | **R** | *P* | | 11166 | **R** | *C* | § |
| 11127 | **R** | *P* | | 11148 | **R** | *P* | | 11167 | **R** | *C* | |
| 11128 | **R** | *P* | | 11149 | **R** | *P* | | 11168 | **R** | *C* | |
| 11129 | **R** | *P* | | 11150 | **R** | *P* | | 420 169-3 | **C** | *C* | § |
| 11130 | **R** | *P* | | 11151 | **R** | *P* | | 11170 | **R** | *C* | |

| | | | |
|---|---|---|---|
| 11171 | **R** | *C* | |
| 11172 | **R** | *C* | * |
| 11173 | **R** | *C* | |
| 11174 | **R** | *C* | |
| 11175 | **R** | *C* | |
| 11176 | **R** | *C* | |
| 11177 | **R** | *C* | |
| 420 178-6 | **C** | *C* | |
| 11179 | **R** | *C* | |
| 11180 | **R** | *C* | |
| 11181 | **R** | *P* | |
| 11182 | **R** | *C* | |
| 11183 | **R** | *C* | |
| 11184 | **R** | *C* | |
| 11185 | **R** | *C* | |
| 420 186-9 | **C** | *C* | |
| 11187 | **R** | *C* | |
| 11188 | **R** | *C* | |
| 11189 | **R** | *C* | |

| | | | | | | | | | | |
|---|---|---|---|---|---|---|---|---|---|---|
| 11190 | **R** *C* | | 11235 | **R** *P* | | 11280 | **R** *C* e | | 11327 | **R** *C* e |
| 11191 | **R** *C* | | 11236 | **R** *P* | | 11281 | **R** *C* e | | 11328 | **R** *C* e |
| 11192 | **R** *C* | | 11237 | **R** *P* | | 11283 | **R** *C* e | | 11329 | **R** *C* e |
| 11193 | **R** *P* | | 11238 | **R** *P* | | 11284 | **R** *C* e | | 11330 | **G** *C* e |
| 11194 | **R** *P* | | 11239 | **R** *P* | | 11285 | **R** *C* e | | 11331 | **R** *C* e |
| 11195 | **R** *P* | | 11240 | **R** *C* e | | 11286 | **R** *C* e | | 11332 | **R** *C* e |
| 11196 | **R** *P* | | 11241 | **R** *P* | | 11287 | **R** *C* e | | 11333 | **R** *C* e |
| 11197 | **R** *P* | | 11242 | **R** *P* | | 11288 | **R** *C* e | | 11334 | **R** *C* e |
| 11198 | **R** *P* | | 11243 | **R** *C* | | 11289 | **R** *C* e | | 11335 | **R** *C* e |
| 11199 | **R** *P* | | 11244 | **R** *P* | | 11290 | **R** *C* e | | 11336 | **R** *C* e |
| 11200 | **R** *P* | | 11245 | **R** *P* | | 11291 | **R** *C* e | | 11337 | **R** *C* e |
| 11201 | **R** *P* | | 11246 | **R** *P* | | 11292 | **R** *C* e | | 11338 | **R** *C* e |
| 11202 | **R** *P* | | 11247 | **R** *P* | | 11293 | **R** *C* e | | 11339 | **R** *C* e |
| 11203 | **R** *P* | | 11248 | **R** *P* | | 11294 | **R** *C* e | | 11340 | **R** *C* e |
| 11204 | **R** *P* | | 11249 | **R** *P* | | 11295 | **R** *C* e | | 11341 | **R** *C* e |
| 11205 | **R** *P* | | 11250 | **R** *P* | | 11296 | **R** *C* e | | 11342 | **R** *C* e |
| 11206 | **R** *P* | | 11251 | **R** *P* | | 11297 | **R** *C* e | | 11343 | **R** *C* e |
| 11207 | **R** *P* | | 11252 | **R** *P* | | 11298 | **R** *C* e | | 420 344-4 | **C** *C* e |
| 11208 | **R** *P* | | 11253 | **R** *P* | | 11299 | **R** *P* | | 11345 | **R** *C* e |
| 11209 | **R** *P* | | 11254 | **R** *P* | | 11300 | **R** *P* | | 420 346-9 | **C** *C* e |
| 11210 | **R** *P* | | 11255 | **R** *P* | | 11301 | **R** *P* | | 11347 | **G** *C* e |
| 11211 | **R** *P* | | 11256 | **R** *P* | | 11302 | **R** *P* | | 11348 | **R** *C* e |
| 11212 | **R** *P* | | 11257 | **R** *P* | | 11303 | **R** *P* | | 11349 | **R** *C* e |
| 11213 | **R** *P* | | 11258 | **R** *P* | | 11304 | **R** *P* | | 11350 | **R** *C* * |
| 11214 | **R** *P* | | 11259 | **R** *P* | | 11305 | **R** *P* | | 11351 | **R** *C* * |
| 11215 | **R** *P* | | 11260 | **R** *P* | | 11306 | **R** *P* | | 11352 | **R** *C* * |
| 11216 | **R** *P* | | 11261 | **R** *P* | | 420 307-1 | **C** *C* | | 11353 | **R** *C* * |
| 11217 | **R** *P* | | 11262 | **R** *P* | | 11308 | **R** *C* | | 11354 | **R** *C* * |
| 11218 | **R** *P* | | 11263 | **R** *P* | | 11309 | **G** *C* | | 11355 | **R** *C* * |
| 11219 | **R** *P* | | 11264 | **R** *P* | | 420 310-5 | **C** *C* | | 11356 | **R** *C* * |
| 11220 | **R** *P* | | 11265 | **R** *C* e | | 11311 | **R** *C* | | 11357 | **R** *C* * |
| 11221 | **R** *P* | | 11266 | **R** *C* e | | 11313 | **R** *C* | | 11358 | **R** *C* * |
| 11222 | **R** *P* | | 11267 | **R** *C* e | | 11314 | **R** *C* | | 11359 | **R** *C* * |
| 11223 | **R** *P* | | 420 268-5 | **C** *C* e | | 11315 | **R** *C* | | 11360 | **R** *C* * |
| 11224 | **R** *P* | | 11269 | **R** *C* e | | 11316 | **R** *C* | | 11361 | **R** *C* * |
| 11225 | **R** *P* | | 11270 | **R** *C* e | | 11317 | **R** *C* | | 11362 | **R** *C* * |
| 11226 | **R** *P* | | 11271 | **R** *C* e | | 11318 | **R** *C* | | 11363 | **R** *C* * |
| 11227 | **R** *P* | | 11272 | **R** *C* e | | 11319 | **R** *C* | | 11364 | **G** *C* * |
| 11228 | **R** *P* | | 11273 | **R** *C* e | | 11320 | **N** *C* e | | 11365 | **R** *C* * |
| 11229 | **R** *P* | | 11274 | **R** *C* e | | 11321 | **R** *C* e | | 11366 | **R** *C* * |
| 11230 | **R** *P* | | 11275 | **R** *C* e | | 11322 | **R** *C* e | | 11367 | **R** *C* * |
| 11231 | **R** *P* | | 420 276-8 | **C** *C* e | | 11324 | **R** *C* e | | 11368 | **R** *C* * |
| 11232 | **R** *P* | | 11277 | **R** *C* e | | 11325 | **R** *C* e | | 11369 | **R** *C* * |
| 11233 | **R** *P* | | 11278 | **R** *C* e | | 11326 | **R** *C* e | | 11370 | **R** *C* * |
| 11234 | **R** *P* | | 11279 | **R** *C* e | | | | | | |

Name: 11239 PORRENTRUY (name taken from 11483 in 1979).

# CLASS Re 421　　　　　ћ. 51　　　　　Bo-Bo

These are Class 420 (Re 4/4ᴵᴵ) locos modified for operation into Germany and allocated to SBB Cargo. Also used on Zürich–Lindau passenger trains. Modifications include changes to fit in the loading gauge, a new Schunk Type WBL 85 pantograph, German radio and signalling equipment. Former numbers 11371 to 11397. 11382 was destroyed in a fire.

Details as Class Re 420 except:

**Maximum Speed:** 140 km/h (120 km/h in Germany).

| | | | | | | | | | | |
|---|---|---|---|---|---|---|---|---|---|---|
| 421 371-6 | **C** *C* | BS | 421 378-1 | **C** *C* | BS | 421 385-6 | **C** *C* | BS | 421 392-2 | **C** *C* | BS |
| 421 372-4 | **C** *C* | BS | 421 379-9 | **C** *C* | BS | 421 386-4 | **C** *C* | BS | 421 393-0 | **C** *C* | BS |
| 421 373-2 | **C** *C* | BS | 421 380-7 | **C** *C* | BS | 421 387-2 | **C** *C* | BS | 421 394-8 | **C** *C* | BS |
| 421 374-0 | **C** *C* | BS | 421 381-5 | **C** *C* | BS | 421 388-0 | **C** *C* | BS | 421 395-5 | **C** *C* | BS |
| 421 375-7 | **C** *C* | BS | 421 382-3 | **C** *C* | BS | 421 389-8 | **C** *C* | BS | 421 396-3 | **C** *C* | BS |
| 421 376-5 | **C** *C* | BS | 421 383-1 | **C** *C* | BS | 421 390-6 | **C** *C* | BS | 421 397-1 | **C** *C* | BS |
| 421 377-3 | **C** *C* | BS | 421 384-9 | **C** *C* | BS | 421 391-4 | **C** *C* | BS | | | |

# CLASS Re 450    ⟨ 𝟝𝟤⟩    Bo-Bo

These are single-ended locos to work push-pull trains on the Zürich S-Bahn, which commenced operation in May 1990. They have 3-phase traction motors, SLM "shifting axle drive", which allows radial adjustment of the axles within the bogies, and regeneration braking. The locos operate in fixed formation sets with two intermediate trailers and a driving trailer. SBB has ordered new low-floor trailers of which one will be added to each set to conform with modern standards of access. The trailers replaced will be formed into hauled sets for use in the peak. Locos/sets 450 067 and 070 were transferred to SZU in 2008 and six more are to follow.

**Built:** 1989–97.
**Builder–Mechanical Parts:** SLM.
**Builder–Electrical. Parts:** ABB.
**Traction Motors:** 4 3-phase axle-hung, nose suspended.
**One Hour Rating:** 3200 kW.    **Weight:** 74 tonnes.
**Maximum Tractive Effort:** 240 kN.    **Length over Buffers:** 18.40 m.
**Wheel Diameter:** 1100 mm.    **Maximum Speed:** 130 km/h.

| | | | | | | |
|---|---|---|---|---|---|---|
| 450 000-5 | S | ZU | Seebach | 450 046-8 S | ZU | Zürich Affoltern |
| 450 001-3 | A | ZU | Schwerzenbach | 450 047-6 S | ZU | Seegräben |
| 450 002-1 | S | ZU | Oberwinterthur | 450 048-4 S | ZU | Elgg ZH |
| 450 003-9 | S | ZU | Zollikon | 450 049-2 S | ZU | Nänikon |
| 450 004-7 | A | ZU | Stettbach | 450 050-0 A | ZU | Wien |
| 450 005-4 | S | ZU | Kilchberg | 450 051-8 S | ZU | Kleinandelfingen |
| 450 006-2 | S | ZU | Rafz | 450 052-6 S | ZU | Lottstetten |
| 450 007-0 | S | ZU | Fehraltorf | 450 053-4 A | ZU | Witikon |
| 450 008-8 | S | ZU | Riesbach | 450 054-2 S | ZU | Oberglatt |
| 450 009-6 | S | ZU | Hedingen | 450 055-9 S | ZU | Küsnacht ZH |
| 450 010-4 | S | ZU | Steinmaur | 450 056-7 S | ZU | Otelfingen |
| 450 011-2 | S | ZU | Oberrieden | 450 057-5 S | ZU | Dielsdorf |
| 450 012-0 | A | ZU | Schwamendingen | 450 058-3 S | ZU | Niederhasli |
| 450 013-8 | S | ZU | Niederglatt | 450 059-1 S | ZU | Knonau |
| 450 014-6 | S | ZU | Männedorf | 450 060-9 A | ZU | Glattfelden |
| 450 015-3 | S | ZU | Erlenbach | 450 061-7 S | ZU | Mönchaltorf |
| 450 016-1 | S | ZU | Altstetten | 450 062-5 A | ZU | Gossau ZH |
| 450 017-9 | S | ZU | Bubikon | 450 063-3 S | ZU | Hombrechtikon |
| 450 018-7 | S | ZU | Hirslanden/Hottingen | 450 064-1 S | ZU | City of Osaka |
| 450 019-5 | S | ZU | Stäfa | 450 065-8 S | ZU | Bonstetten |
| 450 020-3 | S | ZU | Pfäffikon | 450 066-6 S | ZU | Neerach |
| 450 021-1 | S | ZU | Seuzach | 450 068-2 S | ZU | Waltalingen |
| 450 022-9 | S | ZU | Richterswil | 450 069-0 S | ZU | Wiesendangen |
| 450 023-7 | S | ZU | Greifensee | 450 071-6 S | ZU | Altenburg |
| 450 024-5 | S | ZU | Pfungen | 450 072-4 S | ZU | Rheinau |
| 450 025-2 | S | ZU | Winterthur Seen | 450 073-2 S | ZU | Wettswil |
| 450 026-0 | S | ZU | Birmensdorf | 450 074-0 S | ZU | Stadel |
| 450 027-8 | A | ZU | Zürich Enge | 450 075-7 S | ZU | Ossingen |
| 450 028-6 | A | ZU | Uerikon | 450 076-5 S | ZU | Unterstammheim |
| 450 029-4 | S | ZU | Altikon | 450 077-3 A | ZU | Oberstammheim |
| 450 030-2 | S | ZU | Rümlang | 450 078-1 S | ZU | Au ZH |
| 450 031-0 | S | ZU | Wald | 450 079-9 S | ZU | Jestetten |
| 450 032-8 | S | ZU | Mettmenstetten | 450 080-7 S | ZU | Rüschlikon |
| 450 033-6 | S | ZU | Thalheim | 450 081-5 S | ZU | Weiningen |
| 450 034-4 | S | ZU | Oberweningen | 450 082-3 S | ZU | Feuerthalen |
| 450 035-1 | S | ZU | Schöfflisdorf | 450 083-1 S | ZU | Trüllikon |
| 450 036-9 | A | ZU | Dietikon | 450 084-9 S | ZU | Neftenbach |
| 450 037-7 | A | ZU | Niederweningen | 450 085-6 A | ZU | Rickenbach ZH |
| 450 038-5 | S | ZU | Wollishofen | 450 086-4 S | ZU | Benken ZH |
| 450 039-3 | S | ZU | Embrach | 450 087-2 S | ZU | Zell ZH |
| 450 040-1 | S | ZU | Hinwil | 450 088-0 S | ZU | Wangen SZ |
| 450 041-9 | S | ZU | Buchs/Dällikon | 450 089-8 S | ZU | Bäretswil |
| 450 042-7 | S | ZU | Hettlingen | 450 090-6 S | ZU | Turbental |
| 450 043-5 | S | ZU | Rorbas | 450 091-4 S | ZU | Dürnten |
| 450 044-3 | S | ZU | Henggart | 450 092-2 S | ZU | Wila |
| 450 045-0 | S | ZU | Feldbach | 450 093-0 S | ZU | Wil ZH |

| | | | | | |
|---|---|---|---|---|---|
| 450 094-8 **S** | ZU | Hüntwangen | 450 105-2 **S** | ZU | Herrliberg |
| 450 095-5 **S** | ZU | Wasterkingen | 450 106-0 **S** | ZU | Winterthur Töss |
| 450 096-3 **S** | ZU | Winterthur Veltheim | 450 107-8 **S** | ZU | Maschwanden |
| 450 097-1 **S** | ZU | Maur | 450 108-6 **S** | ZU | Uetikon |
| 450 098-9 **S** | ZU | Grüningen | 450 109-4 **A** | ZU | Kappel a./A. |
| 450 099-7 **S** | ZU | Volketswil | 450 110-2 **S** | ZU | Hittnau |
| 450 100-3 **S** | ZU | Rudolfingen | 450 111-0 **S** | ZU | Neuenhof |
| 450 101-1 **S** | ZU | Obfelden | 450 112-8 **S** | ZU | Flurlingen |
| 450 102-9 **S** | ZU | Wangen-Brütisellen | 450 113-6 **S** | ZU | Humlikon/Adlikon |
| 450 103-7 **S** | ZU | Marthalen | 450 114-4 **A** | ZU | Dänikon |
| 450 104-5 **A** | ZU | Zürich Hard | | | |

# CLASS Re 460                    ⌐52                    Bo-Bo

High speed locos built for the "Bahn 2000" project. Originally used on mixed traffic, they are now all passenger locos, very often used in push-pull mode with IC2000 double-deckers or Mark IV single-deck stock. Locos temporarily in advertising livery often do not carry their names – which are thus shown in italics. All are equipped with ETCS Level 2.

**Built:** 1991–6.
**Builders–Mechanical Parts:** SLM/Krauss Maffei.
**Builder–Electrical. Parts:** ABB.
**Traction Motors:** 4 3-phase fully suspended.
**One Hour Rating:** 6100 kW.
**Maximum Tractive Effort:** 275 kN.
**Wheel Diameter:** 1100 mm.
**Weight:** 84 tonnes.
**Length over Buffers:** 18.50 m.
**Maximum Speed:** 230 km/h.

**Non-Standard Livery: X** Red with dark grey lower body and a very large arrowed cross on the side. This may become a new standard livery for SBB passenger locos.

Depot allocations are not shown, as locos of this class are common user.

| | | | |
|---|---|---|---|
| 460 000-3 **R** | Grauholz | 460 036-7 **R** | Franches-Montagnes |
| 460 001-1 **R** | Lötschberg | 460 037-5 **R** | Sempacher See |
| 460 002-9 **R** | Seeland | 460 038-3 **A** | *Hauenstein* |
| 460 003-7 **R** | Milieu de Monde | 460 039-1 **R** | Rochers-de-Naye |
| 460 004-5 **R** | Uetliberg | 460 040-9 **R** | Napf |
| 460 005-2 **A** | *Val d'Anniviers* | 460 041-7 **R** | Mendrisiotto |
| 460 006-0 **R** | Lavaux | 460 042-5 **R** | Albis |
| 460 007-8 **A** | *Junior* | 460 043-3 **R** | Dreispitz |
| 460 008-6 **R** | La Gruyère | 460 044-1 **A** | *Zugerland* |
| 460 009-4 **R** | Le Jet d'Eau | 460 045-8 **R** | Rigi |
| 460 010-2 **R** | Löwenberg | 460 046-6 **R** | Polmengo |
| 460 011-0 **R** | Léman | 460 047-4 **R** | Maderanertal |
| 460 012-8 **A** | *Erguël* | 460 048-2 **R** | Züri Wyland |
| 460 013-6 **R** | Nord Vaudois | 460 049-0 **R** | Pfaffenstiel |
| 460 014-4 **R** | Val-du-Trient | 460 050-8 **R** | Züspa |
| 460 015-1 **A** | *uf u dervo* | 460 051-6 **A** | *Staffelegg* |
| 460 016-9 **X** | Rohrdorferberg Reussta | 460 052-4 **R** | Eigenamt |
| 460 017-7 **R** | Les Diablerets | 460 053-2 **A** | *Suhrental* |
| 460 018-5 **R** | | 460 054-0 **R** | Dreiländereck |
| 460 019-3 **R** | Terre Sainte | 460 055-7 **R** | Lillehammer |
| 460 020-1 **A** | SBB locomotive drivers | 460 056-5 **R** | |
| 460 021-9 **A** | Kambly II | 460 057-3 **R** | Val-de-Ruz |
| 460 022-7 **R** | Sihl | 460 058-1 **R** | La Côte |
| 460 023-5 **R** | Wankdorf | 460 059-9 **R** | La Béroche |
| 460 024-3 **A** | *Rheintal* | 460 060-7 **R** | Val-de-Travers |
| 460 025-0 **R** | Striegel | 460 061-5 **R** | Wiggertal |
| 460 026-8 **A** | *Fricktal* | 460 062-3 **R** | Ergolz |
| 460 027-6 **R** | Joggeli | 460 063-1 **R** | Brunegg |
| 460 028-4 **A** | *Seetal* | 460 064-9 **R** | Mythen |
| 460 029-2 **R** | Eulach | 460 065-6 **A** | *Rotsee* |
| 460 030-0 **R** | Säntis | 460 066-4 **R** | Finse |
| 460 031-8 **R** | Chaumont | 460 067-2 **R** | Hohle Gasse |
| 460 032-6 **R** | | 460 068-0 **R** | Gütsch |
| 460 033-4 **R** | | 460 069-8 **R** | Verkehrshaus |
| 460 034-2 **R** | Aare | 460 070-6 **R** | |
| 460 035-9 **R** | | 460 071-4 **A** | *Mittelland* |

| | | | | |
|---|---|---|---|---|
| 460 072-2 **R** | Reuss | | 460 096-1 **R** | Furttal |
| 460 073-0 **R** | Monte Ceneri | | 460 097-9 **R** | Studenland |
| 460 074-8 **R** | | | 460 098-7 **R** | Balsberg |
| 460 075-5 **A** | *Schafmatt* | | 460 099-5 **R** | Bodensee |
| 460 076-3 **R** | Leventina | | 460 100-1 **A** | *Tösstal* |
| 460 077-1 **R** | Chunnel | | 460 101-9 **A** | *Bözberg* |
| 460 078-9 **R** | Monte Generoso | | 460 102-7 **A** | *Lägern* |
| 460 079-7 **R** | Weissenstein | | 460 103-5 **R** | Heitersberg |
| 460 080-5 **A** | *Tre Valli* | | 460 104-3 **R** | Toggenburg |
| 460 081-3 **R** | Pfänder | | 460 105-0 **R** | Fürstenland |
| 460 082-1 **R** | Ceresio | | 460 106-8 **A** | *Munot* |
| 460 083-9 **R** | | | 460 107-6 **A** | *Glärnisch* |
| 460 084-7 **R** | Helvetia | | 460 108-4 **R** | Engadin |
| 460 085-4 **R** | Pilatus | | 460 109-2 **R** | Alpstein |
| 460 086-2 **R** | Ägerisee | | 460 110-0 **R** | Mariaberg |
| 460 087-0 **A** | *Säuliamt* | | 460 111-8 **R** | Kempt |
| 460 088-8 **R** | Limmat | | 460 112-6 **R** | Thurtal |
| 460 089-6 **R** | Freiamt | | 460 113-4 **R** | Irchel |
| 460 090-4 **A** | *Goffersberg* | | 460 114-2 **A** | Circus Knie |
| 460 091-2 **R** | Werdenberg | | 460 115-9 **R** | Heidiland |
| 460 092-0 **R** | Fridolin | | 460 116-7 **R** | Ostschweiz |
| 460 093-8 **R** | Rhein | | 460 117-5 **R** | Zürichsee |
| 460 094-6 **A** | *Rätia* | | 460 118-3 **R** | Gotthard/Gottardo |
| 460 095-3 **R** | Bachtel | | | |

# CLASS Re 474  Bo-Bo

These locos are the same Siemens ES64F4 design as DB Schenker Class 189 but are configured only for 15 kV AC in Switzerland and 3000 V DC in Italy. They work mainly southwards from Bellinzona and Chiasso. Siemens won this contract by claiming to be able to deliver the locos faster than Class Re 484 from Bombardier. This turned out not to be the case and SBB penalised the builder by refusing to accept six of the locos. The first versions of 474 007 and 008 were damaged during delivery then rebuilt and became MRCE Dispolok 189 919 and 920. 474 001 and 010 plus the second versions of 474 007 and 008 went to Italian operator Del Fungo Giera which went bankrupt. 474 006 and 011 are now with Hector Rail in Sweden as 441 001 and 002. 474 007 has gone to Rail One as 474 103 and 474 008 has gone to NordCargo in Italy as 474 201.

**Built:** 2004.
**Systems:** 15 kV AC 16.7 Hz, 25 kV AC 50 Hz.
**Builder:** Siemens.
**Continuous Rating:** 6400 kW.
**Maximum Tractive Effort:** 300 kN.
**Wheel Diameter:** 1250 mm.
**Weight:** 86 tonnes.
**Length over Buffers:** 19.58 m.
**Maximum Speed:** 140 km/h.

| | | | | | | | | |
|---|---|---|---|---|---|---|---|---|
| 474 002-3 **C** *C* | BE | 474 005-6 **C** *C* | BE | 474 013-0 **C** *C* | BE | 474 016-3 **C** *C* | BE |
| 474 003-1 **C** *C* | BE | 474 009-8 **C** *C* | BE | 474 014-8 **C** *C* | BE | 474 017-1 **C** *C* | BE |
| 474 004-9 **C** *C* | BE | 474 012-2 **C** *C* | BE | 474 015-5 **C** *C* | BE | 474 018-9 **C** *C* | BE |

# CLASS Re 482  Bo-Bo

When SBB Cargo started to expand northwards into Germany, it needed more than just the two dozen Class 421. So the company ordered 10 Class Re 482 locomotives, almost identical to Railion's Class 185, then added 40 more locos to take the total to 50. The main difference compared with Class 185 was the addition of rear-facing mini cameras behind the cab doors to allow the driver to back onto a train without opening the window in the Swiss winter. Like Class 185, the locos have 25 kV AC equipment as standard but this is not used. Class 482 are used throughout Switzerland and into Germany, mainly northwards along the Basel–Köln corridor but also many other places including Aachen and Hamburg daily. The last batch also works to Wien in Austria. In contrast, the class usually come off freights over the Gotthard route at either Basel or Arth-Goldau. Several locos have been hired to other operators in Germany.

**Built:** 2002–2004.
**Systems:** 15 kV AC 16.7 Hz/25 kV AC 50 Hz.
**Builder:** Bombardier Transportation, Kassel.
**Traction Motors:** Nose-suspended.
**Continuous Rating:** 5600 kW.
**Maximum Tractive Effort:** 300 kN.
**Wheel Diameter:** 1250 mm.
**Weight:** 84 tonnes.
**Length over Buffers:** 18.90 m.
**Maximum Speed:** 140 km/h.

All locos multiple fitted within class and with Classes 420 and 620.
b Authorised to operate to Brennero in Italy.

**TRAXX 1 Locos.**

| | | | | | | | | | | |
|---|---|---|---|---|---|---|---|---|---|---|
| 482 000-7 **C** *C* | BS | 482 009-8 **C** *C* | BS | 482 018-9 **C** *C* | BS | 482 027-0 **C** *C* | BS |
| 482 001-5 **C** *C* | BS | 482 010-6 **C** *C* | BS | 482 019-7 **C** *C* | BS | 482 028-8 **A** *C* | BS |
| 482 002-3 **C** *C* | BS | 482 011-4 **A** *C* | BS | 482 020-5 **C** *C* | BS | 482 029-6 **C** *C* | BS |
| 482 003-1 **C** *C* | BS | 482 012-2 **C** *C* | BS | 482 021-3 **C** *C* | BS | 482 030-4 **C** *C* | BS |
| 482 004-9 **C** *C* | BS | 482 013-0 **C** *C* | BS | 482 022-1 **C** *C* | BS | 482 031-2 **C** *C* | BS |
| 482 005-6 **C** *C* | BS | 482 014-8 **C** *C* | BS | 482 023-9 **C** *C* | BS | 482 032-0 **C** *C* | BS |
| 482 006-4 **C** *C* | BS | 482 015-5 **C** *C* | BS | 482 024-7 **C** *C* | BS | 482 033-8 **C** *C* | BS |
| 482 007-2 **C** *C* | BS | 482 016-3 **C** *C* | BS | 482 025-4 **C** *C* | BS | 482 034-6 **C** *C* | BS |
| 482 008-0 **C** *C* | BS | 482 017-1 **C** *C* | BS | 482 026-2 **C** *C* | BS | | |

**Names:**

482 000-7 Köln
482 008-0 Ökotrans

482 033-8 Basler Rheinhafen
482 034-6 Duisburg

**TRAXX 2 Locos.** Authorised for use in Austria.

| | | | | | | | |
|---|---|---|---|---|---|---|---|
| 482 035-3 **C** *C* b BS | 482 039-5 **C** *C* | BS | 482 043-7 **C** *C* b BS | 482 047-8 **C** *C* b BS |
| 482 036-1 **C** *C* | BS | 482 040-3 **C** *C* | BS | 482 044-5 **C** *C* | BS | 482 048-6 **C** *C* b BS |
| 482 037-9 **C** *C* b BS | 482 041-1 **C** *C* | BS | 482 045-2 **A** *C* | BS | 482 049-4 **A** *C* b BS |
| 482 038-7 **C** *C* | BS | 482 042-9 **C** *C* | BS | 482 046-0 **C** *C* | BS | |

# CLASS Re 484       Bo-Bo

In order to expand into Italy, SBB Cargo's Italian subsidiary ordered 18 Class Re 484 locomotives from Bombardier, plus 30 options, in late 2002. Three options have been taken up. These were the first TRAXX locomotives designed to operate under 3000 V DC as well as 15 kV AC. The locos are also pre-equipped to operate off 1500 V DC and 25 kV AC but only have signalling for Switzerland and Italy. The locos are used south of Bellinzona, taking over from straight 15 kV AC machines, running mainly to points such as Novara, Gallarate, Ollegio and Milano although they now also reach Bologna. In 2009, SBB Cargo was also hiring identical locos 484 103, 104 and 105 from MRCE Dispolok. Ten are equipped with ETCS Level 2. 484 013–018 have been hired by Cisalpino during refurbishment of ETR.470 sets and are in a special livery.

**Built:** 2003–.
**Systems:** 3000 V DC; 15 kV AC 16.7 Hz.
**Builder:** Bombardier Transportation, Kassel.
**Traction Motors:** Nose-Suspended.
**Continuous Rating:** 5600 kW.
**Maximum Tractive Effort:** 300 kN.
**Wheel Diameter:** 1250 mm.
**Weight:** 85.6 tonnes.
**Length over Buffers:** 18.90 m.
**Maximum Speed:** 140 km/h.
**Non-Standard Livery:** 484 017 and 018 are in Cisalpino livery.

Name: 484 021-1 Gottardo.

| | | | | | | | |
|---|---|---|---|---|---|---|---|
| 484 001-3 **C** *C* | BE | 484 007-0 **C** *C* | BE | 484 012-0 **C** *C* | BE | 484 017-9 **C** *C* | BE |
| 484 002-1 **C** *C* | BE | 484 008-8 **C** *C* | BE | 484 013-8 **C** *C* | BE | 484 018-7 **C** *C* | BE |
| 484 003-9 **C** *C* | BE | 484 009-6 **C** *C* | BE | 484 014-6 **C** *C* | BE | 484 019-5 **C** *C* | BE |
| 484 004-7 **C** *C* | BE | 484 010-4 **C** *C* | BE | 484 015-3 **C** *C* | BE | 484 020-3 **C** *C* | BE |
| 484 005-4 **C** *C* | BE | 484 011-2 **C** *C* | BE | 484 016-1 **C** *C* | BE | 484 021-1 **C** *C* | BE |
| 484 006-2 **C** *C* | BE | | | | | | |

# CLASS Ae 6/6 (Re 610)            Co-Co

Built for general use on the Gotthard and Simplon lines, this class has been displaced to other routes, being used entirely on freight work. All are now in the Cargo fleet. It was the first SBB type to receive names and emblems and to carry the white cross on the ends. 11403–25 carry chrome decorations and names of cantons. The others carry the names of towns. 11401/2 were pre-series locos with detailed differences and so have been withdrawn. 11402 is now part of the SBB Historic fleet. Although the class is in decline, SBB has upgraded drivers' cabs on 81 locos. Those passing through works are receiving SBB Cargo livery and new numbers. The economic turndown from 2008 and problems with cracked wheels meant that many have gone into store.

**Built:** 1955–66.
**Builder–Mechanical Parts:** SLM.
**Builders–Electrical. Parts:** BBC/MFO.
**Traction Motors:** 6 single phase commutator type, fully suspended with BBC spring drive.
**One Hour Rating:** 4300 kW.       **Weight:** 120 tonnes.
**Maximum Tractive Effort:** 392 kN.       **Length over Buffers:** 18.40 m.
**Wheel Diameter:** 1260 mm.       **Maximum Speed:** 125 km/h.

**Notes:**

Some locos carry names in different languages on opposite sides. However, most nameplates have now been removed. Locos in Cargo livery have stickers for names.
Locos in Cargo livery have been renumbered.
Depot allocations are not shown, as locos of this class are common user.

| No. | | | | Name | No. | | | | Name |
|---|---|---|---|---|---|---|---|---|---|
| 11403 | G | C | S | SCHWYZ | 11459 | G | C | | CHIASSO |
| 11404 | G | C | | LUZERN | 11461 | G | C | S | LOCARNO |
| 11405 | G | C | S | NIDWALDEN | 11462 | G | C | S | BIASCA |
| 11411 | G | C | | ZUG | 610 463-2 | C | C | | GÖSCHENEN |
| 11417 | R | C | S | FRIBOURG/FREIBURG | 11464 | R | C | | ERSTFELD |
| 11419 | R | C | | APPENZELL I.RH | 11465 | G | C | | OERLIKON |
| 610 420-2 | R | | | APPENZELL A.RH | 11466 | R | C | | SURSEE |
| 11422 | R | C | S | VAUD | 11467 | G | C | S | ZOFINGEN |
| 11423 | R | C | | VALAIS/WALLIS | 11469 | G | C | | THALWIL |
| 11424 | R | C | | NEUCHÂTEL | 11470 | R | C | | BRUGG |
| 11425 | R | C | | GENÈVE | 11471 | G | C | S | PRATTELN |
| 11426 | R | C | | STADT ZÜRICH | 11472 | R | C | | BRIG |
| 11427 | G | C | | STADT BERN | 11473 | G | C | | ST MAURICE |
| 11428 | G | C | S | STADT LUZERN | 11474 | G | C | S | VEVEY |
| 11429 | R | C | | ALTDORF | 11477 | R | C | S | MARTIGNY |
| 11430 | R | C | S | GEMEINDE SCHWYZ | 11478 | G | C | S | SIERRE |
| 11431 | R | C | S | SARNEN | 11479 | G | C | | VISP |
| 11432 | R | C | S | STANS | 11480 | G | C | | MONTREUX |
| 11434 | R | C | | STADT ZUG | 610 482-2 | C | C | | DELÉMONT |
| 11435 | G | C | | FRIBOURG | 11483 | G | C | S | JURA |
| 11437 | R | C | | STADT BASEL | 11485 | R | C | | THUN |
| 11438 | G | C | | LIESTAL | 610 486-3 | C | C | | BURGDORF |
| 610 439-2 | C | C | S | SCHAFFHAUSEN | 610 487-1 | C | C | | LANGENTHAL |
| 11440 | R | C | | HERISAU | 11488 | G | C | | MENDRISIO |
| 11442 | R | C | | ST GALLEN | 610 489-7 | C | C | S | AIROLO |
| 11444 | G | C | S | AARAU | 11490 | R | C | S | ROTKREUZ |
| 11445 | R | C | S | FRAUENFELD | 11491 | G | C | S | WOHLEN AG |
| 11446 | R | C | S | BELLINZONA | 610 492-1 | C | C | | ERSTFELD |
| 610 447-5 | C | C | S | LAUSANNE | 11493 | G | C | S | SISSACH |
| 11448 | R | C | | SION | 11494 | G | C | S | SCHLIEREN |
| 11449 | G | C | S | NEUCHÂTEL | 11495 | G | C | | BÜLACH |
| 11450 | R | C | | VILLE DE GENÈVE | 610 496-2 | C | C | | STADT WIL |
| 11451 | G | C | S | WINTERTHUR | 11497 | G | C | S | ST MARGRETHEN |
| 11453 | G | C | | ARTH-GOLDAU | 11498 | G | C | S | BUCHS SG |
| 11454 | R | C | | YVERDON | 11499 | G | C | | SARGANS |
| 11455 | R | C | | BIEL/BIENNE | 11501 | G | C | | RENENS |
| 11456 | R | C | | OLTEN | 11502 | G | C | | NYON |
| 11457 | R | C | S | ROMANSHORN | 11504 | G | C | | LE LOCLE |
| 11458 | G | C | S | RORSCHACH | 11506 | G | C | | GRENCHEN |

| | | | | | | | | |
|---|---|---|---|---|---|---|---|---|
| 11507 | **G** *C* | | WILDEGG | | 11515 | **G** *C* | S | KREUZLINGEN |
| 610 508-4 | **C** *C* | | WETTINGEN | | 11516 | **G** *C* | S | BAAR |
| 11509 | **G** *C* | S | GOSSAU SG | | 11517 | **G** *C* | | BRUNNEN |
| 11511 | **G** *C* | S | DIETIKON | | 11518 | **G** *C* | | FLÜELEN |
| 11512 | **R** *C* | | HORGEN | | 610 519-1 | **C** *C* | | GIUBIASCO |
| 11513 | **G** *C* | | WALLISELLEN | | 11520 | **R** *C* | | LANGNAU I.E |
| 11514 | **G** *C* | | WEINFELDEN | | | | | |

# CLASS Re 620 (Re 6/6)                    Bo-Bo-Bo

Effectively an enlarged and uprated version of the Re4/4ᴵᴵ, this class was built to work on the mountain routes, but also appears elsewhere. The wheel arrangement was selected to provide a total adhesion weight similar to the Ae6/6, but with a better ability to run through curves, and to reduce weight transfer. Four prototypes were built, the first two having a hinged body with the axis of the hinge horizontal; the rigid body design was adopted for the production version. The entry into service of the Re 460 class has seen a reduction of turns on the Gottard route, and the class now appears over a much wider area than previously. 11638 was withdrawn following an accident.

**Built:** 1972*, 1975–80.
**Builder–Mechanical Parts:** SLM.
**Builders–Electrical. Parts:** BBC/SAAS (BBC*).
**Traction Motors:** 6 single phase commutator type, fully suspended with BBC spring drive.
**One Hour Rating:** 7850 kW.              **Weight:** 120 tonnes.
**Maximum Tractive Effort:** 398 kN (394 kN*).    **Length over Buffers:** 19.31 m.
**Wheel Diameter:** 1260 mm.               **Maximum Speed:** 140 km/h.

e  ETCS fitted.

**Notes:**

All locos are mw fitted (can mw with Re4/4ᴵᴵ, Re4/4ᴵᴵᴵ, Re4/4ᴵⱽ, RBe4/4 classes).
Depot allocations are not shown, as locos of this class are common user.

| | | | |
|---|---|---|---|
| 620 001-8 | (11601) | **R** *P* * | WOLHUSEN |
| 620 002-6 | (11602) | **R** *P* * | MORGES |
| 620 003-4 | (11603) | **R** *P* * | WÄDENSWIL |
| 620 004-2 | (11604) | **R** *P* * | FAIDO |
| 620 005-9 | (11605) | **R** *C* e | USTER |
| 620 006-7 | (11606) | **R** *C* e | TURGI |
| 620 007-5 | (11607) | **R** *C* e | WATTWIL |
| 620 008-3 | (11608) | **R** *C* e | WETZIKON |
| 620 009-1 | (11609) | **R** *C* e | UZWIL |
| 620 010-9 | (11610) | **R** *C* e | SPREITENBACH |
| 620 011-7 | (11611) | **R** *C* e | RÜTI ZH |
| 620 012-5 | (11612) | **C** *C* e | REGENSDORF |
| 620 013-3 | (11613) | **R** *C* e | RAPPERSWIL |
| 620 014-1 | (11614) | **R** *C* e | MEILEN |
| 620 015-8 | (11615) | **R** *C* e | KLOTEN |
| 620 016-6 | (11616) | **R** *C* e | ILLNAU-EFFRETIKON |
| 620 017-4 | (11617) | **R** *C* e | HEERBRUGG |
| 620 018-2 | (11618) | **R** *C* e | DÜBENDORF |
| 620 019-0 | (11619) | **R** *C* e | ARBON |
| 620 020-8 | (11620) | **R** *C* e | WANGEN BEI OLTEN |
| 620 021-6 | (11621) | **R** *C* e | TAVERNE-TORRICELLA |
| 620 022-4 | (11622) | **R** *C* e | SUHR |
| 620 023-2 | (11623) | **R** *C* e | RUPPERSWIL |
| 620 024-0 | (11624) | **R** *C* e | ROTHRIST |
| 620 025-7 | (11625) | **R** *C* e | OENSINGEN |
| 620 026-5 | (11626) | **R** *C* e | ZOLLIKOFEN |
| 620 027-3 | (11627) | **R** *C* e | LUTERBACH-ATTISHOLZ |
| 620 028-1 | (11628) | **R** *C* e | KONOLFINGEN |
| 620 029-9 | (11629) | **R** *C* e | INTERLAKEN |
| 620 030-7 | (11630) | **R** *C* e | HERZOGENBUCHSEE |
| 620 031-5 | (11631) | **R** *C* e | DULLIKEN |
| 620 032-3 | (11632) | **R** *C* e | DÄNIKEN |
| 620 033-1 | (11633) | **G** *C* e | MURI AG |
| 620 034-9 | (11634) | **R** *C* e | AARBURG-OFTRINGEN |

| | | | |
|---|---|---|---|
| 620 035-6 | (11635) | R C e | MUTTENZ |
| 620 036-4 | (11636) | R C e | VERNIER-MEYRIN |
| 620 037-2 | (11637) | R C e | SONCEBOZ-SOMBEVAL |
| 620 039-8 | (11639) | R C e | MURTEN |
| 620 040-6 | (11640) | R C | MÜNCHENSTEIN |
| 620 041-4 | (11641) | R C | MOUTIER |
| 620 042-2 | (11642) | C C | MONTHEY |
| 620 043-0 | (11643) | R C | LAUFEN |
| 620 044-8 | (11644) | R C | CORNAUX |
| 620 045-5 | (11645) | R C | COLOMBIER |
| 620 046-3 | (11646) | G C | BUSSIGNY |
| 620 047-1 | (11647) | C C | BEX |
| 620 048-9 | (11648) | R C | AIGLE |
| 620 049-7 | (11649) | R C | AARBERG |
| 620 050-5 | (11650) | R C | SCHÖNENWERD |
| 620 051-3 | (11651) | G C | DORNACH-ARLESHEIM |
| 620 052-1 | (11652) | R C | KERZERS |
| 620 053-9 | (11653) | R C | GÜMLINGEN |
| 620 054-7 | (11654) | R C | VILLENEUVE |
| 620 055-4 | (11655) | C C | COSSONAY |
| 620 056-2 | (11656) | R C | TRAVERS |
| 620 057-0 | (11657) | R C | ESTAVAYER-LE-LAC |
| 620 058-8 | (11658) | C C | AUVERNIER |
| 620 059-6 | (11659) | G C | CHAVORNAY |
| 620 060-4 | (11660) | C C | TAVANNES |
| 620 061-2 | (11661) | C C | GAMPEL-STEG |
| 620 062-0 | (11662) | G C e | REUCHENETTE-PÉRY |
| 620 063-8 | (11663) | G C e | EGLISAU |
| 620 064-6 | (11664) | R C e | KÖNIZ |
| 620 065-3 | (11665) | C C e | ZIEGELBRÜCKE |
| 620 066-1 | (11666) | R C e | STEIN AM RHEIN |
| 620 067-9 | (11667) | R C e | BODIO |
| 620 068-7 | (11668) | R C e | STEIN-SÄCKINGEN |
| 620 069-5 | (11669) | C C e | HÄGENDORF |
| 620 070-3 | (11670) | R C e | AFFOLTERN AM ALBIS |
| 620 071-1 | (11671) | R C e | OTHMARSINGEN |
| 620 072-9 | (11672) | R C e | BALERNA |
| 620 073-7 | (11673) | R C e | CHAM |
| 620 074-5 | (11674) | R C e | MURGENTHAL |
| 620 075-2 | (11675) | C C e | GELTERKINDEN |
| 620 076-0 | (11676) | R C e | ZURZACH |
| 620 077-8 | (11677) | R C e | NEUHAUSEN AM RHEINFALL |
| 620 078-6 | (11678) | R C e | BASSERSDORF |
| 620 079-4 | (11679) | R C e | CADENAZZO |
| 620 080-2 | (11680) | R C e | MÖHLIN |
| 620 081-0 | (11681) | R C e | IMMENSEE |
| 620 082-8 | (11682) | R C e | PFÄFFIKON SZ |
| 620 083-6 | (11683) | R C e | AMSTEG-SILENEN |
| 620 084-4 | (11684) | R C e | UZNACH |
| 620 085-1 | (11685) | R C e | SULGEN |
| 620 086-9 | (11686) | C C e | HOCHDORF |
| 620 087-7 | (11687) | C C e | BISCHOFSZELL |
| 620 088-5 | (11688) | G C e | LINTHAL |
| 620 089-3 | (11689) | R C e | GERRA-GAMBAROGNO |

# 1.3. ELECTRIC MULTIPLE UNITS

New EMUs are are made up of fixed formations. Older railcars (now only Classes 540 and 560) are single motor coaches which are coupled to driving and intermediate trailer cars to make up push-pull trains. Trailers for Classes 540 and 560 are numbered in the carriage series and are not shown here. All units can operate only under 15 kV AC 16.7 Hz in Switzerland unless otherwise shown. Many classes of unit are common user and depot codes are not shown.

Under "accommodation" are shown the number of first and second class seats, followed by the number of toilets. "TD" indicates a disabled toilet. Tip-up seats are shown in brackets. Example: 16/32(8) 1T indicates 16 first class seats, 32 second class seats, 8 tip-up seats and one toilet.

## CLASS RABDe 500                    7-CAR TILTING UNIT

Recent tilting train sets known as ICN – Intercity *Neigezug* (tilting train). Sets are named after famous personalities, either Swiss or with a strong connection to the country. All are equipped with ETCS Level 2, bogies with steerable axles and electric tilt, disc, regenerative and magnetic track brakes. Sets are used on the Basel–Biel/Bienne–Genève Aéroport, Basel–Biel/Bienne–Lausanne, St. Gallen–Zürich–Biel/Bienne–Genève Aéroport and Lausanne–Biel/Bienne–Zürich–St. Gallen services plus since 2008 Zürich/Basel–Lugano.

**Built:** 1998–.
**Builder–Mechanical Parts:** Schindler/FIAT-SIG.
**Builder–Electrical Parts:** ABB.
**Wheel Arrangement:** 1A-A1 + 1A-A1 + 2-2 + 2-2 + 2-2 + 1A-A1 + 1A-A1.
**Length over Couplers:** 27.4 + 26.8 + 26.8 + 26.8 + 26.8 + 26.8 + 27.4 m.
**Formation:** Bt + B + WRA + A + AD + B + Bt.
**Accommodation:** –/70 (3) 1T + –/93 1T + 24/– 26 restaurant + 60/– 1TD + 47/– 1T + –/93 1T + –/70 (3) 1T.
**Traction Motors:** 8 x 650 kW.
**Total Weight:** 355 tonnes.
**Maximum Speed:** 200 km/h.

Sets are known as 500 0xx, and numbered 500 0xx–500 2xx–500 3xx–500 4xx–500 5xx– 500 6xx–500 7xx–500 1xx.

| | | | | | |
|---|---|---|---|---|---|
| 500 000-5 | GE | Le Corbusier | 500 022-9 | GE | Expo 02 |
| 500 001-3 | GE | Jean Piaget | 500 023-7 | GE | Charles Ferdinand Ramuz |
| 500 002-1 | GE | Annemarie Schwarzenbach | 500 024-5 | GE | Ernest Von Stockalper |
| 500 003-9 | GE | Germaine de Staël | 500 025-2 | GE | Xavier Stockmar |
| 500 004-7 | GE | Mani Matter | 500 026-0 | GE | Alfred Escher |
| 500 005-4 | GE | Heinrich Pestalozzi | 500 027-8 | GE | Henry Dunant |
| 500 006-2 | GE | Johanna Spyri | 500 028-6 | GE | Francesco Borromini |
| 500 007-0 | GE | Albert Einstein | 500 029-4 | GE | Eduard Spelterini |
| 500 008-8 | GE | Vincenzo Vela | 500 030-2 | GE | Louis Chevroulet |
| 500 009-6 | GE | Friedrich Dürrenmatt | 500 031-0 | GE | Louis Favre |
| 500 010-4 | GE | Robert Walser | 500 032-8 | GE | Henri Dufaux |
| 500 011-2 | GE | Blaise Cendrars | 500 033-6 | GE | Gallus Jakob Baumgartner |
| 500 012-0 | GE | Jean Rudolf von Salis | 500 034-4 | GE | Gustav Wenk |
| 500 013-8 | GE | Denis de Rougemont | 500 035-1 | GE | Niklaus Riggenbach |
| 500 014-6 | GE | Max Frisch | 500 036-9 | GE | Minister Kern |
| 500 015-3 | GE | Jean-Jacques Rousseau | 500 037-7 | GE | Grock |
| 500 016-1 | GE | Alice Rivaz | 500 038-5 | GE | Arthur Honneger |
| 500 017-9 | GE | Willi Ritschard | 500 039-3 | GE | Auguste Piccard |
| 500 018-7 | GE | Adolf Wölfli | 500 040-1 | GE | Graf Zeppelin |
| 500 019-5 | GE | Friedrich Glauser | 500 041-9 | GE | William Barbey |
| 500 020-3 | GE | Jeanne Hersch | 500 042-7 | GE | Steivan Brunies |
| 500 021-1 | GE | Jeremias Gotthelf | 500 043-5 | GE | Harald Szeemann |

## CLASS RABDe 511          6-CAR DOUBLE-DECK UNIT

On 27 June 2008, Stadler won an order for its first double-deck EMUs. These will be built for the Zürich S-Bahn and will enter service from March 2011. The order is for 50 6-car sets with options for 160 more. The units will be able to operate in multiple with Class 514.

**Built:** 2010–.
**Builder:** Stadler Altenrhein.
**Wheel Arrangement:** Bo-Bo + 2-2 + 2-2 + 2-2 + 2-2 + Bo-Bo.

**Length over Couplers:** 25.36 + 24.82 + 24.82 + 24.82 + 24.82 + 25.36 m.
**Accommodation:** –/70 + 60/42 + –/96 1T + –/95 1TD + 60/42 + –/70.
**Traction Motors:** 5 x 500 kW. **Total Weight:** 297.6 tonnes.
**Maximum Speed:** 160 km/h.

| | | | |
|---|---|---|---|
| 511 001-0 | 511 014-3 | 511 027-5 | 511 039-0 |
| 511 002-8 | 511 015-0 | 511 028-3 | 511 040-8 |
| 511 003-6 | 511 016-8 | 511 029-1 | 511 041-6 |
| 511 004-4 | 511 017-6 | 511 030-9 | 511 042-4 |
| 511 005-1 | 511 018-4 | 511 031-7 | 511 043-2 |
| 511 006-9 | 511 019-2 | 511 032-5 | 511 044-0 |
| 511 007-7 | 511 020-0 | 511 033-3 | 511 045-7 |
| 511 008-5 | 511 021-8 | 511 034-1 | 511 046-5 |
| 511 009-3 | 511 022-6 | 511 035-8 | 511 047-3 |
| 511 010-1 | 511 023-4 | 511 036-6 | 511 048-1 |
| 511 011-9 | 511 024-2 | 511 037-4 | 511 049-9 |
| 511 012-7 | 511 025-9 | 511 038-2 | 511 050-7 |
| 511 013-5 | 511 026-7 | | |

# CLASS RABDe 514    DTZ    4-CAR DOUBLE-DECK UNIT

Recent air-conditioned double-deck EMUs (known as *Doppelstocktriebzüge* – DTZ – or double-deck EMUs) for the Zürich S-Bahn built by Siemens – the company's first double-deck EMUs. The completion of delivery allowed the withdrawal of all Class 510 "Mirage" 3-car RABDe 12/12 EMUs at the end of 2008. Can operate in multiple with Class 450. Used on S-bahn lines S7, S8 & S15.

**Built:** 2006–2009.
**Builder:** Siemens.
**Wheel Arrangement:** Bo-Bo + 2-2 + 2-2 + Bo-Bo.
**Length over Couplers:** 25 + 25 + 25 + 25 m.
**Accommodation:** –/84 + –/118 (12) + –/112 1T + 74/–.
**Traction Motors:** Eight of 400 kW.    **Weight:** 218 tonnes.
**Maximum Speed:** 140 km/h.

Coaches are numbered:

*Set*
514 0xx     514 1xx-x   514 2xx-x   514 3xx-x   514 4xx-x

| Set 514 0xx | | 514 1xx-x | | 514 2xx-x | | 514 3xx-x | | 514 4xx-x | |
|---|---|---|---|---|---|---|---|---|---|
| 514 001-7 | WT | 514 017-3 | WT | 514 032-2 | WT | 514 047-0 | WT | | |
| 514 002-5 | WT | 514 018-1 | WT | 514 033-0 | WT | 514 048-8 | WT | | |
| 514 003-3 | WT | 514 019-9 | WT | 514 034-8 | WT | 514 049-6 | WT | | |
| 514 004-1 | WT | 514 020-7 | WT | 514 035-5 | WT | 514 050-4 | WT | | |
| 514 005-8 | WT | 514 021-5 | WT | 514 036-3 | WT | 514 051-2 | WT | | |
| 514 006-6 | WT | 514 022-3 | WT | 514 037-1 | WT | 514 052-0 | WT | | |
| 514 007-4 | WT | 514 023-1 | WT | 514 038-9 | WT | 514 053-8 | WT | | |
| 514 008-2 | WT | 514 024-9 | WT | 514 039-7 | WT | 514 054-6 | WT | | |
| 514 009-0 | WT | 514 025-6 | WT | 514 040-5 | WT | 514 055-3 | WT | | |
| 514 010-8 | WT | 514 026-4 | WT | 514 041-3 | WT | 514 056-1 | WT | | |
| 514 011-6 | WT | 514 027-2 | WT | 514 042-1 | WT | 514 057-9 | WT | | |
| 514 012-4 | WT | 514 028-0 | WT | 514 043-9 | WT | 514 058-7 | WT | | |
| 514 013-2 | WT | 514 029-8 | WT | 514 044-7 | WT | 514 059-5 | WT | | |
| 514 014-0 | WT | 514 030-6 | WT | 514 045-4 | WT | 514 060-3 | WT | | |
| 514 015-7 | WT | 514 031-4 | WT | 514 046-2 | WT | 514 061-1 | WT | | |
| 514 016-5 | WT | | | | | | | | |

**Names:**

| | | | | |
|---|---|---|---|---|
| 514 006 | Hans Künzi | | 514 022 | Frauenfeld/Weinfelden |
| 514 012 | Russikon | | 514 027 | Lufingen |
| 514 016 | Schaffhausen | | 514 050 | Züri West |

# CLASS RABe 520    3-SECTION ARTICULATED UNIT

This is a version of Stadler's GTW 2/8 EMU with a body 2.65 m wide as compared with 3.00 m as normally used on standard gauge units) for use on the Luzern–Lenzburg *Seetal* line. The unit has two doors per car - more than the usual units of this type. The units were being fitted with forced air traction motor ventilation in late 2008.

**Built:** 2001/2.
**Builder:** Stadler.
**Wheel Arrangement:** 2-Bo-2-2.
**Length over Couplers:** 53.434 m.
**Accommodation:** 12/32 (1) + –/36 (8) 1T + –/48 (2).
**Traction Motors:** 2 x 260 kW.          **Total Weight:** 78.5 tonnes.
**Maximum Speed:** 115 km/h.

| | | | | | | |
|---|---|---|---|---|---|---|
| 520 000-1 | LZ | Seon | | 520 009-2 | LZ | Schloss Heidegg |
| 520 001-9 | LZ | Beinwil am See | | 520 010-0 | LZ | Staufen |
| 520 002-7 | LZ | Hochdorf | | 520 011-8 | LZ | Ballwil |
| 520 003-5 | LZ | Emmen | | 520 012-6 | LZ | Hallwil |
| 520 004-3 | LZ | Mosen | | 520 013-4 | LZ | Lenzburg |
| 520 005-0 | LZ | Eschenbach | | 520 014-2 | LZ | Gelfingen |
| 520 006-8 | LZ | Hitzkirch | | 520 015-9 | LZ | Ermensee |
| 520 007-6 | LZ | Boniswil | | 520 016-7 | LZ | Birrwil |
| 520 008-4 | LZ | Stadt Luzern | | | | |

# CLASS RABe 521 FLIRT 4-SECTION ARTICULATED UNIT

FLIRT (Flinker Leichter Innovativer Regional Triebzug – faster, lighter innovative regional unit) was the first EMU – low floor, air conditioned and articulated – to be built by Stadler for city suburban services and was ordered by SBB in five versions. Class 521 has been built for Line S3 of the Basel S-Bahn network (Olten–Basel–Porrentruy). Set 521 011 is equipped with 25 kV AC to act as a prototype and demonstrator and is often out of the country.

**Built:** 2005–2007.
**Builder:** Stadler.                        **Accommodation:** 20/141 (19) 1T.
**Traction Motors:** Four of 500 kW.         **Weight:** 120 tonnes.
**Wheel Arrangement:** Bo-2-2-2-Bo.          **Maximum Speed:** 160 km/h.
**Length over Couplers:** 74.078 m.          **Floor Height (entrance):** 570 mm.

d   Fitted with signalling equipment to operate in Germany as SBB runs the Basel Bad–Lörrach–Zell (Wiesenthal) line plus its branch Lörrach–Weil (Rhein) under contract to the Baden-Württemberg Land.

| | | | | | | | |
|---|---|---|---|---|---|---|---|
| 521 001-8 | BS | Regio TriRhena | | 521 016-6 | | BS | Sissach |
| 521 002-6 | BS | Riehen | | 521 017-4 | | BS | |
| 521 003-4 | BS | Weil am Rhein | | 521 018-2 | | BS | |
| 521 004-2 | BS | | | 521 019-0 | | BS | |
| 521 005-9 | BS | | | 521 020-8 | | BS | |
| 521 006-7 | BS | | | 521 021-6 | | BS | |
| 521 007-5 | BS | | | 521 022-4 | d | BS | Lausen |
| 521 008-3 | BS | | | 521 023-2 | d | BS | Ajoie |
| 521 009-1 | BS | | | 521 024-0 | d | BS | |
| 521 010-9 | BS | | | 521 025-7 | d | BS | |
| 521 011-7 | BS | Oberdorf-Weissenstein | | 521 026-5 | d | BS | |
| 521 012-5 | BS | | | 521 027-3 | d | BS | |
| 521 013-3 | BS | Delémont | | 521 028-1 | d | BS | Liestal |
| 521 014-1 | BS | | | 521 029-9 | d | BS | |
| 521 015-8 | BS | | | 521 030-7 | d | BS | République et Canton du Jura |

# CLASS RABe 522 FLIRT 4-SECTION ARTICULATED UNIT

These units are basically the same as Class 521 but are equipped to operate under 25 kV AC in France, so as to operate the Basel–Mulhouse section of the Basel S-Bahn which runs through from Basel to Frick and Laufenburg. Unfortunately, Stadler did not take international crashworthiness standards into account and the units were refused by the French. A further 14 sets to be numbered 522 201–214) were ordered for France in 2008. They will be used not only on the Mulhouse service but also on the Biel/Bienne–Belfort line which will reopen in 2011. The first batch will have their 25 kV AC equipment removed, be renumbered 523 032 to 043 and transferred to Swiss-only services. In 2008, 522 001 and 002 were still with Stadler and were tested in France to validate all the other parts of the unit.

Details as Class 521 except:

**Built:** 2008/9.                          **Systems:** 15 kV AC 16.7 Hz/25 kV AC 50 Hz.

**Original batch.**

| | | | | | | | |
|---|---|---|---|---|---|---|---|
| 522 001-7 | BS | 522 004-1 | BS | 522 007-4 | BS | 522 010-8 | BS |
| 522 002-5 | BS | 522 005-8 | BS | 522 008-2 | BS | 522 011-6 | BS |
| 522 003-3 | BS | 522 006-6 | BS | 522 009-0 | BS | 522 012-4 | BS |

**New batch.**

| | | | |
|---|---|---|---|
| 522 201-3 | 522 205-4 | 522 209-6 | 522 212-0 |
| 522 202-1 | 522 206-2 | 522 210-4 | 522 213-8 |
| 522 203-9 | 522 207-0 | 522 211-2 | 522 214-6 |
| 522 204-7 | 522 208-8 | | |

# CLASS RABe 523 FLIRT 4-SECTION ARTICULATED UNIT

These units are basically the same as Class 521 but are not equipped to operate in Germany. They also have a slightly different livery. The first 12 are used on the Zug S-Bahn network and a further 12 were ordered in 2007. Seven more are to be ordered. 520 013 to 031 (which will have a special leather-seated first class area, will be used on the RER Vaudois network around Lausanne whilst 523 032 to 043 will be used on the Luzern S-Bahn. The first batch of units had to receive new traction motors and couplings from Stadler in late 2008.

**Accommodation:** –/44 + –/44 + –/28 (14) 1T + 20/19.

**New batch.**

| | | | | | | |
|---|---|---|---|---|---|---|
| 523 001-6 | LZ | 523 009-9 | LZ | 523 017-2 | 523 025-5 | |
| 523 002-4 | LZ | 523 010-7 | LZ | 523 018-0 | 523 026-3 | |
| 523 003-2 | LZ | 523 011-5 | LZ | 523 019-8 | 523 027-1 | |
| 523 004-0 | LZ | 523 012-3 | LZ | 523 020-6 | 523 028-9 | |
| 523 005-7 | LZ | 523 013-1 | | 523 021-4 | 523 029-7 | |
| 523 006-5 | LZ | 523 014-9 | | 523 022-2 | 523 030-5 | |
| 523 007-3 | LZ | 523 015-6 | | 523 023-0 | 523 031-3 | |
| 523 008-1 | LZ | 523 016-4 | | 523 024-8 | | |

**Rebuilt sets.**

| | | |
|---|---|---|
| 523 032-1 (522 001-7) | 523 036-2 (522 005-8) | 523 040-4 (522 009-0) |
| 523 033-9 (522 002-5) | 523 037-0 (522 006-6) | 523 041-2 (522 010-8) |
| 523 034-7 (522 003-3) | 523 038-8 (522 007-4) | 523 042-0 (522 011-6) |
| 523 035-4 (522 004-1) | 523 039-6 (522 008-2) | 523 043-8 (522 012-4) |

# CLASS RABe 524   FLIRT   4/6-SECTION ARTICULATED UNIT

These units are very similar to Class 521 but have only one entrance door instead of two in the outer cars and are equipped for operation under 3000 V DC in Italy as well as 15 kV AC in Switzerland. The units are being used on services around Bellinzona and into Italy under the branding TILO, which combines the letters representing Ticino canton and the Lombardia region. These units are known as Class ETR.150 in Italy. It was expected in late 2008 that SBB would order 11 more units which would be 6-car with ETCS for use on services to Milano.

Details as Class 521 except:

**Built:** 2007/8.
**Systems:** 3000 V DC/15 kV AC 16.7 Hz.
**Accommodation:** 28/16 + –/32 (14) 1T + –/48 + –/40 (8).
**Weight:** 133 tonnes.

**Class 524.0 4-Section Units.**

| | | | |
|---|---|---|---|
| 524 001-5 | 524 006-4 | 524 011-4 | 524 016-3 |
| 524 002-3 | 524 007-2 | 524 012-2 | 524 017-1 |
| 524 003-1 | 524 008-0 | 524 013-0 | 524 018-9 |
| 524 004-9 | 524 009-8 | 524 014-8 | 524 019-7 |
| 524 005-6 | 524 010-6 | 524 015-5 | |

**Names:**

| | |
|---|---|
| 524 002-3 Ticino | 524 003-1 Tre Valli |

**Class 524.1 6-Section Units.**

| | | | |
|---|---|---|---|
| 524 101-3 | 524 104-7 | 524 107-0 | 524 110-4 |
| 524 102-1 | 524 105-4 | 524 108-8 | 524 111-2 |
| 524 103-9 | 524 106-2 | 524 109-6 | |

# CLASS RABe 526.6   FLIRT   4-SECTION ARTICULATED UNIT

This version of the FLIRT was delivered to SBB subsidiary SBB Gmbh (Deutschland) for the "Seehas" service operated by the company from Konstanz to Engen in Germany, under contract with the Baden-Württemberg Land. The units are therefore very similar to those used on the Basel S-Bahn but have only one door instead of two in the outer cars and more space for bikes. They are numbered in the Thurbo number series as this was the company which won the originalcontract.

Details as Class 521 except:

**Built:** 2006.
**Accommodation:** 16/32 + –/30 1T + –/32 + –/52.

| | | | |
|---|---|---|---|
| 526 651-5 | 526 654-9 | 526 656-4 | 526 658-0 |
| 526 652-3 | 526 655-6 | 526 657-2 | 526 659-8 |
| 526 653-1 | | | |

# CLASS RBe 540                                                    Bo-Bo

Originally built for longer distance push-pull workings, these motor coaches are still mainly used around Zürich, and most have been formed into 6-coach formations now. Rebuilt with thyristor control and renumbered from RBe 4/4 in 1990–97 with new doors and capability for one person operation. Both ends gangwayed. 540 059 is now used on e.c.s. in Basel.

**Built:** 1963–66.
**Builder–Mechanical Parts:** SIG/SWS.
**Builder–Electrical Parts:** BBC/MFO.
**Traction Motors:** 4 single phase, commutator type of 497 kW fully suspended with BBC spring drive.
**Length over Buffers:** 23.70 m.                     **Weight:** 72 tonnes.
**Accommodation:** –/60 1T.                           **Maximum Speed:** 125 km/h.

All are push-pull & mw fitted (can mw with Re4/4$^{II}$, Re4/4$^{III}$, Re4/4$^{IV}$ & Re6/6 classes).

| | | | | | |
|---|---|---|---|---|---|
| 540 006-4 (1407) | N | 540 030-4 (1432) | N | 540 056-9 (1459) | N |
| 540 007-2 (1408) | N | 540 031-2 (1433) | N | 540 057-7 (1460) | N |
| 540 009-8 (1410) | N | 540 032-0 (1434) | N | 540 058-5 (1461) | N |
| 540 010-6 (1411) | N | 540 034-6 (1436) | N | 540 059-3 (1462) | N |
| 540 011-4 (1412) | N | 540 035-3 (1437) | N | 540 060-1 (1463) | N |
| 540 012-2 (1413) | N | 540 036-1 (1438) | N | 540 061-9 (1464) | N |
| 540 013-0 (1414) | N | 540 037-9 (1439) | N | 540 062-7 (1465) | N |
| 540 014-8 (1415) | N | 540 038-7 (1440) | N | 540 063-5 (1466) | N |
| 540 015-5 (1416) | N | 540 039-5 (1441) | N | 540 064-3 (1467) | N |
| 540 016-3 (1417) | N | 540 040-3 (1442) | N | 540 065-0 (1468) | N |
| 540 017-1 (1418) | N | 540 043-7 (1445) | N | 540 066-8 (1469) | N |
| 540 018-9 (1420) | N | 540 045-2 (1447) | N | 540 067-6 (1470) | N |
| 540 020-5 (1422) | N | 540 046-0 (1448) | N | 540 068-4 (1471) | N |
| 540 021-3 (1423) | N | 540 047-8 (1449) | N | 540 069-2 (1472) | N |
| 540 022-1 (1424) | N | 540 048-6 (1450) | N | 540 071-8 (1474) | N |
| 540 024-7 (1426) | N | 540 050-2 (1452) | N | 540 075-9 (1478) | N |
| 540 027-0 (1429) | N | 540 052-8 (1455) | N | 540 077-5 (1480) | N |
| 540 028-8 (1430) | N | 540 053-6 (1456) | N | 540 078-3 (1481) | N |
| 540 029-6 (1431) | N | 540 055-1 (1458) | N | | |

# CLASS Bem 550                                        2-CAR UNIT

Lightweight articulated railcars for the "Rhône Express Régional" (RER) on the Genève–La Plaine line which is electrified at 1500 V DC. They also work through to Bellegarde in France. They have a diesel engine to allow access under their own power to the depot. Units are very similar to those used by TL Line 1 (formerly TSOL) in Lausanne. The units started to be replaced by Class 524 FLIRT EMUs on the Genève–La Plaine service in September 2009. They will continue to be used on the Genève–Bellegarde service.

**Built:** 1994.
**Builder–Mechanical Parts:** ACMV/Duewag.
**Builder–Electrical Parts:** ABB.
**Diesel engine:** 88 kW.
**Wheel Arrangement:** Bo-2-Bo.
**Length over Couplers:** 15.70 + 15.70 m.
**Maximum Speed:** 100 km/h.

**System:** 1500 V DC.

**Accommodation:** –/38 + –/40.
**Traction Motors:** 2 x 300 kW.
**Weight:** 45 tonnes.

| | | | |
|---|---|---|---|
| 550 000-4 **N** | Mouille-Galand | 550 003-8 **N** | Le Mandement |
| 550 001-2 **N** | La Donzelle | 550 004-6 **N** | La Grôle |
| 550 002-0 **N** | Nant d'Avril | | |

# CLASS RBDe 560                    VARIOUS FORMATIONS

This design for local services is formally known as the "NPZ" – *Neue Pendel Zug* or "new shuttle train" – and informally, though officially, as *Kolibri* or "humming bird". Four prototypes 2100 to 2103 (later 560 000 to 003) were delivered in 1984 with series production beginning in 1987. They are equipped with solid state control. Operating in sets of varying length, with driving and intermediate trailers, they can also multiple with other members of the class. Gangwayed at the non-driving end only. Operate throughout Switzerland. Class 565, 566 and 567, operated by private companies are similar.

Prototypes 560 000 to 003 were withdrawn in 2007/8. 560 001 and 003 were sold to the Montafonerbahn in Austria, 560 000 to OeBB and 560 002 to CJ.

In 2008, the units started to be refurbished, with air conditioning, and receiving one or more new, central low-floor coaches. Refurbished 3-car units for Regionalps are being renumbered in the 560 400 series and other units in the 560 200 series. The first of these are 6-car units for Glarus Sprinter services. The Bombardier "Inova" centre cars are being built in three versions: four Type AB 24/37 1T, 95 Type B with toilet –/61 1T and 41 Type B without toilet –/68.

**Built:** 1987–90, 1993–96§.
**Builder–Mechanical Parts:** FFA/SIG/SWP/ABB (SWG-A/SWG-P/SIG §).
**Builder–Electrical Parts:** BBC (ABB).
**Wheel Arrangement:** Bo-Bo.
**Length over Couplers:** 25.00 m.
**Accommodation:** –/56 [refurbished –/48 (6).
**Non-Standard Livery:** X 2-car unit in a special yellow livery for Vevey-Puidoux-Chexbres "Train des Vignes".

**Traction Motors:** Four of 412.5 kW.
**Weight:** 78 tonnes.
**Maximum Speed:** 140 km/h.

**Notes:**

560 000–083 were renumbered from 2100–83 respectively. 2184/5 are now with PBr as 568 384/5.

**CLASS 560.1**

| | | | |
|---|---|---|---|
| 560 005-1 **N** | Untersiggental | 560 040-8 **N** | Tecknau |
| 560 006-9 **N** | Wünnewil/Flammatt | 560 041-6 **N** | Wassen |
| 560 011-9 **N** | Aesch | 560 042-4 **N** | Saint Gingolph |
| 560 012-7 **N** | Zwingen | 560 043-2 **N** | Pully |
| 560 013-5 **N** | Oberbuchsiten | 560 044-0 **N** | Twann |
| 560 014-3 **N** | Näfels/Mollis | 560 045-7 **N** | Glovelier |
| 560 018-4 **N** | Les Hauts-Geneveys | 560 046-5 **N** | Muralto |
| 560 024-2 **N** | Bauma | 560 047-3 **N** | Les Eplatures |
| 560 025-9 **N** | Düdingen | 560 048-1 **N** | Frick |
| 560 026-7 **N** | Versoix | 560 049-9 **N** | Reinach |
| 560 027-5 **N** | Tenero-Contra | 560 050-7 **N** | La Neuveville |
| 560 028-3 **N** | Saint-Ursanne | 560 051-5 **N** | Egerkingen |
| 560 030-9 **N** | Amriswil | 560 052-3 **N** | Dagmersellen |
| 560 031-7 **N** | Rolle | 560 053-1 **N** | Boncourt/Delle |
| 560 032-5 **N** | Birr/Lupfig | 560 054-9 **N** | Küssnacht am Rigi |
| 560 033-3 **N** | Avenches | 560 055-6 **N** | Saint-Blaise |
| 560 034-1 **N** | Cressier NE | 560 056-4 **N** | Niederwichtrach/Oberwichtrach |
| 560 035-8 **N** | Niederbipp | 560 057-2 **N** | Reconvilier |
| 560 036-6 **N** | Andelfingen | 560 058-0 **N** | Saxon |
| 560 037-4 **N** | Brügg BE | 560 059-8 **N** | Gurtnellen |
| 560 038-2 **N** | Münchenbuchsee | 560 060-6 **N** | Kaiseraugst |
| 560 039-0 **N** | Steinhausen | 560 061-4 **N** | Sins |

| | | | | | | |
|---|---|---|---|---|---|---|
| 560 062-2 | **N** | | Deitingen | 560 104-2 | **N** § | Arth |
| 560 063-0 | **N** | | Giornico | 560 106-7 | **N** § | Egnach |
| 560 064-8 | **N** | | Koblenz | 560 107-5 | **N** § | Hunzenschwil |
| 560 065-5 | **N** | | Laufenburg | 560 108-3 | **N** § | Beinwil am See |
| 560 066-3 | **N** | | Schüpfheim | 560 109-1 | **N** § | Bazenheid |
| 560 067-1 | **N** | | Mägenwil | 560 110-9 | **N** § | Lichtensteig |
| 560 068-9 | **N** | | Gisikon/Root | 560 111-7 | **N** § | Triengen |
| 560 069-7 | **N** | | Sirnach | 560 112-5 | **N** § | Hasle LU |
| 560 070-5 | **N** | | Trubschachen | 560 113-3 | **N** § | Port-Valais |
| 560 071-3 | **N** | | Leuk | 560 114-1 | **N** § | Ouchy |
| 560 072-1 | **N** | | Vernayaz | 560 115-8 | **N** § | Thal/Staad/Altenrhein |
| 560 073-9 | **N** | | Gland | 560 116-6 | **N** § | Matt/Mâche-Bözingen/Boujean |
| 560 074-7 | **N** | | Gorgier/Saint Aubin | 560 117-4 | **N** § | Lucens |
| 560 075-4 | **N** | | Grellingen | 560 118-2 | **N** § | Ittigen |
| 560 076-2 | **N** | | Orbe | 560 119-0 | **N** § | Rubigen |
| 560 077-0 | **N** | | Puidoux/Chexbres | 560 120-8 | **N** § | Netstal |
| 560 078-8 | **N** | | Grand-Saconnex | 560 121-6 | **N** § | Mels |
| 560 079-6 | **N** | | Moudon | 560 122-4 | **N** § | Walenstadt |
| 560 080-4 | **N** | | Palézieux | 560 123-2 | **N** § | Braunwald |
| 560 081-2 | **N** | | Busswil | 560 124-0 | **N** § | Algetshausen-Henau |
| 560 082-0 | **N** | | Schüpfen | 560 125-7 | **N** § | Goldach |
| 560 083-8 | **N** | | Courtelary | 560 126-5 | **N** § | Lengnau |
| 560 100-0 | **N** | § | Luino | 560 129-9 | **N** § | Sonvillier |
| 560 101-8 | **N** | § | Mesocco | 560 130-7 | **N** § | Les Geneveys-sur-Coffrane |
| 560 102-6 | **N** | § | Melide/Bissone/Morcote | 560 131-5 | **X** § | Saint-Saphorin |
| 560 103-4 | **N** | § | Studen | 560 132-3 | **N** § | Noiraigue |

## CLASS 560.2

| | | | |
|---|---|---|---|
| 560 201-6 (560 029-1) | 560 237-0 ( ) | 560 273-5 ( ) |
| 560 202-4 (560 007-7) | 560 238-8 ( ) | 560 274-3 ( ) |
| 560 203-2 ( ) | 560 239-6 ( ) | 560 275-0 ( ) |
| 560 204-0 ( ) | 560 240-4 ( ) | 560 276-8 ( ) |
| 560 205-7 ( ) | 560 241-2 ( ) | 560 277-6 ( ) |
| 560 206-5 ( ) | 560 242-0 ( ) | 560 278-4 ( ) |
| 560 207-3 ( ) | 560 243-8 ( ) | 560 279-2 ( ) |
| 560 208-1 ( ) | 560 244-6 ( ) | 560 280-0 ( ) |
| 560 209-9 ( ) | 560 245-3 ( ) | 560 281-8 ( ) |
| 560 210-7 ( ) | 560 246-1 ( ) | 560 282-6 ( ) |
| 560 211-5 ( ) | 560 247-9 ( ) | 560 283-4 ( ) |
| 560 212-3 ( ) | 560 248-7 ( ) | 560 284-2 ( ) |
| 560 213-1 ( ) | 560 249-5 ( ) | 560 285-9 ( ) |
| 560 214-9 ( ) | 560 250-3 ( ) | 560 286-7 ( ) |
| 560 215-6 ( ) | 560 251-1 ( ) | 560 287-5 ( ) |
| 560 216-4 ( ) | 560 252-9 ( ) | 560 288-3 ( ) |
| 560 217-2 ( ) | 560 253-7 ( ) | 560 289-1 ( ) |
| 560 218-0 ( ) | 560 254-5 ( ) | 560 290-9 ( ) |
| 560 219-8 ( ) | 560 255-2 ( ) | 560 291-7 ( ) |
| 560 220-6 ( ) | 560 256-0 ( ) | 560 292-5 ( ) |
| 560 221-4 ( ) | 560 257-8 ( ) | 560 293-3 ( ) |
| 560 222-2 ( ) | 560 258-6 ( ) | 560 294-1 ( ) |
| 560 223-0 ( ) | 560 259-4 ( ) | 560 295-8 ( ) |
| 560 224-8 ( ) | 560 260-2 ( ) | 560 296-6 ( ) |
| 560 225-5 ( ) | 560 261-0 ( ) | 560 297-4 ( ) |
| 560 226-3 ( ) | 560 262-8 ( ) | 560 298-2 ( ) |
| 560 227-1 ( ) | 560 263-6 ( ) | 560 299-0 ( ) |
| 560 228-9 ( ) | 560 264-4 ( ) | 560 300-6 ( ) |
| 560 229-7 ( ) | 560 265-1 ( ) | 560 301-4 ( ) |
| 560 230-5 ( ) | 560 266-9 ( ) | 560 302-2 ( ) |
| 560 231-3 ( ) | 560 267-7 ( ) | 560 303-0 ( ) |
| 560 232-1 ( ) | 560 268-5 ( ) | 560 304-8 ( ) |
| 560 233-9 ( ) | 560 269-3 ( ) | 560 305-5 ( ) |
| 560 234-7 ( ) | 560 270-1 ( ) | 560 306-3 ( ) |
| 560 235-4 ( ) | 560 271-9 ( ) | 560 307-1 ( ) |
| 560 236-2 ( ) | 560 272-7 ( ) | |

**CLASS 560.4 3-car units for Regionalps services around Martigny**

| | | |
|---|---|---|
| 560 401-2 (560 004-4) | 560 406-1 (560 023-4) | 560 410-3 (560 016-8) |
| 560 402-0 (560 008-5) | 560 407-9 (560 021-8) | 560 411-1 (560 017-6) |
| 560 403-8 (560 019-2) | 560 408-7 (560 022-6) | 560 412-9 (560 010-1) |
| 560 404-6 (560 015-0) | 560 409-5 (560 020-0) | 560 413-7 (560 011-9) |
| 560 405-3 (560 009-3) | | |

# CLASS RBDe 561                                             EMU

Units 561 001 to 005 were Class 560 equipped to operate in Germany on the Basel Bad–Zell line but have since reverted to normal Swiss duties after delivery of Class 521. Details as Class 560 except built in 1994. All are to be refurbished as Class 560 sets.

| | | | | | |
|---|---|---|---|---|---|
| 561 001-9 (560 127-3) | BS | 561 003-5 (560 128-1) | BS | 561 005-0 (560 134-9) | BS |
| 561 002-7 (560 105-9) | BS | 561 004-3 (560 133-1) | BS | 561 006-8 (560 135-6) | BS |

Units 561 171 to 174 were formerly THURBO (ex MThB) 566 631 to 634 and are now part of the normal SBB fleet. They are also equipped for use in Germany, having previously operated the Konstanz–Engen service. They are usually used on the Luzern-Langenthal service.

| | | | | | |
|---|---|---|---|---|---|
| 561 171-0 (566 631-8) | LZ | 561 173-6 (566 633-4) | LZ | 561 174-4 (566 634-2) | LZ |
| 561 172-8 (566 632-6) | LZ | | | | |

# CLASS RBDe 562                                       5-CAR EMUs

Six Class 560 class were rebuilt for dual voltage operation for use on through local services from Basel to Mulhouse in France. They will shortly be replaced by Class 522. Also to be refurbished as Class 560. Details as Class 560 except:

**Rebuilt:** 1997.
**Systems:** 15 kV AC 16.7 Hz/25 kV AC 50 Hz.

| | | | |
|---|---|---|---|
| 562 000-0 (560 136-4) | N | BS | Kleinhüningen |
| 562 001-8 (560 137-2) | N | BS | Basel St. Johann |
| 562 002-6 (560 138-0) | N | BS | Ville de Mulhouse |
| 562 003-4 (560 139-8) | N | BS | |
| 562 004-2 (560 140-6) | N | BS | St-Louis |
| 562 005-9 (560 141-4) | N | BS | |

# 1.4. DIESEL LOCOMOTIVES

## CLASS Bm 4/4 (Bm 840) 　　　　　　　　　　　Bo-Bo

Locos for shunting and trip working on non-electrified tracks.

**Built:** 1960–70.
**Builder–Mechanical Parts:** SLM.　　　**Maximum Tractive Effort:** 216 kN.
**Builder–Electrical Parts:** SAAS.　　　**Wheel Diameter:** 1040 mm.
**Engine:** SLM 12YD20TrTH of 895 kW.　**Weight:** 72 tonnes.
**Transmission:** Electric.　　　　　　　**Length over Buffers:** 12.65 m. (13.15 m†).
**Maximum Speed:** 75 km/h.

§ Fitted with signalling and radio for operation over RBS lines.
Infrastructure locos are used for fire-fighting and rescue trains.
z Equipped with ZUB/ETM signalling.

| | | | | | | | | | | | | | | | | | |
|---|---|---|---|---|---|---|---|---|---|---|---|---|---|---|---|---|---|
| 18403 | **P** | *I* | | BE | 18416 | **P** | *C* | | W | 18429 | **R** | *C* | † | O | 18438 | **R** | *I* | † | GE |

18403 **P** *I*　　BE | 18416 **P** *C*　W | 18429 **R** *C* † O | 18438 **R** *I* † GE
18405 **R** *C*　　S | 18419 **P** *C*　O | 18430 **R** *C* † S | 18439 **R** *I* † LS
18406 **P** *I*　　RW | 18420 **P** *C*　O | 18431 **R** *C* † O | 18440 **R** *I* † BS
18407 **R** *C*　　O | 18422 **R** *C*　O | 18432 **R** *C* *† W | 18441 **R** *I* † W
18408 **R** *C* §　W | 18423 **P** *C*　O | 18433 **R** *C* † O | 18442 **R** *I* † ER
18410 **P** *C*　　W | 18424 **R** *C*　O | 18434 **R** *C* † S | 18443 **R** *I* † BI
18412 **P** *I*　　RE | 18425 **P** *I*　SG | 18435 **R** *C* † S | 18444 **R** *C* † BS
18413 **P** *C*　　W | 18426 **R** *C*　O | 18436 **R** *I* † LS | 18445 **R** *I* † AI
18414 **P** *C* §　W | 18427 **R** *C* †　O | 18437 **R** *I* † GO | 18446 **R** *I* † ER
18415 **P** *P*　　BS | 18428 **P** *C* *†　O |

## CLASS Bm 6/6 (Bm 861) 　　　　　　　　　　　Co-Co

Centre cab diesels used for yard shunting and trip working. Each bonnet contains its own engine and generator set.

**Built:** 1954–61.
**Builder–Mechanical Parts:** SLM.　　　　　**Maximum Tractive Effort:** 334 kN.
**Builder–Electrical Parts:** BBC/SAAS.　　　**Wheel Diameter:** 1040 mm.
**Engine:** Two Sulzer 6LDA25 of 635 kW each.　**Weight:** 106 tonnes.
**Transmission:** Electric.　　　　　　　　　**Length over Buffers:** 17.00 m. (17.56 m*).
**Maximum Speed:** 75 km/h.

18505 **R** *P*　　BR　|

## CLASS Bm 6/6 (Am 863) 　　　　　　　　　　　Co-Co

Heavy shunting locos, built specifically for use in Limmattal yard near Zürich. They have three phase traction motors supplied from a fixed frequency alternator via frequency conversion equipment tested on the Henschel DE 2500 prototype. The engine is the same as that in SNCF's Class BB 67400.

**Built:** 1976.
**Builder–Mechanical Parts:** Thyssen Henschel.　**Maximum Tractive Effort:** 393 kN.
**Builder–Electrical Parts:** BBC.　　　　　　　**Wheel Diameter:** 1260 mm.
**Engine:** SEMT Pielstick 16 PA4 V-185 VG of 1840 kW.
**Transmission:** Electric.　　　　　　　　　　　**Weight:** 111 tonnes.
**Maximum Speed:** 85 km/h.　　　　　　　　　　**Length over Buffers:** 17.40 m.

Infrastructure locos are used in marshalling yards.

18521 **P** *I*　　ZU | 18523 **P** *I*　ZU | 18525 **P** *I*　ZU | 18526 **P** *I*　ZU
18522 **P** *I*　　ZU

# CLASS Em 3/3 (Em 830)                                    C

General purpose shunting locos found throughout the system.

**Built:** 1959* 1962–3.
**Builder–Mechanical Parts:** SLM.
**Builder–Electrical Parts:** BBC/SAAS.
**Engine:** SLM 6VD20TrTH of 450 kW. (SLM 8YD20TrD of 450 kW*).
**Transmission:** Electric.
**Maximum Speed:** 65 km/h.

**Maximum Tractive Effort:** 124 kN (118 kN*).
**Wheel Diameter:** 1040 mm.
**Weight:** 49 tonnes.
**Length over Buffers:** 10.02 m.

| 18807 **R** *C* | O | 18816 **P** *C* | W | 18824 **R** *P* | OL | 18832 **P** *C* | O |
| 18808 **P** *C* | W | 18818 **P** *C* | W | 18825 **P** *C* | W | 18835 **P** *C* | O |
| 18809 **P** *C* | O | 18819 **P** *C* | W | 18827 **P** *C* | O | 18836 **P** *I* | HD |
| 18810 **P** *C* | W | 18820 **P** *C* | W | 18828 **P** *C* | O | 18837 **P** *C* | W |
| 18813 **P** *C* | W | 18821 **R** *C* | O | 18829 **P** *C* | O | 18838 **P** *I* | BU |
| 18814 **P** *C* | W | 18822 **P** *P* | BS | 18830 **P** *C* | O | 18840 **P** *I* | BS |
| 18815 **P** *C* | W | 18823 **P** *P* | BS | 18831 **P** *P* | CH | 18841 **P** *I* | BS |

**Name:** 18824 EMMA.

# CLASS Em 831                                              Co

The prototypes of a new generation of diesel shunters of which no more have been built.

**Built:** 1992.
**Builder–Mechanical Parts:** RACO.
**Builder–Electrical Parts:** ABB.
**Engine:** Cummins of 900 kW.
**Transmission:** Electric.
**Maximum Speed:** 80 km/h.

**Maximum Tractive Effort:** kN.
**Wheel Diameter:** mm.
**Weight:** 60 tonnes.
**Length over Buffers:** 9.84 m.

831 000-5 **R** *C*    O   | 831 001-3 **R** *C*    O   | 831 002-1 **R** *C*    R   |

# CLASS Am 840                                              B-B

SBB Cargo set up a subsidiary in Italy in January 2003 and started services with diesel locomotives. Class Am 840 are standard Vossloh Type G2000-2. The locos also carry a separate number for the benefit of the Italian authorities. The locos work freight from the border stations at Chiasso and Luino to various destinations in northern Italy. SBB Cargo also hired three more G2000s from Angel Trains Cargo when launching its activities (Am 840 901 to 903). These are now with DB Schenker Italia.

**Built:** 2003.
**Builder:** Vossloh. Type G2000-2.
**Engine:** Caterpillar 3516 B-HD of 2240 kW.
**Transmission:** Hydraulic. Voith L620 re U2.
**Maximum Speed:** 120 km/h.

**Wheel Diameter:** 1000 mm.
**Maximum Tractive Effort:** 282 kN.
**Length Over Buffers:** 17.40 m.
**Weight:** 87.3 tonnes.

| SBB No. | Italian No. | Vossloh Works No. | Depot |
|---|---|---|---|
| 840 001-2 | G2000 05 SR | 1001453 | CH |
| 840 002-0 | G2000 06 SR | 1001481 | CH |
| 840 003-8 | G2000 07 SR | 1001482 | CH |

# CLASS Am 841                                              Bo-Bo

A centre-cab diesel locomotive for use on shunting and trip work. Similar on the outside to RENFE Class 311 and SNCF Class BB 60000. Five locos are equipped with ETCS Level 2. Divided between Cargo and Infra activities.

**Built:** 1996–97.
**Builder:** GEC-Alsthom (Type GA-DE 900 AS).
**Engine:** One MTU 8V 396 TB14 of 920 kW at 1800 r.p.m.
**Transmission:** Electric. Four 6 FRA 3055 asynchronous traction motors.
**Maximum Tractive Effort:** 190 kN.       **Weight:** 72 tonnes.
**Wheel Diameter:** 1100 mm.               **Length over Buffers:** 14.12 m.
**Maximum Speed:** 80 km/h.

e Fitted with ETCS.
f Equipped with particle filter.

| | | | | | | | | | | | |
|---|---|---|---|---|---|---|---|---|---|---|---|
| 841 000-3 | R C | W | 841 010-2 | R C | O | 841 020-1 | R C | W | 841 030-0 | R P | O |
| 841 001-1 | R C | W | 841 011-0 | R C | O | 841 021-9 | R C | W | 841 031-8 | R C | O |
| 841 002-9 | R C | W | 841 012-8 | R C | O | 841 022-7 | R I | ef S | 841 032-6 | R I | S |
| 841 003-7 | R C | W | 841 013-6 | R C | W | 841 023-5 | R I | S | 841 033-4 | R I | S |
| 841 004-5 | R C | W | 841 014-4 | R C | W | 841 024-3 | R I | S | 841 034-2 | R I | f S |
| 841 005-2 | R I | ef S | 841 015-1 | R I | S | 841 025-0 | R I | S | 841 035-9 | R I | S |
| 841 006-0 | R I | ef S | 841 016-9 | R I | S | 841 026-8 | R I | S | 841 036-7 | R I | S |
| 841 007-8 | R I | ef S | 841 017-7 | R I | S | 841 027-6 | R I | S | 841 037-5 | R C | W |
| 841 008-6 | R I | S | 841 018-5 | R I | ef S | 841 028-4 | R I | S | 841 038-3 | R C | W |
| 841 009-4 | R I | S | 841 019-3 | R I | S | 841 029-2 | R I | S | 841 039-1 | R I | GE |

# CLASS Am 842                                                        B-B

The first of these locos are MaK Type G1004 BB - a pair of diesel locomotives purchased in 1993/94 from permanent way contractor Sersa. They were formerly known as "Corinne" and "Daniela" respectively – MaK works numbers 1001878 and 1001879. Only 18 of this type were built and these were the last two. A third Sersa G1204 "Bettina" numbered Am 847 953 was sold to a German operator and is now owned by Vossloh and hired out in Germany.

The second batch are similar locos, but are the more recent Vossloh G1000 BB, on hire from Angel Trains Cargo and used in Italy, for which they carry a second number. SBB Cargo also had two Vossloh G1206 locos on hire in 2009 for use in Germany. They are not numbered in the SBB series and are not included here.

**Class 842.00.**

**Built:** 1991.
**Builder:** MaK. Type G 1204.
**Engine:** MTU 12V 396 TC13 of 1120 kW.    **Wheel Diameter:** 1000 mm.
**Transmission:** Hydraulic. Voith L5r4U2.    **Weight:** 80 tonnes.
**Maximum Tractive Effort:** ?    **Length over Buffers:** 12.50 m.
**Maximum Speed:** 90 km/h.
**Class 842.01.**

These locos are used for rolling stock management.

| | | | | | | | |
|---|---|---|---|---|---|---|---|
| 842 000-2 | R I | ZU | Corinne | 842 001-0 | R I | ZU | Daniele |

**Class 842.01.**

As Class 842.00 except:

**Builder:** Vossloh Type G 1000 B.
**Engine:** MTU 8V 4000 R41L of 1100 kW.    **Maximum Tractive Effort:** 259 kN.
**Transmission:** Hydraulic. Voith L4r4.    **Length over Buffers:** 14.13 m.
**Maximum Speed:** 100 km/h.

| SBB No. | Italian No. | Vossloh Works No. | Built | Depot |
|---|---|---|---|---|
| 842 011-9 | D.100.003 SR | 5001736 | 2007 | CH |
| 842 012-7 | D.100.001 SR | 5001612 | 2005 | CH |
| 842 013-5 | D.100.002 SR | 5001613 | 2005 | CH |

# CLASS Am 843                                                        B-B

In July 2002, SBB ordered 59 Class Am 843 diesel-hydraulic locos based on Vossloh's G1700-2 design. This was followed by options taking the total to 73 locos. The locos are split between the Infrastructure and Cargo divisions, the Infra locos being all red and the Cargo locos red and blue. Infra locos originally had the name of the activity in big letters on the bonnet side but this was changed to the SBB logo in 2009. Originally, five locos (843 031–035) were ordered for the Passenger activity but there was a change of heart and these became Cargo's 843 091–095. Infra locos are used for yard shunting and rescue trains whilst Cargo locos work mainly trip freights and some shunting. 843 015 was renumbered from 840 051 in autumn 2005. In May 2008, SBB's Passenger division ordered three more locos to be numbered 843 041 to 043. Two will go to Basel and one to Chiasso.

**Built:** 2003–2005.
**Builder:** Vossloh. Type G 1700-2 BB.
**Engine:** Caterpillar CAT 3512 B of 1500 kW.
**Transmission:** Hydraulic. Voith L5r4zseU2. **Length Over Buffers:** 15.20 m.
**Wheel Diameter:** 1000 mm. **Weight:** 80 tonnes.
**Maximum Tractive Effort:** 250 kN. **Maximum Speed:** 100 km/h.

843 026–28 are equipped with ETCS Level 2 for use on the Rothrist–Mattstetten line.
d equipped to operate in Germany.

| | | | | | | | |
|---|---|---|---|---|---|---|---|
| 843 001-9 **R** / | BS | Muttenz | | 843 015-9 **R** / | ZU | Limmattal |
| 843 002-7 **R** / | BN | Bern | | 843 016-7 **R** / | CH | Chiasso |
| 843 003-5 **R** / | BS | Muttenz | | 843 017-5 **R** / | BU | Buchs |
| 843 004-3 **R** / | BU | Buchs | | 843 018-3 **R** / | BS | Muttenz |
| 843 005-0 **R** / | OL | Olten | | 843 019-1 **R** / | BS | Muttenz |
| 843 006-8 **R** / | CH | Chiasso | | 843 020-9 **R** / | BS | Muttenz |
| 843 007-6 **R** / | CH | Chiasso | | 843 021-7 **R** / | OL | Olten |
| 843 008-4 **R** / | CH | Chiasso | | 843 022-5 **R** / | CH | Chiasso |
| 843 009-2 **R** / | BS | Muttenz | | 843 023-3 **R** / | ZU | Limmattal |
| 843 010-0 **R** / | CH | Chiasso | | 843 024-1 **R** / | RK | Rotkreuz |
| 843 011-8 **R** / | BS | Muttenz | | 843 025-8 **R** / | ZU | Limmattal |
| 843 012-6 **R** / | CH | Chiasso | | 843 026-6 **R** / | BN | Bern |
| 843 013-4 **R** / | BS | Muttenz | | 843 027-4 **R** / | OL | Olten |
| 843 014-2 **R** / | BS | Muttenz | | 843 028-2 **R** / | OL | Olten |

| | | | | | | | | | | |
|---|---|---|---|---|---|---|---|---|---|---|
| 843 041-5 | P | | 843 060-5 **B** *C* | W | 843 072-0 **B** *C* | W | 843 084-5 **B** *C* | O |
| 843 042-3 | P | | 843 061-3 **B** *C* | W | 843 073-8 **B** *C* | W | 843 085-2 **B** *C* | O |
| 843 043-1 | P | | 843 062-1 **B** *C* | O | 843 074-6 **B** *C* | O | 843 086-0 **B** *C* | O |
| 843 050-6 **B** *C* | O | 843 063-9 **B** *C* | O | 843 075-3 **B** *C* | S | 843 087-8 **B** *C* | W |
| 843 052-2 **B** *C* | O | 843 064-7 **B** *C* | W | 843 076-1 **B** *C* | O | 843 088-6 **B** *C* | O |
| 843 053-0 **B** *C* | O | 843 065-4 **B** *C* | W | 843 077-9 **B** *C* | O | 843 089-4 **B** *C* | O |
| 843 054-8 **B** *C* | W | 843 066-2 **B** *C* | W | 843 078-7 **B** *C* | S | 843 090-2 **B** *C* | O |
| 843 055-5 **B** *C* | O | 843 067-0 **B** *C* | O | 843 079-5 **B** *C* | O | 843 091-0 **B** *C* d O |
| 843 056-3 **B** *C* | O | 843 068-8 **B** *C* | O | 843 080-3 **B** *C* | O | 843 092-8 **B** *C* d O |
| 843 057-1 **B** *C* | O | 843 069-6 **B** *C* | O | 843 081-1 **B** *C* | W | 843 093-6 **B** *C* d O |
| 843 058-9 **B** *C* | W | 843 070-4 **B** *C* | O | 843 082-9 **B** *C* | O | 843 094-4 **B** *C* d O |
| 843 059-7 **B** *C* | W | 843 071-2 **B** *C* | W | 843 083-7 **B** *C* | O | 843 095-1 **B** *C* d O |

**Name:** 843 074-6 Uristei.

# CLASS 203     ex-DR TYPE V100     B-B

These are former DR Class 110, then rebuillt as Class 112 then renumbered as Class 202 by DB, on hire to SBB Cargo from Alstom. The numbers given by SBB Cargo correspond to the former DB number rather than the EVN – 203 383 is former DB 202 383, and so on.

**Built:** 1964–1978 for Deutsche Reichsbahn as Class 112.
**Builder:** LEW. Rebuilt by Alstom, Stendal.
**Engine:** Caterpillar CAT 3512 B of 1305 kW.
**Transmission:** Hydraulic. **Length Over Buffers:** 14.24 m.
**Wheel Diameter:** 1000 mm. **Weight:** 72 tonnes.
**Maximum Tractive Effort:** 206 kN. **Maximum Speed:** 100 km/h.

| Loco | Built | Works No. | EVN |
|---|---|---|---|
| 203 383-5 | 1971 | 12892 | 92 80 1203 149-0 D-ALS |
| 203 405-6 | 1971 | 12914 | 92 80 1203 151-6 D-ALS |
| 203 406-4 | 1971 | 12915 | 92 80 1203 153-2 D-ALS |
| 203 558-2 | 1973 | 13876 | 92 80 1203 126-8 D-ALS |
| 203 652-3 | 1974 | 14079 | 92 80 1203 125-0 D-ALS |

▲ SBB 540 021 arrives at Winterthur on 18 April 2006. Most of this class are now used only in the peaks, mainly around Zürich.                                                                          **Brian Denton**

▼ SBB 1500 V DC "light rail" EMU 550 004 is pictured in the bay platform at Genève Cornavin on 20 March 2009 with a service to La Plaine on the line to Bellegarde in France. Class 522 FLIRT EMUs have now taken over this service and Class 550 now work all trains to Bellegarde.     **David Haydock**

▲ SBB "NPZ" EMU 560 141 is the only 2-car set of its class and carries a special livery. The unit works the Montreux–Puidoux-Chexbres "Train des Vignes", the line actually being owned by MOB. The unit is seen leaving Montreux on 14 April 2009. **David Haydock**

▼ SBB is now modernising Class 560 as "Domino" sets. In this view, power car 560 402 and a driving trailer are seen on test at Bettlach on 8 September 2008. **Mario Stefani**

▲ SBB Cargo Class Re 421 locos work deep into Germany on freight but also stand in on passenger trains from Zürich to Lindau. 421 373 is seen at St. Margrethen with a EuroCity service on 18 April 2009. **Matthias Müller**

▼ Class Ae 6/6 (610) are now in decline with many locomotives either withdrawn on stored. All names have been removed. This is 11515 "KREUZLINGEN" at Ems Werk, near Chur, on 24 April 2009. The loco was withdrawn shortly after. **Brian Denton**

▲ 450 112 "Flurlingen" and 450 013 "Niederglatt" stand at Rapperswil on 14 May 2009 with Zürich
S-Bahn services.                                                                    **David Haydock**

▼ SBB 460 081 "Pfänder" is seen at Rivaz with train IR 1723 from Genève Aéroport to Brig on
17 July 2009.                                                                    **Philip Wormald**

▲ SBB Cargo electric loco E 474 016 SR is seen at an open day even at Biasca on 9 September 2007, with Ae 6/6 610 496-2 in the background. **Keith Fender**

▼ SBB Cargo Class 482 locos work deep into Germany. 482 031 is seen here on 9 October 2009 at Bopparder Hamm in the Rhine valley with a northbound intermodal service. **Matthias Muller**

▲ SBB Bm 4/4 18415 is the only one of the class to be used by the Passenger division – for empty stock movements at Basel. This is where it is seen on 21 May 2006.                    **David Haydock**

▼ SBB Am 6/6 18521, used for hump shunting, is seen stabled at the depot next to Limmattal yard on 6 September 2007.                                                                      **Brian Garvin**

▲ SBB diesel Am 841 024 is seen stabled at Palézieux on 20 March 2009, with Tm 234 120 in the background. **David Haydock**

▼ Both SBB and BLS have bought Vossloh G1700 diesel locos in recent years. This is SBB Cargo Am 843 054 with a short freight at Arnex on 15 April 2009. **Mario Stefani**

▲ The first of SBB's new electric shunters, Ee 922 001, is seen on a test run at Onnens on 27 June 2009.                                                                                    **Mario Stefani**

▼ SBB Ee 3/3 electric shunter 16412 sparkles in the sun at Altdorf on 19 April 2006. The different version of Ee 3/3 are all very similar.                                                    **Brian Denton**

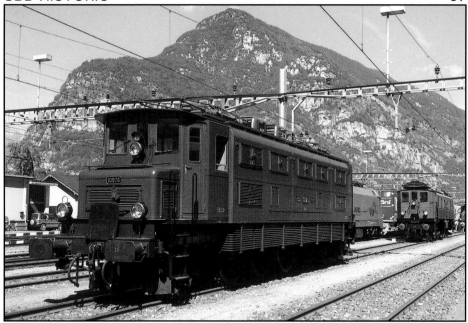

▲ SBB Historic Class Ae 4/7 2-Do-1 electric loco 10976 is seen on show at Biasca on 9 September 2007. In the background is Be 4/6 12320. **Keith Fender**

▼ SBB Historic 2-10-0 C 5/6 2978 is seen at Erstfeld depot on 8 September 2007 being prepared for a special train. **Brian Garvin**

▲ BLS Re 4/4 locos 163 "GRENCHEN", 165 "MOUTIER", 186 "LEISSIGEN" and 177 "ZWEISIMMEN" quadruple-head an intermodal service through Hohtenn station in May 2005. **David Cable**

▼ BLS electric loco 485 019 plus a second member of the class head a RoLa service carrying complete lorries for Novara in Italy through Spiez on 11 June 2009. **Brian Denton**

▲ The first of the new BLS "Lötschberger" EMUs, 535 101, arrives at Zweisimmen on 16 April 2009 with a local service from Spiez. **David Haydock**

▼ BLS EMU 565 742 "St-BLAISE" was one of the first to be equipped with the new "Jumbo" articulated low-floor trailers and finished in the new livery. The unit is seen at Boudry on 16 October 2004 with a Neuchâtel–Gorgier St. Aubin service. **Mario Stefani**

▲ SOB electric loco 456 093 arrives at Romanshorn with the "Voralpern Express" from Luzern on 10 June 2006. The loco has an all-over advertising livery for track contractor Sersa.     **Brian Denton**

▼ THURBO EMUs 526 762-0 (3-car) and 738-0 (2-car) arrive at Rheineck with a train to St. Gallen and Wil on 20 May 2006.     **David Haydock**

▲ MGB HGe 4/4 II loco 106 "St. Gotthard" awaits departure from Brig with a Glacier Express train from Zermatt to St. Moritz on 25 July 2009. On the left is Stadler EMU 2012 with a train to Zermatt.
**David Haydock**

▼ MGB motor luggage van Deh 4/4 I 53 "URSEREN" approaches Göschenen with a train from Andermatt on 15 May 2008. **Philip Wormald**

▲ RhB electro-diesel 802 "Murmultier" and electric railcar ABe 4/4 II 56 "Corviglia" head a St. Moritz–Tirano service at the summit station of Ospizio Bernina (2253 metres a.s.l.) on 19 July 2009. The mountains are sprinkled with the previous day's snow!                          **David Haydock**

▼ RhB still has two "crocodile" electric locos used on charters. Here, Ge 6/6 414 is seen at Filisur with a special on 12 September 2009.                                              **Mario Stefani**

▲ 60-year-old RhB Class Ge 4/4 I are mainly used on the Pontresina to Scuol-Tarasp service. 604 "Calanda" is seen in superb conditions at Bever on 5 February 2008.          **Brian Denton**

▼ RhB locos 161, built in 1911, and 151, built in 1909, both by SIG Alioth, prepare for shunting duties at Poschiavo on 19 July 2009.          **David Haydock**

▲ Zentralbahn electric loco HGe 101 964 "Sachseln" coincidentally passes Sachseln station with a Luzern–Interlaken service on 17 July 2007.                                    **Thierry Leleu**

▼ Zentralbahn EMU 130 008 arrives at Giswil on 17 July 2007. On the right is loco 120 008, now withdrawn.                                                                        **Thierry Leleu**

# 1.5. ELECTRIC SHUNTING LOCOMOTIVES

## CLASS Ee 922

h 5b(uther)    **Bo**

In mid 2009, SBB received the first of 21 new two-axle dual-voltage shunting locomotives from Stadler for shunting passenger stock. These will replace all of the 38 Ee 3/3 and seven Ee 3/3" currently in passenger use around Switzerland. Only the eight Class Ee 934 used in Genève and Chiasso will remain from the old classes.

**Built:** On order 2009/10.
**Systems:** 15 kV AC 16.7 Hz, 25 kV AC 50 Hz.
**Builder:** Stadler.
**Power Rating:** 600 kW.
**Maximum Tractive Effort:** 120 kN.
**Wheel Diameter:**

**Weight:** 44 tonnes.
**Length over Buffers:** 8.80 m.
**Maximum Speed:** 100 km/h; shunting 40 km/h.

| | | | |
|---|---|---|---|
| 922 001-3 | 922 007-0 | 922 013-8 | 922 018-7 |
| 922 002-1 | 922 008-8 | 922 014-6 | 922 019-5 |
| 922 003-9 | 922 009-6 | 922 015-3 | 922 020-3 |
| 922 004-7 | 922 010-4 | 922 016-1 | 922 021-1 |
| 922 005-4 | 922 011-2 | 922 017-9 | 922 022-9 |
| 922 006-2 | 922 012-0 | | |

## CLASS Ee3/3 (CLASS Ee 930)

h 56 (lower)    **C**

This development of the standard electric shunter of the 1930s, which all had a single motored geared to a layshaft and driving through a jack and coupling rods, has a centre cab, and shunter's platforms at both ends.

**Built:** 1932–47.
**Builder–Mechanical Parts:** SLM.
**Builder–Electrical. Parts:** BBC.
**Traction Motors:** 1 single phase frame mounted with jackshaft/side rod drive.
**One Hour Rating:** 428 kW.
**Maximum Tractive Effort:** 88 kN.
**Wheel Diameter:** 1040 mm.

**Weight:** 45 tonnes.
**Length over Buffers:** 9.75 m.
**Maximum Speed:** 40 km/h.

| | | | | | | | | | | | |
|---|---|---|---|---|---|---|---|---|---|---|---|
| 16351 | R | P | ZU | 16375 | R | P | BR | 16390 | R | P | ZU | 16404 | P | C | O |
| 16358 | R | C | O | 16381 | R | P | BR | 16391 | R | C | O | 16406 | P | P | LS |
| 16362 | R | P | RH | 16382 | R | P | LS | 16393 | R | P | BI | 16408 | P | P | ZU |
| 16363 | R | P | ZU | 16383 | P | P | BN | 16396 | R | C | O | 16409 | R | P | LZ |
| 16365 | R | P | RH | 16386 | R | C | W | 16398 | P | P | ZU | 16410 | R | P | LZ |
| 16368 | P | P | BR | 16387 | R | C | W | 16401 | R | C | O | 16411 | P | P | RW |
| 16371 | R | P | BR | 16388 | R | P | SG | 16402 | R | P | RW | 16412 | P | C | O |

## CLASS Ee3/3 (CLASS Ee 930)

**C**

The final development of the Ee3/3.

**Built:** 1951–66.
**Builder–Mechanical Parts:** SLM.
**Builder–Electrical. Parts:** BBC/MFO/SAAS.
**Traction Motors:** 1 single phase frame mounted with jackshaft/side rod drive.
**One Hour Rating:** 502 kW.
**Maximum Tractive Effort:** 118 kN.
**Wheel Diameter:** 1040 mm.

**Weight:** 45 tonnes (44 tonnes*).
**Length over Buffers:** 9.51 m.
**Maximum Speed:** 45 km/h.

| | | | | | | | | | | | | | | | | | | |
|---|---|---|---|---|---|---|---|---|---|---|---|---|---|---|---|---|---|---|
| 16422 | R | I | | LT | 16436 | R | P | | ZU | 16448 | R | P | * | BE | 16455 | R | I | * | LT |
| 16423 | R | C | | W | 16437 | R | P | | ZU | 16450 | R | I | * | RK | 16456 | R | I | * | BI |
| 16425 | R | P | | BN | 16440 | R | P | | BI | 16451 | R | P | * | BN | 16457 | R | C | * | W |
| 16427 | R | P | | CH | 16442 | R | P | * | LZ | 16452 | R | P | * | BN | 16458 | R | P | * | BN |
| 16428 | R | P | | CH | 16445 | P | I | * | OL | 16453 | R | C | * | S | 16459 | P | C | * | O |
| 16430 | P | P | | ZU | 16446 | P | P | * | BR | 16454 | P | C | * | O | 16460 | R | C | * | W |
| 16433 | R | C | | O | 16447 | P | P | * | BE | | | | | | | | | | |

# Ee3/3 II (CLASS Ee 932) C

The dual-voltage version of the Ee 3/3, which can be used under the 25 kV 50 Hz wires in Basel where the SNCF AC electrification extends into the SBB station. 16511–9 were built for SNCF (C 20151–9) for use around Basel, but were sold to the SBB in 1971. All are fitted for work in multiple but this facility is not used any more.

**Built:** 1957–63
**Systems:** 15 kV 16.7 Hz/25kV 50Hz.
**Builder–Mechanical Parts:** SLM.
**Builders–Electrical. Parts:** SAAS.
**Traction Motors:** 1 single phase frame mounted with jackshaft/side rod drive.
**One Hour Rating:** 506 kW.           **Weight:** 52 tonnes.
**Maximum Tractive Effort:** 132 kN.   **Length over Buffers:** 9.42 m.
**Wheel Diameter:** 1040 mm.           **Maximum Speed:** 45 km/h.

All mw fitted.

16512 **R** *P*    BS    | 16513 **R** *P*    BS    | 16515 **R** *P*    BS    | 16517 **R** *P*    BS

# CLASS Ee 934 (Ee3/3 IV) C

The four-voltage version of the Ee 3/3, for use at border stations. It differs from the others in having two DC motors, one geared directly to the centre and one to the end axle, there being no intermediate jackshaft. They are to be found at Genève where the SNCF 1500 V DC system extends into the station, and at Chiasso for use under the FS 3000 V DC wires. The 25 kV AC facility is not used at present.

**Built:** 1962–3.
**Systems:** 1500 V DC/3000 V DC/15 kV AC 16.7 Hz/25 kV AC 50 Hz.
**Builder–Mechanical Parts:** SLM.
**Builder–Electrical. Parts:** SAAS.
**Traction Motors:** 2 DC series wound, axle suspended with side rod drive.
**One Hour Rating:** 390 kW.           **Weight:** 48 tonnes.
**Maximum Tractive Effort:** 118 kN.   **Length over Buffers:** 10.02 m.
**Wheel Diameter:** 1040 mm.           **Maximum Speed:** 60 km/h.

| | | | | | | | |
|---|---|---|---|---|---|---|---|
| 934 551-3 (16551) **R** *P* | GE | 934 555-4 (16555) **R** *P* | GE | 934 559-6 (16559) **R** *P* | CH |
| 934 553-9 (16553) **R** *P* | GE | 934 556-2 (16556) **R** *P* | GE | 934 560-4 (16560) **R** *P* | GE |
| 934 554-7 (16554) **R** *P* | GE | 934 558-8 (16558) **R** *P* | CH | | |

# Ee6/6 II (CLASS Ee 962) C-C

A modern design of heavy yard loco which replaced some converted "Crocodiles" previously used for such work; fitted with 3-phase traction motors supplied through an inverter. They can be radio controlled and are to be found in the yards at Biel/Bienne, Denges (Lausanne), Limmattal (Zürich) and Muttenz (Basel).

**Built:** 1980.
**Builder–Mechanical Parts:** SLM.
**Builder–Electrical. Parts:** BBC.
**Traction Motors:** Six 3-phase axle hung, nose suspended.
**One Hour Rating:** 730 kW.           **Weight:** 111 tonnes.
**Maximum Tractive Effort:** 360 kN.   **Length over Buffers:** 17.40 m.
**Wheel Diameter:** 1260 mm.           **Maximum Speed:** 85 km/h.

| | | | | | | | |
|---|---|---|---|---|---|---|---|
| 16811 **P** / | ZU | 16814 **P** / | LT | 16816 **P** / | LT | 16817 **P** / | LS |
| 16813 **P** / | LT | 16815 **P** / | BI | | | | |

# 1.6. SBB HISTORIC STOCK

Swiss Federal Railways now has a department specifically set up to look after heritage stock. Most of the locomotives shown are in working order and may move around. The "allocations" shown here are the last base known to us. The code VHS means **Verkehrshaus** – the Swiss national transport museum in Luzern.

# 1.6.1. STEAM LOCOMOTIVES

## CLASS D 1/3                                                     4-2-0

**Built:** 1947. Replica to original plans of Kessler (original loco built 1847, works number 78).
**Builder:** SLM (works no. 3937)/HW Zürich.

| | |
|---|---|
| **Power Rating:** 125 kW. | **Boiler Pressure:** 6 bar. |
| **Cylinders:** Two 360 x 560 mm. | **Driving Wheel Diameter:** 1500 mm. |
| **Valve Gear:** Stephenson. | **Length over Buffers:** 11.6 m. |
| **Weight (loco):** 21 tonnes. | **Maximum Speed:** 40 km/h. |
| **(tender):** 14 tonnes. | |

LIMMAT     VHS

## CLASS Ec 3/3                                                    0-6-0T

**Built:** 1936. Ex HWB.

| | |
|---|---|
| **Power Rating:** 240 kW. | **Builder:** SLM. |
| **Cylinders:** Two 400 x 550 mm. | **Boiler Pressure:** 13 bar. |
| **Valve Gear:** | **Driving Wheel Diameter:** 1030 mm. |
| **Weight:** 40.5 tonnes. | **Length over Buffers:** 9.12 m. |
| | **Maximum Speed:** 60 km/h. |

5          ER

## CLASS Ec 2/5                                                    0-4-6T

In 2009, this loco was based at the Verkehrshaus in Luzern.

| | |
|---|---|
| **Built:** 1858. Ex SCB. | **Builder:** Esslingen. |
| **Power Rating:** 296 kW. | **Boiler Pressure:** 10 bar. |
| **Cylinders:** Two 408 x 561 mm. | **Driving Wheel Diameter:** 1375 mm. |
| **Valve Gear:** Stephenson. | **Length over Buffers:** 9.54 m. |
| **Weight:** 47 tonnes. | **Maximum Speed:** 55 km/h. |

28 GENF     VHS

## CLASS Ed 2x2/2          MALLET              0-4-0+0-4-0T

**Built:** 1893. Ex SCB.
**Power Rating:** 515 kW.
**Cylinders:** Four HP: 350 x 610 mm; LP 540 x 610 mm.
**Driving Wheel Diameter:** 1200 mm.
**Length over Buffers:** 10.4 m.
**Maximum Speed:** 55 km/h.
**Builder:** Maffei.
**Boiler Pressure:** 14 bar.
**Valve Gear:** Walschaerts.
**Weight:** 59 tonnes.

196 (SBB 7696)     OeBB depot, Balsthal

## CLASS A 3/5          COMPOUND                 4-6-0

**Built:** 1904.
**Power Rating:** 1000 kW.
**Cylinders:** Four HP: 360 x 660 mm; LP: 570 x 660 mm.
**Driving Wheel Diameter:** 1780 mm.
**Length over Buffers:** 18.60 m.
**Weight (loco):** 67 tonnes.
**(tender):** 43 tonnes.
**Builder:** SLM.
**Boiler Pressure:** 15 bar.
**Valve Gear:** Walschaerts/Joy.
**Maximum Speed:** 100 km/h.

705       Brugg

## CLASS B 3/4                                    2-6-0

**Built:** 1916.
**Power Rating:** 730 kW.
**Cylinders:** Two 540 x 600 mm.
**Valve Gear:** Walschaerts.
**Weight (loco):** 57 tonnes.
      **(tender):** 37 tonnes.

**Builder:** SLM.
**Boiler Pressure:** 12 bar.
**Driving Wheel Diameter:** 1520 mm.
**Length over Buffers:** 16.28 m.
**Maximum Speed:** 75 km/h.

1367      Brugg

## CLASS C 5/6          COMPOUND          2-10-0

**Built:** 1917.
**Power Rating:** 1200 kW.
**Cylinders:** Four. HP: 470 x 640 mm; LP: 690 x 660 mm.
**Driving Wheel Diameter:** 1330 mm.
**Weight (loco):** 86 tonnes.
      **(tender):** 42 tonnes.

**Builder:** SLM.
**Boiler Pressure:** 15 bar.
**Valve Gear:** Walschaerts.
**Length over Buffers:** 19.20 m.
**Maximum Speed:** 65 km/h.

2978      Delémont

## CLASS Eb 3/5                                  2-6-2T

**Built:** 1912
**Power Rating:** 730 kW.
**Cylinders:** Two 520 x 600 mm.
**Valve Gear:** Walschaerts.
**Weight:** 74 tonnes.

**Builder:** SLM
**Boiler Pressure:** 12 bar.
**Driving Wheel Diameter:** 1520 mm.
**Length over Buffers:** 12.74 m.
**Maximum Speed:** 75 km/h.

5819      Brugg

## CLASS Eb 2/4                                  4-4-0T

Built for the Jura-Simplon Bahn (JS) in 1891 (Class A2 no. 35) for Genève–Lausanne shuttle services. Taken over by SBB in 1903 as Class Eb 2/4 number 5469. Looked after by Dampfgruppe OeBB.

**Built:** 1891
**Power Rating:** 407 kW.
**Cylinders:** Two 410 x 612 mm.
**Valve Gear:**
**Weight (loco):** 49 tonnes.

**Builder:** Esslingen
**Boiler Pressure:** 10 bar.
**Driving Wheel Diameter:** 1555 mm.
**Length over Buffers:** 10.2 m.
**Maximum Speed:** 75 km/h.

35 (SBB 5469)      OeBB depot, Balsthal

# 1.6.2. STEAM RAILCAR

## CLASS CZm 1/2                                 A1

**Built:** 1902. Ex UeBB.
**Power Rating:** 74 kW
**Cylinders:** .
**Valve Gear:** .
**Weight:** 23 tonnes.
**Accommodation:** –/38.

**Builder:** Esslingen.
**Boiler Pressure:** .
**Driving Wheel Diameter:** 1000 mm.
**Length over Buffers:** 11.00 m.
**Maximum Speed:** 45 km/h.

31 Brugg

# 1.6.3. ELECTRIC LOCOMOTIVES

## CLASS Re 4/4¹                                           Bo–Bo

A development of the RFe 4/4 motor luggage vans (later De 4/4 of the SOB and SZU), the Re 4/4¹ was introduced to work light expresses. It was the first production design to omit carrying wheels and to have a maximum speed of over 110 km/h. 10001 to 10026 were built in 1946–48, were fitted for push-pull operation and had corridor connections in the front ends. 10027 to 10050 were built 1950/51 and do not have the connections. Various liveries have been carried, the most significant variation being TEE red and cream applied to 10033, 34, 46 and 50 in 1972. Apart from the two SBB Historic locos, others have been preserved and some are still in use with private operators. The German magazine Eisenbahn Kurier owns one loco which operates regularly in Germany.

**Built:** 1946 10001; 1951 10044.
**Builder–Mechanical Parts:** SLM.
**Builder–Electrical Parts:** BBC/MFO/SAAS.
**Traction Motors:** 4 single phase commutator type, fully suspended with BBC spring drive.
**Power Rating:** 1830 kW 10001; 1854 kW 10044.
**Maximum Tractive Effort:** 137 kN.          **Weight:** 57 tonnes.
**Wheel Diameter:** 1040 mm.                   **Length over Buffers:** 14.70  (14.90*) m.
**Maximum Speed:** 125 km/h.

| 10001 | OL | | 10044 * | Rapperswil |

## CLASS Ae 3/5                                           1Co1

The last survivor of a class once totalling 26.

**Built:** 1924.
**Builder–Mechanical Parts:** SLM.
**Builder–Electrical Parts:** SAAS.
**Traction Motors:** 6 single phase commutator type, body mounted with hollow axle drive.
**One Hour Rating:** 1340 kW.                  **Maximum Tractive Effort:** 137 kN.
**Driving Wheel Diameter:** 1610 mm.           **Pony Wheel Diameter:** 950 mm.
**Weight:** 81 tonnes.                         **Length over Buffers:** 12.32 m.
**Maximum Speed:** 90 km/h.

10217  **G**   OL

## CLASS Ae 3/6¹¹¹                                        2Co1

This class is a lengthened version of Class Ae 3/5, with a bogie at one end instead of a pony truck.

**Built:** 1926.
**Builder–Mechanical Parts:** SLM.
**Builder–Electrical Parts:** SAAS.
**Traction Motors:** 6 single phase commutator type, body mounted with hollow axle drive.
**One Hour Rating:** 1340 kW.                  **Maximum Tractive Effort:** 137 kN.
**Driving Wheel Diameter:** 1610 mm.           **Pony Wheel Diameter:** 950 mm.
**Weight:** 89 tonnes.                         **Length over Buffers:** 13.76 m.
**Maximum Speed:** 90 km/h.

10264  **B**   LS

# CLASS Ae3/6 II                                           2C1

This class differs from the other Ae 3/6 series in having rod drive. Once a class of 60 locos, others survive as heating units.

**Built:** 1925.
**Builder–Mechanical Parts:** SLM.
**Builder–Electrical Parts:** MFO.
**Traction Motors:** 2 single phase commutator type, body mounted with jackshaft/side rod drive.
**One Hour Rating:** 1490 kW.     **Maximum Tractive Effort:** 147 kN.
**Driving Wheel Diameter:** 1610 mm.     **Pony Wheel Diameter:** 950 mm.
**Weight:** 98 tonnes.     **Length over Buffers:** 14.15 m.
**Maximum Speed:** 100 km/h.

10439 **B**   OL

# CLASS Ae 3/6 I                                          2Co1

Once a class of 114 units, this was the most successful of several general purpose types introduced in the early years of electrification. The powered wheels are rigid with the frame and are each driven by a motor mounted above in the locomotive body through a "Büchli" drive. This is carried in a circular casing outside the wheels on one side only, completely obscuring them on that side. The class was finally withdrawn from regular service in 1994.

**Built:** 1926/7.
**Builder–Mechanical Parts:** SLM.
**Builder–Electrical Parts:** BBC 10664, MFO 10700.
**Traction Motors:** 3 single phase commutator type, frame mounted with BBC Büchli flexible drive.
**One Hour Rating:** 1560 kW.     **Maximum Tractive Effort:** 147 kN.
**Driving Wheel Diameter:** 1610 mm.     **Pony Wheel Diameter:** 950 mm.
**Weight:** 95.5 t .     **Length over Buffers:** 14.70 m.
**Maximum Speed:** 110 km/h.

10664 **G**   Rapperswil     | 10700 **B**   OL |

# CLASS Ae 4/7                                            2Do1

An enlargement of the Ae 3/6I class, this was for many years the most numerous type in Switzerland until exceeded by the Re 4/4 II, and formed the mainstay of SBB main line passenger power well into the 1960s. The class was finally withdrawn from regular service in 1996, the survivors being retained as museum locos. In 2007, two locos owned by Classic Rail returned to service with rail4chem but the hire ended in 2008. 10949 also belongs to SBB but is on long term loan to Bahnpark in Augsburg, Germany.

**Built:** 1927 and 1931 respectively.
**Builder–Mechanical Parts:** SLM.
**Builder–Electrical Parts:** BBC 10905, MFO 10976.
**Traction Motors:** 4 single phase commutator type, frame mounted with BBC Büchli flexible drive.
**One Hour Rating:** 2300 kW.     **Maximum Tractive Effort:** 196 kN.
**Driving Wheel Diameter:** 1610 mm.     **Pony Wheel Diameter:** 950 mm.
**Weight:** 118 t 10905, 123 t 10976.     **Length over Buffers:** 16.76 m; 10976 17.1 m..
**Maximum Speed:** 100 km/h.

10905 **G**   RS     | 10976 **G**   LS

# CLASS Ae 6/6                                            Co-Co

Built for general use on the Gotthard and Simplon lines, this class has been displaced to other routes, being used entirely on freight work. Most locos are still in service with SBB Cargo as Class 610. 11401/2 were pre-series locos with detailed differences and so have been withdrawn.

**Built:** 1953.
**Builder–Mechanical Parts:** SLM.
**Builder–Electrical Parts:** BBC/MFO.
**Traction Motors:** 6 single phase commutator type, fully suspended with BBC spring drive.
**One Hour Rating:** 4300 kW.     **Maximum Tractive Effort:** 324 kN.
**Driving Wheel Diameter:** 1260 mm.     **Weight:** 124 tonnes.
**Length over Buffers:** 18.40 m.     **Maximum Speed:** 125 km/h.

11402 **G**   ER     URI

# CLASS Ae 8/14                        1AA1AA1 + 1AA1AA1

This loco is effectively two Ae 4/7s permanently coupled with the wheels and electrical equipment rearranged. Regenerative braking is fitted. It was the first of three high power, twin units built for the Gotthard route between 1931 and 1940; experience showed smaller, single units to be more practical.

**Built:** 1931.
**Builder–Mechanical Parts:** SLM.
**Builder–Electrical Parts:** BBC.
**Traction Motors:** 8 single phase commutator type, frame mounted with BBC Büchli flexible drive.
**One Hour Rating:** 4650 kW.          **Maximum Tractive Effort:** 490 kN.
**Driving Wheel Diameter:** 1610 mm.   **Pony Wheel Diameter:** 950 mm.
**Weight:** 240 tonnes.                **Length over Buffers:** 34.00 m.
**Maximum Speed:** 100 km/h.

11801 **G** ER

# CLASS Be 4/6                         1B–B1

One of a class of 40 built for passenger use when the Gotthard line was electrified. Each bogie carries two motors geared to a single layshaft connected to the driving wheels by coupling rods. 12332 and 12339 are also preserved.

**Built:** 1911.
**Builder–Mechanical Parts:** SLM.
**Builder–Electrical Parts:** BBC.
**Traction Motors:** 4 single phase commutator type, frame mounted with jackshaft/side rod drive.
**One Hour Rating:** 1520 kW.
**Maximum Tractive Effort:** 177 kN.   **Driving Wheel Diameter:** 1530 mm.
**Pony Wheel Diameter:** 950 mm.       **Weight:** 110 tonnes.
**Length over Buffers:** 16.56 m.      **Maximum Speed:** 100 km/h.

12320 **B** WT

# CLASS Be 4/7                         1Bo1Bo1

The only survivor of a class of six locos, a design from the early years of electrification which never went into series production.

**Built:** 1922.
**Builder–Mechanical Parts:** SLM.
**Builder–Electrical Parts:** MFO.
**Traction Motors:** 8 single phase commutator type, body mounted with hollow axle drive.
**One Hour Rating:** 1790 kW.          **Maximum Tractive Effort:** 196 kN.
**Driving Wheel Diameter:** 1610 mm.   **Pony Wheel Diameter:** 950 mm.
**Weight:** 111 tonnes.                **Length over Buffers:** 16.30 m.
**Maximum Speed:** 80 km/h.

12504 **B** ER

# CLASS Ce 6/8 <sup>II</sup>          1C–C1

The "Crocodile" configuration arose from the need to build a locomotive with high power, adequate adhesion weight and the ability to negotiate tight curves. Two motors in each frame are geared to a single shaft connected to the driving wheels by coupling rods. This loco was modernised and uprated in 1947, being reclassified Be 6/8$^{II}$ and renumbered 13253. It reverted to its original classification and number on becoming a museum loco. The specification is from rebuilding. Four others are preserved including 14270 plinthed at Erstfeld depot.

**Built:** 1919.
**Builder–Mechanical Parts:** SLM.
**Builder–Electrical Parts:** MFO.
**Traction Motors:** 4 single phase commutator type, bogie mounted with jackshaft/side rod drive.
**One Hour Rating:** 2688 kW.          **Maximum Tractive Effort:** 294 kN.
**Driving Wheel Diameter:** 1350 mm.   **Pony Wheel Diameter:** 950 mm.
**Weight:** 126 tonnes.                **Length over Buffers:** 19.46 m.
**Maximum Speed:** 65 km/h.

14253 **B** ER

# CLASS Ce 6/8 III                                    1C–C1

This loco represents the second series of 18 "Crocodiles". Renumbered 13305 in 1956, it also reverted to its original number on becoming a museum loco. Loco 13302 is also preserved.

**Built:** 1926.
**Builder–Mechanical Parts:** SLM.
**Builder–Electrical Parts:** MFO.
**Traction Motors:** 4 single phase commutator type, bogie mounted with jackshaft/side rod drive.
**One Hour Rating:** 1820 kW.                **Maximum Tractive Effort:** 294 kN.
**Driving Wheel Diameter:** 1350 mm.         **Pony Wheel Diameter:** 950 mm.
**Weight:** 131 tonnes.                       **Length over Buffers:** 20.06 m.
**Maximum Speed:** 65 km/h.

14305  **G**   OL |

# 1.6.4. ELECTRIC RAILCARS

## CLASS RAe 2/4   "ROTER   PFEIL"   SINGLE RAILCAR

One of a number of lightweight, single units built during the 1930s, known as "Red Arrows" (Roter Pfeil) because of their livery. 1001 and 1002 were pre-series and 1003–1007 series units built 1936–38. When built this unit was numbered CLe 2/4 201 and the others 202 to 207. They were then renumbered 601 to 607 then 1001 to 1007 (602 and 606 exchanged numbers in 1954). In 1952, 601 was involved in a collision after which it was rebuilt with a longer chassis and new bogies. 203 is a static exhibit at the Verkehrshaus. 1001 is normally used on charter work.

**Built:** 1935.
**Builder–Mechanical Parts:** SLM.
**Builder–Electrical Parts:** BBC/MFO/SAAS.
**Traction Motors:** 2 single phase commutator type, fully suspended with BBC spring drive.
**One Hour Rating:** 400 kW.                 **Maximum Tractive Effort:** 25 kN.
**Driving Wheel Diameter:** 900 mm.          **Weight:** 41 tonnes.
**Length over Buffers:** 25.20 m.            **Maximum Speed:** 100 km/h.
**Wheel Arrangement:** 2–Bo.                 **Accommodation:** 60/– 1T.

1001   **R**   OL

## CLASS RAe                                    5-CAR UNIT

These four-voltage six-car units were built for use on international TEE trains, and at one time could be seen as far afield as Brussels, Paris and Genova. They were later refurbished for use on EuroCity services from Zürich, Genève & Lausanne to Milano. This resulted in the installation of second class seats (meaning reclassification as RABe) in these once first class only units which are unusual in having separate toilet facilities for ladies and gentlemen. Sets 1051–4 were built as 5-car units, and lengthened to six cars in 1967 when the fifth unit was delivered.

**Built:** 1961.
**Builder–Mechanical Parts:** SIG.
**Builder–Electrical Parts:** MFO.
**Traction Motors:** 4 single phase commutator type, fully suspended with BBC spring drive.
**One Hour Rating:** 2345 kW.                **Maximum Tractive Effort:** 157 kN.
**Wheel Arrangement:** 2–2 + 2–2 + A1A–A1A + 2–2 + 2–2 + 2–2.
**Accommodation:** 42/– 2T + 42/– 2T + baggage/kitchen + 39/- 15R + 42/- 2T + 42/- 2T.
**Driving Wheel Diameter:** 1110 mm.         **Weight:** 296 tonnes.
**Length over Buffers:** 149.76 m.           **Maximum Speed:** 160 km/h.
**System:** 1500 V DC, 3000 V DC, 15 kV AC 16.7 Hz/25 kV AC 50 Hz.

1053     BS

# CLASS BDe 4/4                    SINGLE UNIT

These railcars, bearing a distinct resemblance to Re 4/4[1] locos, were used on local and branch line services in the north and west of the country.

**Built:** 1954/5.
**Builder–Mechanical Parts:** SLM/SWP.
**Builder–Electrical Parts:** BBC/MFO/SIG.
**Traction Motors:** 4 single phase commutator type, axle suspended.
**One Hour Rating:** 1195 kW.               **Maximum Tractive Effort:** 98 kN.
**Wheel Diameter:** 940 mm.                **Weight:** 57 tonnes.
**Length over Buffers:** 22.70 m.          **Maximum Speed:** 110 km/h.
**Wheel Arrangement:** Bo–Bo.              **Accommodation:** –/40 1T.

Rheostatic brake and push-pull fitted.

1643   **G**   WT                    | 1646 **G**   ER

# CLASS De 4/4             MOTOR LUGGAGE VAN

Once a class of 25 motor luggage vans originally built for use on local services. Eleven (1661–71) were rebuilt with new bodies in 1966–71 and used for many years on the Seetalbahn and Pont Brassus line, but have now been withdrawn. The last survivor is in unrebuilt condition.

**Built:** 1928.
**Builder–Mechanical Parts:** SIG/SWS.
**Builder–Electrical Parts:** MFO.
**Traction Motors:** 4 single phase commutator type, axle suspended.
**One Hour Rating:** 820 kW.                **Maximum Tractive Effort:** 86 kN.
**Wheel Diameter:** 1040 mm.               **Weight:** 59 tonnes.
**Length over Buffers:** 15.20 m.          **Maximum Speed:** 85 km/h.
**Wheel Arrangement:** Bo–Bo.

1679   **G**   ?

# 1.6.5. DIESEL LOCOMOTIVE
## CLASS Bm 4/4 [II]                          Bo–Bo

The survivor of pair of elderly diesels, originally Am 4/4 1001 and 1002, which had a varied life, being moved around as electrification progressed. Withdrawn in 1990.

**Built:** 1939.
**Builder–Mechanical Parts:** SLM.            **Engine:** Sulzer 8-cylinder of 820 kW.
**Builder–Electrical Parts:** BBC.            **Transmission:** Electric.
**Maximum Tractive Effort:** 112 kN.          **Wheel Diameter:** 1040 mm.
**Weight:** 66 tonnes.                        **Length over Buffers:** 14.90 m.
**Maximum Speed:** 75 km/h.

18451   **G**   OL

# 2. INDEPENDENT STANDARD GAUGE MAIN LINE OPERATORS

## 2.1. BLS LÖTSCHBERGBAHN                    BLS

The BLS Group of railways is second only in route mileage to the metre gauge RhB among Swiss private railways. The Lötschberg Pass forms part of the Basel–Bern–Milano main line, and extensive joint through working occurs with the SBB. In 2007, a partially completed base tunnel opened on this route, considerably accelerating long-distance passenger trains. The base tunnel is equipped with ETCS Level 2 cab signalling and all locos used on long-distance services have therefore been equipped.

Since the last edition of this book, very major changes have affected BLS. The former subsidiaries Bern Lötschberg Simplon (BLS), Bern Neuenburg (BN), Gürbetal Bern Schwarzenburg (GBS), Moutier–Lengnau Bahn (MLB) and Spiez Erlenbach Zweisimmen (SEZ) have been integrated into the whole and the company has been renamed BLS Lötschbergbahn. The "new" BLS adopted a livery of light grey, highlighted in apple green and dark blue. At the same time the company was divided into passenger, cargo and infrastructure subsidiaries.

BLS Cargo is now owned to the tune of 45% by Deutsche Bahn and cooperation is significant. BLS Cargo Class 485 locos operate through to Mannheim in Germany and DB Schenker Class 185 operate from Basel to Domodossola over the BLS main line. Thanks to open access, BLS Cargo and DB Schenker also operate over the Gotthard route to Chiasso as well as across the rest of Switzerland.

Another major change was a "swap" of responsibility for certain services between BLS and SBB. The latter has taken over long-distance passenger trains and wagonload freight in exchange for BLS running the entire standard gauge part of the Bern S-Bahn. BLS now operates no express passengers services, being limited to regional and S-Bahn services.

BLS has also absorbed Regionalverkehr Mittelland (RM, itself the merger of EBT, SMB and VHB) in which the Bern canton was also majority shareholder. The freight section of RM became Crossrail.

**Routes:**

* Thun–Spiez–Kandersteg–Brig (73.8 km)
* Wengi–Raron (Lötschberg base tunnel) (34.6 km)
* Bern–Neuchâtel (42.9 km)
* Bern–Schwarzenburg (20.9)
* Bern–Belp–Thun (34.5 km)
* Lengnau–Moutier (13.0 km)
* Spiez–Interlaken Ost (28.0 km)
* Spiez–Zweisimmen (34.9 km).

**Ex RM network:**

* Moutier–Solothurn (22.1 km)
* Solothurn–Burgdorf–Hasle-Rüegsau–Ramsei–Obermatt (39.5 km)
* Hasle-Rüegsau–Konolfingen–Thun (34.5 km)
* Ramsei–Sumiswald-Grünen (4.6 km)
* Langenthal–Huttwil (14.1 km)
* Huttwil–Wohlhusen (25.2 km).

**Works:** Bönigen (Interlaken), Spiez, Oberburg (EBT).
**Depots:** Bern Holligen, Brig, Schwarzenburg, Erlenbach, Zweisimmen, Huttwil (ex VHB).

All motive power is, in principal, allocated to Spiez, the works and principal depot.

**Liveries:**

The standard livery is now grey with apple green front ends and blue highlights. All stock is in this livery unless indicated otherwise.

| | | | |
|---|---|---|---|
| A | Advertising livery. | N | Brown. |
| B | Dark blue. | O | Orange. |
| G | SBB dark green. | R | Red (mainly former RM stock) |

# 2.1.1. ELECTRIC LOCOMOTIVES

## CLASS Re 420        Bo–Bo

These locos were obtained from SBB as part of the deal when work was divided between the two companies. They are used on push-pull passenger services from Bern to Neuchâtel and Luzern with ex SBB Mark III stock. For details, see SBB Class 420. All locos have single arm pantographs except those marked.

d diamond pantographs.

| | | |
|---|---|---|
| 420 501-9 (11110) | 420 505-0 (11137) **G** | 420 509-2 (11103) |
| 420 502-7 (11117)   d | 420 506-8 (11142) | 420 510-0 (11104)   d |
| 420 503-5 (11119) | 420 507-6 (11107) | 420 511-8 (11105) **G** d |
| 420 504-3 (11123) | 420 508-4 (11102) **G** d | 420 512-6 (11106) |

## CLASS Re 4/4 (Re 425)        Bo–Bo

The standard BLS electric loco, found everywhere on all types of work. 161–165 were Ae 4/4 II 261–265 until 1969. All are with BLS Cargo except 191–195 which are used on the Spiez–Zweisimmen service, although most of this work will be lost with the arrival of Class 535 EMUs.

**Built:** 1964/5 161/2; 1967 163–165; 1970 166–173; 1972 174–189; 1982/83 190–195.
**Builder–Mechanical Parts:** SLM.                    *p, 58*
**Builder–Electrical Parts:** BBC.
**Traction Motors:** Four DC type, fully suspended with BBC spring drive.
**One Hour Rating:** 4980 kW.       **Maximum Tractive Effort:** 314 kN.
**Wheel Diameter:** 1250 mm.      **Weight:** 80 tonnes.
**Length over Buffers:** 15.47 (15.10 m *).      **Maximum Speed:** 140 km/h.
**Full Numbers:** Re 425.161–195.

All locos multiple fitted.
e   Equipped with ETCS Level 2 for Lötschberg base tunnel.
p   Push-pull and door control equipped.

| | | | | | | | |
|---|---|---|---|---|---|---|---|
| 161 | **N** * | | DOMODOSSOLA | 179 | **N** | e | STADT BERN |
| 162 | **N** * | | COURT | 180 | **N** | e | VILLE DE NEUCHÂTEL |
| 163 | **N** * | | GRENCHEN | 181 | **N** | e | INTERLAKEN |
| 164 | **N** * | | LENGNAU | 182 | **N** | e | KANDERGRUND |
| 165 | **N** * | | MOUTIER | 183 | **N** | e | KANDERSTEG |
| 166 | **N** * | | AESCHI | 184 | **N** | e | KRATTIGEN |
| 167 | **N** * | | AUSSERBERG | 185 | **N** | e | LALDEN |
| 168 | **N** * | | BALTSCHIEDER | 186 | **N** | e | LEISSIGEN |
| 169 | **N** * | | BÖNIGEN | 187 (U) | **N** | | MUND |
| 170 | **N** * | e | BRIG-GLIS | 188 | **N** | e | NATERS |
| 171 | **N** * | e | DÄRLIGEN | 189 | **N** | e | NIEDERGESTELN |
| 172 | **N** * | e | EGGERBERG | 190 | **N** | e | RARON |
| 173 | **N** * | e | LÖTSCHENTAL | 191 | **N** | p | REICHENBACH |
| 174 | **N** | e | FRUTIGEN | 192 | **N** | p | SPIEZ |
| 175 | **N** | e | GAMPEL | 193 | **N** | p | STEG |
| 176 | **N** | e | HOHTENN | 194 | **N** | p | THUN |
| 177 | **N** | e | ZWEISIMMEN | 195 | **N** | p | UNTERSEEN |
| 178 | **N** | e | SCHWARZENBURG | | | | |

## CLASS Re 456        Bo–Bo

BLS owns electric locos Re 456 142 and 143, acquired from Regionalverkehr Mittelland, but has never used them. They are on long-term hire to SOB. See SOB for details.

## CLASS Re 465        Bo–Bo

General purpose locos based on the SBB 460 class. They are now used on a few passenger services but are mainly used on Basel–Domodossola freights, especially RoLa services carrying complete lorries.

**Built:** 1994–7.
**Builder–Mechanical Parts:** SLM.
**Builder–Electrical Parts:** ABB (001–8), ADtranz (009–18).

**Traction Motors:** 4 3-phase fully suspended.
**One Hour Rating:** 7000 kW.                    **Maximum Tractive Effort:** 320 kN.
**Wheel Diameter:** 1100 mm.                     **Weight:** 82 tonnes.
**Length over Buffers:** 18.50 m.                **Maximum Speed:** 230 km/h.

All locos are push-pull & multiple fitted (can work with BLS Re 4/4, plus SBB Re 460, Re 4/4 II, Re 4/4 III, Re 6/6). All are equipped with ETCS Level 2. EVNs are 91 85 4465 001-6 upwards.

| | | | | | |
|---|---|---|---|---|---|
| 465 001-6 | B | Simplon / Sempione | 465 010-7 | B | Mont Vully |
| 465 002-4 | B | Gornergrat | 465 011-5 | B | Wisenberg |
| 465 003-2 | B | 3454 m JUNGFRAUJOCH | 465 012-3 | B | Eurotunnel |
| | | TOP OF EUROPE | 465 013-1 | B | Stockhorn |
| 465 004-0 | B | Saas Fee / Mittelallalin | 465 014-9 | B | Spalenberg |
| 465 005-7 | B | Niesen | 465 015-6 | B | Vue-des-Alpes |
| 465 006-5 | B | Lauchernalp-Lötschental | 465 016-4 | B | Centovalli |
| 465 007-3 | B | Schilthorn / Piz Gloria | 465 017-2 | B | Schrattenflue |
| 465 008-1 | B | Niederhorn / Beatenberg | 465 018-0 | B | Brienz Rothorn Bahn |
| 465 009-9 | B | Napf | | | |

# CLASS Re 485            TRAXX                        Bo-Bo

These are Bombardier TRAXX F140 AC locomotives which are identical to Railion Class 185 with which they interwork, and operate in multiple. These were the first locos in the new BLS livery of grey and apple green. The locos haul freight from Basel to the Italian border over both the Lötschberg and Gotthard routes and as far north as Mannheim in Germany. They also work over several other routes in Switzerland in open access mode. All are equipped with ETCS Level 2. BLS Cargo has hired additional locos of this type – numbered Class 185 – from Angel Trains Cargo but with the delivery of Class 486 returned the last ones in mid 2009.

**Built:** 2003/4.
**Systems:** 15 kV AC 16.7 Hz; 25 kV AC 50 Hz.
**Builder:** Bombardier Transportation, Kassel.
**Maximum Rating:** 5600 kW.
**Weight:** 84 tonnes.                            **Length over Buffers:** 18.90 m.
**Wheel Diameter:** 1250 mm.                      **Maximum Speed:** 140 km/h.
**Maximum Tractive Effort:** 300 kN.             **Electric Brake:** Regenerative.
**Multiple Working:** Within class and with Class Re 486.

**EVN Numbers:** 91 85 4485 001 to 4485 020 CH-BLSC

| | | | |
|---|---|---|---|
| 485 001-2 | 485 006-1 | 485 011-1 | 485 016-0 |
| 485 002-0 | 485 007-9 | 485 012-9 | 485 017-8 |
| 485 003-8 | 485 008-7 | 485 013-7 | 485 018-6 |
| 485 004-6 | 485 009-5 | 485 014-5 | 485 019-4 |
| 485 005-3 | 485 010-3 | 485 015-2 | 485 020-2 |

**Name:** 485 001-2 Haltingen.

# CLASS Re 486            TRAXX            Bo-Bo

In 2007 BLS Cargo ordered ten TRAXX MS multi-voltage electric locos to be numbered 486 501 to 510. Locos carry the last three figures on their front ends. They are the DACHI version, equipped to operate in Germany, Austria, Switzerland and Italy and have the relevant national signalling systems plus ETCS Level 2. 486 501 was delivered in autumn 2008 and all will be in service by the end of 2009. Locos carry numbers 486 501 upwards on the front end as well as 501 upwards in large blue numbers, inviting confusion with Class 420.

Details as Class Re 485 except:

**Systems:** 3000 V DC; 15 kV AC 16.7 Hz.
**Weight:** 85 tonnes.
**Multiple Working:** Within class and with Class Re 485.

| | | | |
|---|---|---|---|
| 486 501-0 | 486 504-4 | 486 507-7 | 486 509-3 |
| 486 502-8 | 486 505-1 | 486 508-5 | 486 510-1 |
| 486 503-6 | 486 506-9 | | |

# 2.1.2. ELECTRIC RAILCARS

## CLASS RABe 525  "NINA"  3- or 4-CAR ARTICULATED EMU

Articulated EMUs with a 80% low floor for the Bern S-Bahn, Class 525 are known as "NINA" meaning *Niederflür NAhverkehr* – low-floor local services. The first batch of eight work Line S5 Bern–Neuchâtel whilst the 18 in the second batch were ordered to take over Lines S1 and S3 from SBB Class 560 EMUs when BLS took over the whole Bern S-Bahn. The first batch was supplied without toilets but retrofitted in 2002. The names are mainly rivers, lakes and streams on Bern S-Bahn lines. 4-car sets work Bern S-Bahn Line 1. 3-car sets work S5 and S44. 525 037 and 038 are former TRN sets 527 321 and 322.

**Built:** 1998/9 001–008: 2003–6 009–036.
**Builder–Mechanical Parts:** Vevey/Talbot 001–008; Bombardier 009–036
**Builder–Electrical Parts:** Traxis 001–008; Alstom 009–036

| | |
|---|---|
| **Wheel Arrangement:** Bo-2-2-Bo. | **Continuous Rating:** 1000 kW. |
| **Maximum Tractive Effort:** | **Driving Wheel Diameter:** 750 mm. |
| **Total Weight:** 78 tonnes. | **Length Overall:** 47.74 m. |
| **Maximum Speed:** 140 km/h. | |

**Accommodation:** 3-car 16/32 + –/54 + –/46 1T.
4-car 16/32 + –/54 + –/54 + 16/32

525 015 to 027 are 4-car, the others 3-car. Units carry numbers NINA 01 to 36 on their front ends.

| | | | | |
|---|---|---|---|---|
| 525 001-4 | Thielle/Zihl | 525 020-4 | | Scherlibach |
| 525 002-2 | Schwarzwasser | 525 021-2 | | Worble |
| 525 003-0 | Emme | 525 022-0 | | |
| 525 004-8 | La Broye | 525 023-8 | | |
| 525 005-5 | Aare | 525 024-6 | | |
| 525 006-3 | Gürbe | 525 025-3 | | |
| 525 007-1 | Gäbelbach | 525 026-1 | | Chräbsbach |
| 525 008-9 | La Sarine/Saane | 525 027-9 | | Glütschbach |
| 525 009-7 | Schwarzsee | 525 028-7 | | La Bibera/Bibere |
| 525 010-5 | Gerzensee | 525 029-5 | | |
| 525 011-3 | | 525 030-3 | | |
| 525 012-1 | | 525 031-1 | | |
| 525 013-9 | | 525 032-9 | | |
| 525 014-7 | Wohlensee | 525 033-7 | | Wankdorf |
| 525 015-4 | | 525 034-6 | | |
| 525 016-2 | | 525 035-2 | | |
| 525 017-0 | | 525 036-0 | A | |
| 525 018-8 | Thunersee | 525 037-8 | | |
| 525 019-6 | | 525 038-6 | | Anton |

## CLASS RABe 526      GTW      2- AND 3-CAR EMUs

These units were originally ordered by RM and are still used on former RM lines around Solothurn and Kerzers. 526 260–265 are 2-car sets but are due to be extended to 3-car by December 2009. See Thurbo Class 526 for technical details except:

**Accommodation:** 15/38 (4) + –/56 (4) + –/43 (2) 1T.

| | | | | | |
|---|---|---|---|---|---|
| 526 260-5 | R | Luzerner Hinterland | 526 265-4 | R | Wankdorf |
| 526 261-3 | R | Gotthelf | 526 280-3 | R | Aare |
| 526 262-1 | R | Weissenstein | 526 281-1 | R | Pierre Pertuis |
| 526 263-9 | R | Emme | 526 282-9 | R | Oberaargau |
| 526 264-7 | R | Napf | | | |

# CLASS RABe 535 "Lötschberger" 4-CAR ARTICULATED UNIT

These are a modified version of the NINA design with larger windows for use on the Brig–Spiez Lötschberg summit line plus Spiez–Zweisimmen, with trains eventually all being extended to Bern. They were supposed to replace loco-hauled trains on these routes from December 2008 but were not ready to enter service. *h59*

**Built:** 2008/9.
**Power rating:** 1000 kW.
**Accommodation:** -/44 (3) + –/44 (3) + 28/– + –/32 (11) 1T.
**Driving Wheel Diameter:** 750 mm.
**Wheel Arrangement:** Bo-2-2-2-Bo.

**Builder:** Bombardier/Alstom.
**Length over Couplers:** 62.7 m.
**Weight:** 107 tonnes.
**Maximum Speed:** 160 km/h.

| | | | |
|---|---|---|---|
| 535 101-0 | Züri West | 535 112-7 | |
| 535 102-8 | | 535 113-5 | |
| 535 103-6 | | 535 114-3 | |
| 535 104-4 | | 535 115-0 | |
| 535 105-1 | | 535 116-8 | |
| 535 106-9 | | 535 117-6 | |
| 535 107-7 | | 535 118-4 | |
| 535 108-5 | | 535 119-2 | |
| 535 109-3 | | 535 120-0 | |
| 535 110-1 | | 535 121-8 | |
| 535 111-9 | | | |

# CLASS RBDe 565 (RBDe 4/4)     *h59*     EMU

Modern railcars, very similar to SBB Class 560, found on Bern S-Bahn services S2 and S3. Fitted with thyristor control. They have recently been equipped with pairs of articulated low-floor centre cars known as "Jumbo". Units carry the 721–742 series numbers on the front end but the number of the driving trailer on the other end!

**Built:** 721–738 1982–85; 739–742 1991.
**Builder–Mechanical Parts:** SIG/SWP.
**Builder–Electrical Parts:** BBC (565 721–738) ABB (565 739–742).
**One Hour Rating:** 1700 kW.
**Maximum Tractive Effort:** 186 kN.
**Weight:** 69.7 tonnes.
**Maximum Speed:** 125 km/h.
**Accommodation:** –/54 (1).

**Driving Wheel Diameter:** 940 mm.
**Length over Couplers:** 25.0 m.
**Wheel Arrangement:** Bo-Bo.

| | | | | |
|---|---|---|---|---|
| 565 721-8 | | 565 732-5 | | ERLENBACH |
| 565 722-6 | | 565 733-3 | | BOLTIGEN |
| 565 723-4 | | 565 734-1 | | INS/ANET |
| 565 724-2 | | 565 735-8 | A | BELP |
| 565 725-9 | | 565 736-6 | | TOFFEN |
| 565 726-7 | | 565 737-4 | | FERENBALM/MÜHLEBERG |
| 565 727-5 | | 565 738-2 | | KERZERS/RIED |
| 565 728-3 | | 565 739-0 | | WIMMIS |
| 565 729-1 | | 565 740-8 | | UETENDORF |
| 565 730-9 | | 565 741-6 | | MARIN-ÉPAGNIER |
| 565 731-7 | BUMPLITZ/HOLLIGEN | 565 742-4 | | ST-BLAISE |

# CLASS RBDe 566 (RBDe 4/4)     2- & 3-CAR EMU

Very similar to Class 565, but formerly with RM. 566 220 to 227 are the first generation of the class (566.1) and 566 230 to 242 are the second generation 566.2. Many of the names have been removed. It is not known whether they will be restored.

**Built:** 1973/74 566.1; 1984/85 566.2.
**Builder–Mechanical Parts:** SWS.
**Builder–Electrical Parts:** SAAS 566.1; BBC 566.2.
**Power Rating:** 1340 kW.
**Maximum Tractive Effort:** 186 kN.
**Weight:** 69–71 tonnes.
**Maximum Speed:** 125 km/h.
**Accommodation:** –/54 (1).

**Driving Wheel Diameter:** 940 mm.
**Length over Couplers:** 25.0 m.
**Wheel Arrangement:** Bo-Bo.

| | | | |
|---|---|---|---|
| 566 220-0 (VHB 261) | Walkringen | 566 232-5 (EBT 232) | Grosshöchstetten |
| 566 221-8 (EBT 221) | | 566 233-3 (EBT 233) | Lützelfluh |
| 566 222-6 (EBT 222) | | 566 234-1 (EBT 227) | Trachselwald/Emmental |
| 566 223-4 (EBT 223) | | 566 235-8 (EBT 228) | Gerlafingen |
| 566 224-2 (EBT 224) | | 566 236-6 (EBT 229) | Hasle/Rüegsau |
| 566 225-9 (EBT 225) | Konolfingen | 566 237-4 (VHB 262) | Sumiswald |
| 566 226-7 (EBT 226) | Utzensdorf | 566 238-2 (VHB 263) | Rohrbach |
| 566 227-5 (SMB 281) | Crémines/Gänsbrunnen | 566 239-0 (VHB 264) | Zell |
| 566 230-9 (EBT 230) | Oberdiessbach | 566 240-8 (VHB 265) | Madiswil |
| 566 231-7 (EBT 231) | Kirchberg/Alchenflüh/ | 566 241-6 (SMB 282) | Langendorf |
| | Rüdtlingen | 566 242-4 (SMB 283) | Lommiswil |

# 2.1.3. DIESEL LOCOMOTIVES

## CLASS Em 836          C

These are Henschel shunters with CAT engines absorbed from the RM fleet and originally EBT 15 (ex Essener Steinkohlwerke no. 1) and VHB 57 (ex Rheinische Kalksteinwerke) respectively.

**Built:** 1958/65.
**Builder:** Henschel.
**Engine:** Caterpillar of 412 kW.
**Maximum Tractive Effort:** 145 kN
**Length over Buffers:** 8.90 m.

**Transmission:** Hydraulic. Voith.
**Wheel Diameter:** 1250 mm.
**Weight:** 51 t (361); 45 t (362).
**Maximum Speed:** 60 km/h.

836 361-6      | 836 362-4      |

## CLASS Am 843          B-B

These are Vossloh G1700-2 diesels equipped with ETCS Level 2 for rescue and maintenance trains in the Lötschberg base tunnel. Works numbers 5001645, 646 and 647 respectively.

Details as SBB Class Am 843.

843 501-8      | 843 502-6      | 843 503-4      |

## CLASS Am 845          B-B

Vossloh G1000BB loco on hire from Angel Trains Cargo and used for shunting at Cornaux.

Details as SBB Class 842.01

845 002-5 (Vossloh 1001323, 2003)

# 2.1.4. ELECTRIC SHUNTERS

## CLASS Eea 935/936          Co

Electric shunters with auxiliary batteries for use in non-electrified sidings, based on Class Ee 3/3 for the PTT. BLS 402 (ex GBS) was allocated the new number 935 402 but has never carried it. The loco's name "Susi" has been painted out. 936 132–135 were built at the same time, originally being EBT 132–134 and VHB 151, then absorbed by BLS.

**Built:** 1991/92.
**Builder–Mechanical Parts:** SLM.
**Continuous Rating:** 663 kW.
**Driving Wheel Diameter:** 1040 mm.
**Length over Buffers:** 11.20 m.

**Builder–Electrical Parts:** ABB.
**Maximum Tractive Effort:** 130 kN.
**Weight:** 48 t (402 50 t).
**Maximum Speed:** 75 km/h.

402      **R**      | 936 133-8  **0**      | 936 134-6  **0**      | 936 135-3  **0**
936 132-0  **0**      |

## CLASS Eea 936          C

Although in the same number series as the above locos, this a completely different type, being the same as SBB's Class Ee 3/3 16422–16460 batch. For technical details see SBB section.

936 131-2 **R**

# 2.1.5. TRACTORS

A varied selection of tractors are in use for light shunting and departmental operation. Many do not carry the full number.

| Number | Notes | Builder | km/h | Tonnes | kW | Built |
|---|---|---|---|---|---|---|
| Te 215 011-8 | h | SLM/MFO | 55 | 15 | 95 | 1950 |
| Te 216 301-2 (S) | Te$^{III}$ 121 EBT | SLM/SAAS | 60 | 29 | 257 | 1945 (88) |
| Te 216 302-0 (S) | Te$^{III}$ 122 EBT§ | SLM/SAAS | 60 | 29 | 257 | 1945 (88) |
| Te 216 303-8 | Te$^{III}$ 123 EBT | SLM/SAAS | 60 | 29 | 257 | 1952 (88) |
| Te 216 304-6 | Te$^{III}$ 124 EBT | SLM/SAAS | 60 | 29 | 257 | 1952 (86) |
| Te 216 361-6 | Te$^{I}$ 61 VHB | SLM/MFO | 45 | 13 | 90 | 1963 |
| Tem 225 041-3 | | SLM/MFO/BBC/SAAS | 75 | 30 | 260/145 | 1960 (92) |
| Tem 225 042-1 | | SLM/MFO/BBC/SAAS | 75 | 30 | 260/145 | 1960 (93) |
| Tem 225 043-9 | | BLS/MFO/BBC/SAAS | 75 | 30 | 260/145 | 1965 (93) |
| Tem 225 045-4 | | BLS/SLM/MFO/SAAS/DZ | 75 | 30 | 260/145 | 1960 (74) |
| Tem 225 046-2 | | BLS/SLM/MFO/SAAS/DZ | 75 | 30 | 260/145 | 1960 (74) |
| Tem 225 055-3 | | BLS/MFO/BBC/SAAS/DZ | 75 | 31 | 260/145 | 1967 |
| Tem 225 056-1 | | BLS/MFO/BBC/SAAS | 75 | 31 | 260/145 | 1967 |
| Tem 225 057-9 | | BLS/MFO/BBC/SAAS | 75 | 31 | 260/145 | 1967 (72) |
| Tem 225 058-7 | | BLS/MFO/BBC/SAAS | 75 | 31 | 260/145 | 1967 (80) |
| Tm 235 064-3 | h | BLS/SLM/DZ | 45 | 9 | 75 | 1962 (94) |
| Tm 235 079-1 | | RACO/DZ | 75 | 19 | 175 | 1993 |
| Tm 235 080-9 | | RACO/DZ | 75 | 19 | 176 | 1993 |
| Tm 235 081-7 | | RACO/DZ | 75 | 19 | 176 | 1992 |
| Tm 235 082-5 | | RACO/DZ | 75 | 19 | 176 | 1977 |
| Tm 235 083-3 | | RACO/DZ | 75 | 19 | 176 | 1980 |
| Tm 235 084-1 | | RACO/DZ | 75 | 19 | 176 | 1980 |
| Tm 235 086-6 | | RACO/DZ | 75 | 19 | 176 | 1983 |
| Tm 235 087-4 | | RACO/DZ | 75 | 19 | 176 | 1983 |
| Tm 235 088-2 | | RACO/DZ | 75 | 27 | 176 | 1983 |
| Tm 235 089-0 | | RACO/DZ | 75 | 28 | 176 | 1991 |
| Tm 235 091-6 | | STAD/MB/BBC | 80 | 40 | 700 | 1980 |
| Tm 235 092-4 | | STAD/MB/BBC | 80 | 40 | 700 | 1980 |
| Tm 235 093-2 | | STAD/MB/BBC | 80 | 40 | 700 | 1981 |
| Tm 235 094-0 | | STAD/MB/BBC | 80 | 40 | 700 | 1981 |
| Tm 235 095-7 | | STAD/MB/BBC | 80 | 29 | 350 | 1984 |
| Tm 235 096-5 | | STAD/MB/BBC | 80 | 29 | 350 | 1984 |
| Tm 235 097-3 | | STAD/MB/BBC | 80 | 29 | 350 | 1984 |
| Tm 235 098-1 | | STAD/MB/BBC | 80 | 29 | 350 | 1985 |
| Tm 235 100-5 | | STAD/MB/BBC | 80 | 38 | 550 | 1996 |
| Tm 235 201-1 | | STAD | 100 | 37 | 660 | 2007 |
| Tm 235 202-9 | | STAD | 100 | 37 | 660 | 2007 |
| Tm 235 203-7 | | STAD | 100 | 37 | 660 | 2007 |
| Tm 235 204-5 | | STAD | 100 | 37 | 660 | 2007 |
| Tm 235 205-2 | | STAD | 100 | 37 | 660 | 2008 |
| Tm 235 206-0 | | STAD | 100 | 37 | 660 | 2008 |
| Tm 235 207-8 | | STAD | 100 | 37 | 660 | 2008 |
| Tm 235 208-6 | | STAD | 100 | 37 | 660 | 2008 |
| Tm 235 209-4 | | STAD | 100 | 37 | 660 | 2008 |
| Tm 235 210-2 | | STAD | 100 | 37 | 660 | 2008 |
| Tm 236 310-9 | 10 EBT | MAX DIEMA/DZ | 40 | 24 | 140 | 1978 |
| Tm 236 311-7 | 11 EBT | MAX DIEMA/DZ | 40 | 24 | 140 | 1978 |
| Tm 236 312-5 (S) | 12 EBT | RACO/SAU | 45 | 10 | 74 | 1962 |
| Tm 236 313-3 (S) | 13 EBT | RACO/SAU | 45 | 10 | 74 | 1972 |
| Tm 236 315-8 | 15 EBT | RACO/SAU | 45 | 10 | 74 | 1975 |
| Tm 236 340-6 | * | HEN | - | - | - | 1959 |
| Tm 236 352-1 | 52 VHB | RACO/SAU | 45 | 10 | 74 | 1971 |
| Tm 236 353-9 | 53 VHB | RACO/SAU | 45 | 10 | 74 | 1971 |
| Tm 236 354-7 | 54 VHB | RACO/SAU | 45 | 10 | 74 | 1972 |
| Tm 236 355-4 | 55 VHB | RACO/SAU | 45 | 10 | 74 | 1972 |

| | | | | | | |
|---|---|---|---|---|---|---|
| Tm 236 356-2 | 56 VHB | RACO/DZ | 75 | 19 | 177 | 1980 |
| Tm 236 371-1 | 71 SMB | RACO/SAU | 45 | 10 | 74 | 1964 |
| Tm 236 372-9 | 72 SMB | RACO/DZ | 75 | 19 | 177 | 1983 |
| Tea 245 021-1 | | STAD/ABB | 80 | 34 | 400 | 1993 |
| Tea 245 022-9 | | STAD/ABB | 80 | 34 | 400 | 1993 |
| Tea 245 023-7 | | STAD/ABB | 80 | 34 | 400 | 1993 |
| Tea 245 024-5 | | STAD/ABB | 80 | 34 | 400 | 1994 |

§ ex SBB 137
* ex Preussen Elektra No. 3 in 2000.

# 2.1.6. BLS HISTORIC FLEET

## ELECTRIC LOCOMOTIVES

### CLASS Be 4/4                           Bo-Bo

These are typical electric locos built for secondary networks in the 1930s, SOB also having two preserved examples. They were absorbed from RM – 102 is ex EBT and 171 ex SMB.

**Built:** 1932.
**Builder–Mechanical Parts:** SLM.
**Builder–Electrical Parts:** SAAS.
**Power Rating:** 1177 kW.
**Weight:** 63 tonnes.

**Length over Buffers:** 12.40 m.
**Wheel Diameter:** 1060 kW.
**Maximum Tractive Effort:** 85 kN.
**Maximum Speed:** 80 km/h.

102            |

### CLASS Ae 6/8                     1Co-Co1

This elderly loco was one of a class of eight (201 to 208) built for main line work on the Lötschberg route. It is retained as an historic loco. 206 and 208 are also preserved.

**Built:** 1939.
**Builder–Mechanical Parts:** SLM.
**Builder–Electrical Parts:** SAAS.
**Traction Motors:** 12 single phase, fully suspended with SAAS spring drive.
**Power Rating:** 4146 kW.     **Maximum Tractive Effort:** 353 kN.
**Wheel Diameter:** 1350 mm (driven); 950 mm (pony)
**Weight:** 140 tonnes.     **Maximum Speed:** 100 km/h.

**Length over Buffers:** 20.26 m.

Rheostatic brake fitted.

205     **N**     |

### CLASS Ae 4/4                        Bo–Bo

A very advanced design at the time of its introduction, this was the first electric type to achieve 1000 h.p. per axle. Now in reserve and due for early withdrawal. 253–6 were rebuilt as Class Ae 8/8 locos, detailed next. 251 is now a historic locomotive. 258 was on show in the Verkehrshaus in 2007.

**Built:** 1944–55.
**Builder–Mechanical Parts:** SLM.
**Builder–Electrical Parts:** BBC.
**Traction Motors:** 4 single phase fully suspended with BBC flexible disc drive.
**Power Rating:** 2980 kW.     **Maximum Tractive Effort:** 235 kN.
**Weight:** 80 tonnes.     **Maximum Speed:** 125 km/h.

**Length over Buffers:** 15.60 m.
**Wheel Diameter:** 1250 mm.

Both locos m.w. and push-pull fitted, rheostatic brake fitted.

251     **N**     | 258     **N**  (U)

## CLASS Ae 8/8          Bo-Bo+Bo-Bo

The last of five double locos (271 to 275), in effect a pair of Ae 4/4s permanently coupled, with the cabs at the inner ends removed. 275 was a rebuild of 255 and 256 in 1966.

**Built:** 1959–63.
**Builder–Mechanical Parts:** SLM.
**Builder–Electrical Parts:** BBC.
**Traction Motors:** 8 single phase fully suspended with BBC flexible disc drive.
**One Hour Rating:** 6476 kW.
**Weight:** 160 tonnes.
**Length over Buffers:** 30.23 m.
**Wheel Diameter:** 1250 mm.
**Maximum Tractive Effort:** 471 kN.
**Maximum Speed:** 125 km/h.

273      N      |

## CLASS Ce 4/4          B-B

A class built for mixed traffic duties at the time of electrification. The survivors are used on local freight work around Bern and Thun. They were built as 1BB1, rebuilt to BB in the 1950s. An unrebuilt example of the class (307) is an operational preserved loco. 311, 312 and 315 are also preserved.

**Built:** 1920–4, rebuilt 1954–6.
**Builder–Mechanical Parts:** SLM.
**Builder–Electrical Parts:** BBC.
**Traction Motors:** 4 single phase bogie mounted with jackshaft/side rod drive.
**One Hour Rating:** 736 kW.
**Weight:** 64 tonnes.
**Length over Buffers:** 12.34 m.
**Wheel Diameter:** 1230 mm.
**Maximum Tractive Effort:** 108 kN.
**Maximum Speed:** 65 km/h.

313      N      | 316      N      |

## CLASS Ee 3/3          C

A classic centre-cab jackshaft drive shunter, similar to the SBB locos.

**Built:** 1943.
**Builder–Mechanical Parts:** SLM.
**Builder–Electrical Parts:** SAAS.
**Traction Motors:** 1 single phase frame mounted with jackshaft/side rod drive.
**One Hour Rating:** 452 kW.
**Weight:** 38 tonnes.
**Length over Buffers:** 9.2 m
**Wheel Diameter:** 1040 mm.
**Maximum Tractive Effort:** 88 kN.
**Maximum Speed:** 40 km/h.

401   N      LISI      |

# ELECTRIC RAILCAR

## CLASS Be 4/4          Bo-Bo

The last of three motor coaches which were made up into sets as required with driving and intermediate trailers.

**Built:** 1953–6.
**Builder–Mechanical Parts:** SIG.
**Builder–Electrical Parts:** SAAS.
**One Hour Rating:** 1472 kW.
**Weight:** 68 tonnes.
**Wheel Arrangement:** Bo–Bo.
**Length over Buffers:** 23.70 m.
**Wheel Diameter:** 1040 mm.
**Maximum Tractive Effort:** 128 kN.
**Maximum Speed:** 120 km/h.
**Accommodation:** 60S 1L.

761      |

# 2.2. SÜDOSTBAHN (670, 671, 672, 853, 870)
# SOB

This railway was formed in 2002 from the merger of the Bodensee Toggenburg (BT) and the Schweizerische Südost Bahn (SOB).

The old SOB forms the eastern section of the Romanshorn–Luzern route from Romanshorn to Wattwil. A joint SOB/Thurbo Wil–Wattwil–Nesslau service also operates. The former BT line runs from Rapperswil to Arth Goldau on the Gotthard line, providing the middle section of the Romanshorn–Luzern route. There are also branches to Einsiedeln and Wädenswil. SOB's main service is the "Voralpen Express" over the 147 km route from Romanshorn to Luzern. This is worked by SOB Class 456 or SBB Class Re 4/4". Hauled stock is soon to be replaced by new EMUs.

Sadly most names have been removed from SOB stock.

**Routes:**
* Romanshorn–St. Gallen–Wattwil (53.2 km)
* Ebnat-Kappel–Nesslau-Neu St. Johann (7.9 km)
* Rapperswil–Pfäffikon SZ–Samstagern–Biberbrugg–Arth-Goldau (38.6 km)
* Wädenswil–Samstagern (5.4 km)
* Biberbrugg–Einsiedeln (5.2 km).
**Electrical System:** 15 kV AC 16.7 Hz.
**Depots:** Herisau, Nesslau-Neu St. Johann, Samstagern (ex BT).

## CLASS Re 446 (Re 4/4$^{IV}$)     Bo-Bo
Formerly numbered Re 446 445 to 448 by SOB.

**Built:** 1982 (as SBB Re 4/4 $^{IV}$ 10101 to 10104)    **Builders:** SLM/BBC.
**Hourly Rating:** 4960 kW.    **Weight:** 80 tonnes.
**Length over Buffers:** 15.80 m.    **Maximum Tractive Effort:** 210 kN.
**Maximum Speed:** 160 km/h.    **Wheel Diameter:** 1260 mm.

| 446 015-0 | 446 016-8 | 446 017-6 | 446 018-4 |
|---|---|---|---|

## CLASS Re 456     Bo-Bo

Former BT locos 91–96 (the short version of the number is shown on the front) are used in push-pull mode on the Voralpern Express service between Romanshorn and Luzern. Locos 142 and 143 are on long term loan (almost certainly permanent) from BLS having been absorbed from RM, originally VHB 142 and 143. They are used only on freight.

**Built:** 1987/88 (142/143 1993).    **Builders:** SLM/BBC.
**One Hour Rating:** 3000 kW.    **Weight:** 68 tonnes.
**Length over Buffers:** 16.60 metres.    **Continuous Tractive Effort:** 140 kN.
**Maximum Speed:** 130 km/h.    **Wheel Diameter:** 1100 mm.

*(handwritten: p 60)*

**Ex BT Locos**

| 456 091-0 | Romanshorn | 456 094-2 | Herisau |
|---|---|---|---|
| 456 092-6 | Wittenbach | 456 095-9 | Degersheim |
| 456 093-4 | St. Gallen | 456 096-7 | Wattwil |

**Locos on loan from BLS**

| 456 142-9 | Gutenburg | 456 143 -7 | Menznau |
|---|---|---|---|

## CLASS RABe 526   FLIRT   4-CAR ARTICULATED EMU
Details as SBB Class 526.6 except:

**Built:** 2007/8.    **Weight:** 118 tonnes.
**Accommodation:** 24/148.

| 526 041-9 | 526 044-3 | 526 047-6 | 526 050-0 |
|---|---|---|---|
| 526 042-7 | 526 045-0 | 526 048-4 | 526 051-8 |
| 526 043-5 | 526 046-8 | 526 049-2 | |

*(handwritten: VHB → RM — BLS who loaned them to SOB; now parked at Samstagern + Herisau awaiting another lessee  1993  2011)*

# CLASS RBDe 566 NPZ 4-CAR ARTICULATED EMU

These power cars are formed with trailers to form 3- or 4-car EMUs. Some names have been removed recently. Details as BLS Class 565 except:
**Built**: 1982 by FFA/SIG/BBC 566 071 to 076 (ex BT);
1995 by SWG/SIG/ABB 566 077 to 080 (formerly SOB 566 400–403)..
**Accommodation:** –/48 566 071–076; –/76 566 077–080.

| | | | | |
|---|---|---|---|---|
| 566 071-7 | Muolen | | 566 076-6 | Lichtensteig |
| 566 072-5 | Haggenschwil | | 566 077-4 | Bezirk Schwyz |
| 566 073-3 | Roggwil-Berg | | 566 078-2 | Bezirk Hoff |
| 566 074-1 | Mogelsberg | | 566 079-0 | Richterswil-Samstagern |
| 566 075-8 | Brunnadern | | 566 080-8 | Rothenthurm |

## OTHER ROLLING STOCK

| | Number | Class | Notes | Builder | Seats | km/h | tonnes | kW | Built |
|---|---|---|---|---|---|---|---|---|---|
| Te | 216 035-6 | Te$^{III}$ | ex BT 35 | SLM/MFO | - | 65 | 28 | 239 | 1966 |
| Te | 216 036-4 | Te$^{III}$ | ex SOB 51 | SLM/SAAS | - | 60 | 28.5 | 260 | 1943 |
| Te | 216 037-2 | Te$^{I}$ | ex SOB 52 § | SLM/MFO | - | 45 | 12 | 90 | 1950 |
| Te | 216 038-0 | Te$^{I}$ | ex SOB 53 § | SLM/MFO | - | 45 | 12 | 90 | 1950 |
| Te | 216 039-8 | Te$^{I}$ | ex SOB 54 § | SLM/MFO | - | 45 | 12 | 90 | 1950 |
| Tm | 236 001-4 | Tm$^{I}$ | ex BT 1 | RACO/SAU | - | 45 | 10 | 70 | 1962 |
| Tm | 236 002-2 | Tm$^{I}$ | ex BT 2 | RACO/SAU | - | 45 | 10 | 70 | 1964 |
| Tm | 236 004-8 | Tm | ex BT 4 | RACO/DZ | - | 80 | 18 | 200 | 1977 |
| Tm | 236 005-5 | Tm | ex BT 5 | RACO/DZ | - | 80 | 27 | 176 | 1992 |
| Tm | 236 006-3 | Tm$^{IV}$ | a ex BT 6 | SLM/MAN | - | 60 | 30 | 280 | 1972 |
| Tm | 236 007-1 | Tm$^{IV}$ | a ex BT 7 | SLM/MAN | - | 60 | 30 | 280 | 1973 |
| Tm | 236 008-9 | Tm | ex SOB 34 * | JUNG/KAEL | - | 45 | 16 | 95 | 1960 |
| Tm | 236 009-7 | Tm | ex SOB 33 | STAD/CAT | - | 60 | 37.7 | 565 | 1983 |
| Tm | 236 010-5 | Tm$^{III}$ | ex SBB 9517 | RACO | - | 60 | 24 | 165 | 1977 |
| Tm | 236 011-3 | Tm$^{III}$ | ex SBB 9596 | RACO | - | 60 | 24 | 165 | 1988 |
| Be | 11 | Be 4/4 | h | SLM/SAAS | - | 80 | 66 | 1180 | 1931 |
| Be | 556 043-8 | Be 3/4 | h | SIG/SAAS | 46 | 80 | 68 | 885 | 1938 |
| BDe | 576 058-2 | BDe 4/4 | Wollerau | SIG/BBC | 32 | 110 | 72 | 2135 | 1979 |
| BDe | 576 059-0 | BDe 4/4 | Freienbach | SIG/BBC | 32 | 110 | 72 | 2135 | 1979 |
| Am | 846 033-9 | Am 4/4 | ex SOB 61 † | KRUPP/AEG/CAT | - | 100 | 68 | 990 | 1963 |
| Eea | 936 031-4 | # | | HEN/AEG | - | 50 | 60 | 530 | 1966 |
| Eea | 936 032-2 | # | | HEN/AEG | - | 50 | 60 | 530 | 1966 |

576 049, 055, 056 and 057 were sold to the company Makies in Gettnau. See Open Access Operators.

a   ex Von Roll 26 & 28. As SBB Type Tm$^{IV}$ 8751–8797.
h   Historic stock.
*   ex DB 323 812 in 1984.
#   Ex Ruhrkohle AG, Germany locos 281 and 283 in 1995. Henschel Type Ea 800.
†   Unique loco originally demonstrator DE1500, on loan to DB as 201 001, then WLE DE 0901, then DEG VE 151. To SOB in 1991.
§   52, 53, 54 ex SBB Te$^{I}$ 951, 959 and 952 respectively.

# 2.3. THURBO

THURBO was originally set up as a joint subsidiary of SBB, Mittel Thurgau Bahn (MThB) and the Thurgau canton for the operation of regional services in north-eastern Switzerland from December 2002. MThB then went bankrupt so the company is now basically a subsidiary of SBB, Thurgau canton owning just 10%. All services are operated by Stadler EMUs of the GTW type – mostly 2-car (GTW 2/6) but some are 3-car (GTW 2/8). These have eliminated all EMUs previously operated in the area by MThB. Thurbo also took over the first Stadler GTW 2/6 DMUs (Bm 596 671–673) from MThB but sold them to an Italian dealer in 2007. Livery is white with doors of various colours and coloured blobs along the roof line.

**Depot:** Weinfelden, but some work carried out at SBB's Oberwinterthur depot.

# ELECTRIC MULTIPLE UNITS

## CLASS RABe 526.6                    2-CAR EMUS

This small class is the earliest version of the Stadler GTW 2/6 EMU. They differ from the later series units in having a rather flat front end but have the same short, central two-axle power unit with a driving trailer supported by just one bogie on each side. The units operate a variety of services, including Weinfelden to Wil and Gossau.

**Built:** 1998/99.
**Builder:** Stadler/FIAT-SIG/Adtranz.
**Traction motors:** Two of 380 kW.
**Weight:** 57 tonnes.                      **Overall Length:** 37.80 m.
**Maximum Speed:** 130 km/h.               **Wheel arrangement:** 2-Bo-2.
**Accommodation:** 12/90.

| | | | |
|---|---|---|---|
| 526 680-4 | | 526 685-3 | Ostwind |
| 526 681-2 | Weinfelden | 526 686-1 | |
| 526 682-0 | Amriswil | 526 687-9 | |
| 526 683-8 | | 526 688-7 | |
| 526 684-6 | | 526 689-5 | |

## CLASS RABe 526.7                    2- or 3-CAR EMUS

Used on all regional services in north-east Switzerland. 3-car sets are employed on S29 Winterthur–Stein am Rhein, S33 Winterthur–Schaffhausen and S35 Winterthur–Wil. The original order was altered several times and eventually 51 2-car ( 526 701–751) and 29 3-car sets (526 752–780) were delivered. 526 709 to 718 were then converted to 3-car in 2008 and renumbered in order as 526 781 to 790. Units 720 to 751 were fitted with pantographs and safety equipment to work in Germany from 2005. The first unit to be dealt with, 526 706, became 526 720 and the original 526 720 became 706. The others were not renumbered.

**Built:** 2003–2007.
**Builder:** Stadler.
**Traction Motors:** Two of 350 kW.
**Overall Length:** 39.40 m (2-car); 54.447 m (3-car).
**Wheel Arrangement:** 2-Bo-2 (2-car); 2-Bo-2-2 (3-car).
**Accommodation:** –/56 (6) (+ –/56 (6) + 16/34 (6) 1T.
**Weight:** 63 tonnes (2-car); 82 tonnes (3-car).   **Maximum Speed:** 140 km/h.
**Floor height:** 585 mm.

| | | | |
|---|---|---|---|
| 526 701-8 | Kanton Thurgau | 526 723-2 | |
| 526 702-6 | Frauenfeld | 526 724-0 | Connyland Express |
| 526 703-4 | Kanton St. Gallen | 526 725-7 | Theater St. Gallen |
| 526 704-2 | | 526 726-5 | Rorschach/Rorschacherberg |
| 526 705-9 | | 526 727-3 | Napoleon III |
| 526 706-7 • | Simone Niggli | 526 728-1 | |
| 526 707-5 | TOP-Blitz | 526 729-9 | Kanton Thurgau |
| 526 708-3 | Steinach | 526 730-7 | Wil |
| 526 719-0 | | 526 731-5 | |
| 526 720-8 | Spieleland Express | 526 732-3 | |
| 526 721-6 | | 526 733-1 | |
| 526 722-4 | | 526 734-9 | |

| | |
|---|---|
| 526 735-6 | Rumikon AG |
| 526 736-4 | |
| 526 737-2 | |
| 526 738-0 | |
| 526 739-8 | |
| 526 740-6 | |
| 526 741-4 | |
| 526 742-2 | Flawil |
| 526 743-0 | |
| 526 744-8 | |
| 526 745-5 | Stein am Rhein |
| 526 746-3 | Sirnach |
| 526 747-1 | Elgg |
| 526 748-9 | Elsau |
| 526 749-7 | |
| 526 750-5 | Zürcher Weinland |
| 526 751-3 | |
| 526 752-1 | |
| 526 753-9 | |
| 526 754-7 | |
| 526 755-4 | Rheinfall |
| 526 756-2 | |
| 526 757-0 ✎ | St. Galler Rheintal |
| 526 758-8 | Sargans |
| 526 759-6 | |
| 526 760-4 | |
| 526 761-2 | |
| 526 762-0 | |

| | |
|---|---|
| 526 763-8 | |
| 526 764-6 | |
| 526 765-3 | |
| 526 766-1 | |
| 526 767-9 | Kreuzlingen |
| 526 768-7 | |
| 526 769-5 | |
| 526 770-3 | |
| 526 771-1 | |
| 526 772-9 | |
| 526 773-7 | |
| 526 774-5 | |
| 526 775-2 | |
| 526 776-0 | |
| 526 777-8 | |
| 526 778-6 | |
| 526 779-4 | |
| 526 780-2 | Bussnang |
| 526 781-0 | Schaffhausen |
| 526 782-8 | Alstätten |
| 526 783-6 | Bodensee |
| 526 784-4 | |
| 526 785-1 | Eschlikon |
| 526 786-9 | Bad Zurzach |
| 526 787-7 | Barockes Bischofszell |
| 526 788-5 | Romanshorn |
| 526 789-3 | Aadorf |
| 526 790-1 | Zihlschacht-Sitterdorf |

✎ *in Jaros hi 778 uthur*

# 3. METRE-GAUGE MAIN LINE RAILWAYS

## 3.1. MATTERHORN GOTTHARD BAHN    MGB

This railway was formed in 2003 through the merger of two mountain railways with similar features features which met in Brig:

| | |
|---|---|
| **BRIG–VISP–ZERMATT (139, 140, 141)** | **BVZ** |
| **FURKA OBERALP (142, 143)** | **FO** |

The former BVZ provides the transport link to Zermatt where "normal" road traffic is not permitted. In addition to the main service from Brig, the frequent "Zermatt Shuttle" runs from Täsch, the end of the valley road. Through coaches from Zermatt also operate as the Glacier Express to Chur and St. Moritz over the MGB to Disentis/Muster then via the RhB.

Forming the only east–west rail link across the south of the country, for many years the section over the Furka pass, from which the Rhône glacier could be seen, was only open during the summer. However, in 1982 the Furka base tunnel was opened, facilitating all-year-round operation, but eliminating the spectacular section over the pass itself which is now operated by the DFB with steam. Several stretches of rack remain on this scenic line.

Following the merger no fleet renumbering was necessary except for Gm 4/4 70 which was ex FO 71. Stock now operates in a pool. Names of locos are confusing, often being different on each side.

**Electrical System:** 11 kV 16.7 Hz AC
**Rack system:** Abt.
**Routes:**
• Brig–Visp–Zermatt (44.0 km) (ex BVZ).
• Brig–Andermatt–Disentis/Muster (96.9 km) (ex FO).
• Andermatt–Göschenen (3.7 km) (ex FO).
**Depots:** Andermatt (ex FO), Brig Glisergrund (BVZ and FO).

## 3.1.1. ELECTRIC LOCOMOTIVES

### CLASS HGe 4/4ᴵᴵ                  h61 after R                  Bo-Bo

These rack-fitted locos are very similar to ZB Class HGe 101. They are mainly used on Glacier Express trains from Zermatt via Brig and Andermatt to Disentis-Muster but also power coaches on some Zermatt–Brig services. 1–5 are ex BVZ while 101–108 are ex FO. 104 and 105 were SBB Brünig line 1951 and 1952 respectively, acquired in 1990. 108 was originally named "Nufenen" but was renamed in an "exchange" with Eurotunnel whose loco 9026 is named "FURKATUNNEL 1982".

**Built:** 1986 (101–105), 1989 (106–108), 1990 (1–5).
**Builder–Mechanical Parts:** SLM.
**Builder–Electrical Parts:** BBC/ABB.
**One Hour Rating:** 1932 kW.
**Wheel Diameter:** 943 mm.
**Length over Couplers:** 14.78 m.

**Maximum Tractive Effort:** 140 kN.
**Weight:** 64 tonnes.
**Maximum Speed:** 90 km/h (35 km/h on rack).

| | | | | |
|---|---|---|---|---|
| 1 | MATTERHORN | | 103 | CHUR/MARCAU DE CUERA |
| 2 | MONTE ROSA | | 104 | Furka |
| 3 | DOM | | 105 | Oberalp/Alpsu |
| 4 | TÄSCHHORN | | 106 | St. Gotthard/S. Gottardo |
| 5 | MOUNT FUJI | | 107 | Grimsel |
| 101 | SITTEN/VILLE DE SION | | 108 | CHANNEL TUNNEL |
| 102 | ALTDORF | | | |

## CLASSES Deh 4/4, 4/4$^I$ & 4/4$^{II}$      Bo-Bo

These are not locomotives but motor luggage vans which power all local push-pull trains from Visp to Brig, Andermatt and Göschenen plus Andermatt to Disentis/Muster. Ex BVZ Deh 4/4 † and former FO Deh 4/4$^I$§ look very similar but have slightly different technical details. Deh 4/4$^I$ §and Deh 4/4$^{II}$, both ex FO, have almost identical technical details but the later units look very different due to their ribbed sides. The 60 or 65 km/h limit is a handicap to improving services over the Visp–Andermatt section which has many quite level, straight sections.

**Built:** 1972 51–55§ 1975/76†, 1979–84.
**Builder–Mechanical Parts:** SLM plus SIG Deh 4/4 & 4/4$^I$.
**Builder–Electrical Parts:** BBC (SAAS †).
**One Hour Rating:** 1032 kW (1094 kW †).    **Maximum Tractive Effort:** 118 kN (104 kN †).
**Wheel Diameter:** 790 mm.    **Weight:** 48–49 tonnes.
**Length over Couplers:** 11.59 m (12.79 m †§)
**Maximum Speed:** 65 km/h (35 km/h on rack) †, 60/30 km/h rest.

| | | | | | | |
|---|---|---|---|---|---|---|
| 21 | † | STALDEN | | 55 | § | BRIG |
| 22 | † | ST. NIKLAUS | | 91 | | GÖSCHENEN |
| 23 | † | RANDA | | 92 | | REALP |
| 24 | † | TÄSCH | | 93 | | OBERWALD |
| 51 | § | DISENTIS/MUSTER | | 94 | | FIESCH |
| 52 | § | SEDRUN/TAVETSCH/TUJETSCH* | | 95 | | ANDERMATT |
| 53 | § | URSERN | | 96 | | MUNSTER |
| 54 | § | GOMS | | | | |

\*   52 has names TAVETSCH and TUJETSCH on opposite sides, plus SEDRUN on both sides.

# 3.1.2. ELECTRIC MULTIPLE UNITS

## CLASSES ABDeh 4/8 & ABDeh 4/10     3- & 4-CAR EMUs

These units are the Stadler "Komet" (*Komfortabler Meterspur Zug*) design. The central power car has all four axles powered, a high floor and no access doors. The end cars have only one bogie, at the outer end. The intermediate trailer in the 4-car version also has just one bogie. These units have only one pair of doors in each outer car and first class accommodation.

They were ordered to operate an upgraded service on the Brig–Visp–Zermatt line in connection with the opening of the Lötschberg base tunnel and the new station at Visp. They share these duties with Class HGe 4/4 plus hauled stock.

**Built:** 2007/8.      **Builder:** Stadler/Bombardier.
**Continuous Rating:** 1000 kW.
**Wheel Arrangement:** 2-Bo-Bo(- 2)-2.
**Accommodation:** –/36 (3) 1T + –/72 (+ 15/27) + 26/– (4) 1T.
**Length over Couplers:** 18.607 + 18.869 (+18.064) + 18.607 m.
**Weight:** 17 + 45 (+ 16) + 17 tonnes.
**Maximum Speed:** 80 km/h (adhesion); 35 km/h (rack).

**3-car units**

| 2011 | 2012 | 2013 | |
|---|---|---|---|

**4-car units**

| 2021 | 2022 | |
|---|---|---|

## CLASS BDSeh 4/8      3-CAR EMUs

These "Komet" units were delivered before the above class and are a second class only version for the "Zermatt Shuttle" between Täsch and Zermatt. They have two pairs of doors in the outer cars which only have seats in the outer end, the rest being space for standees and baggage. Details as for ABDeh 4/8 except:

**Built:** 2003–2005.
**Accommodation:** –/20 + –/80 + –/20.

| | | | | | | |
|---|---|---|---|---|---|---|
| 2051 | Castor | | 2053 | Albatros | | 2054 | Eagle |
| 2052 | Pollux | | | | | |

# 3.1.3. OTHER ROLLING STOCK

| Class | No. | Name | Former Rly. | Builder | Seats | km/h | tonnes | kW | Built |
|---|---|---|---|---|---|---|---|---|---|
| HGe 4/4[I] | 15 | | FO | SLM/SWS/MFO | - | 50/25 | 46.6 | 736 | 1930 |
| HGe 4/4 | 32 | | FO | SLM/MFO | - | 55/30 | 48 | 912 | 1941 |
| HGe 4/4 | 33 | | FO | SLM/MFO | - | 55/30 | 48 | 912 | 1941 |
| HGe 4/4 | 36 | | FO | SLM/MFO | - | 55/30 | 48 | 912 | 1948 |
| BDeh 2/4 | 41 | h | FO | SLM/BBC | 40 | 55/30 | 37 | 427 | 1941 |
| HGm 4/4 | 61 | | FO | SLM/BBC/MFO/CUM | – | 50/30 | 54 | 644 | 1967 |
| HGm 4/4 | 62 | | FO | SLM/BBC/MFO/CUM | – | 50/30 | 54 | 644 | 1968 |
| Gm 4/4 | 70 | § ELCH | FO | JUNG/MWM | – | 40 | 37.6 | 652 | 1966 (80) |
| Gm 3/3 | 71 | | VBZ | MOY/DZ | – | 49 | 26 | 191 | 1975 |
| Gm 3/3 | 72 | | VBZ | MOY/DZ | – | 49 | 26 | 191 | 1975 |
| Tm 2/2 | 73 | † | VBZ | SCH/DZ | – | 40 | 21 | 158 | 1972 |
| Tm 2/2 | 74 | * | VBZ | RUHR/MWM | – | 30 | 25 | 184 | 1958 |
| HGm 2/2 | 75 | NIKLAUS | VBZ | STAD/MTU/ABB | - | 65/30 | 23 | 550 | 2002 |
| Ge 4/4[III] | 81 | n | FO | SLM/BBC | - | 90 | 50 | 1700 | 1980 |
| Ge 4/4[III] | 82 | n | FO | SLM/BBC | - | 90 | 50 | 1700 | 1980 |
| BDeh 6/6 | 2031 | | VBZ | SIG/SLM/SAAS | 92 | 55/30 | 71 | 882 | 1960 |
| ABDeh 8/8 | 2041 | BRIG | VBZ | SIG/SLM/SAAS | 12/96 | 55/30 | 88 | 1176 | 1964 |
| ABDeh 8/8 | 2042 | VISP | VBZ | SIG/SLM/SAAS | 12/96 | 55/30 | 88 | 1176 | 1965 |
| ABDeh 8/8 | 2043 | ZERMATT | VBZ | SIG/SLM/SAAS | 12/96 | 55/30 | 88 | 1176 | 1965 |
| Tm 2/2 | 2921 | | VBZ | RACO/SLM | – | 30 | 9.8 | 40 | 1957 |
| Tm 2/2 | 2922 | | VBZ | RACO/DZ | – | 30 | 10.2 | 40 | 1959 |
| Tm 2/2 | 4971 | ‡ | FO | DIEMA/ASPER | – | 45 | 21.8 | 170 | 1961 |
| Tm 2/2 | 4972 | ‡ | FO | SCH/DZ | – | 45 | 21.8 | 170 | 1961 |
| Tm 2/2 | 4973 | * | FO | RUHR/MWM | – | 45 | 23.3 | 176 | 1958 |
| Ta 2/2 | 4982 | | FO | | – | 15 | 6.5 | | 1994 |

n 81 and 82 are officially WALLIS and URI but actually only carry shields from these cantons.
h historic stock.
§ 70 ex Lojo works, Virkby, Finland in 1972.
† 73 ex Tauern Scheiteltunnel DL 11 in 1980.
‡ 4971 and 4972 ex Itzehoe cement works 11 and 12 in 1980.
* 74 and 4973 ex DB 333 901 and 902 respectively, originally Kerkerbachbahn 18 and 19. 74 acquired in 1991, 4973 in 1984.

# 3.2. RHÄTISCHE BAHN                RhB

In terms of route mileage the RhB is the largest of the Swiss private railways. It operates all the lines in south east Switzerland (mainly in the Graubünden canton), connecting with the SBB at Chur and Landquart, and serving the major tourist centres of St. Moritz, Davos and Klosters. Branches also serve Disentis-Mustér (where there is an end-on connection with the MGB allowing through Glacier Express trains to Zermatt), Arosa, Scuol-Tarasp and Tirano (Italy). The main system is electrified at 11 kV 16.7 Hz AC whilst the Berninabahn (St. Moritz–Tirano), once a separate company, is 1000 V DC. The Chur–Arosa line was converted from 2000 V DC to 11 kV AC in 1997.

Of the physically separate 1500 V DC 31.3 km Bellinzona–Mesocco (BM) line, only the 12.7 km Castione-Arbedo–Cama section is still open, but only to tourist trains operated by a presevation group. All the lines of the RhB are very scenic, particularly the Berninabahn and the Albula pass. Until now the only trains which could operate on both the main system and the Berninabahn were two electro-diesels. RhB has now ordered dual-voltage EMUs from Stadler. The Romantsch language (as well as German) is used in this region and this explains some of the double place names. The network carries a remarkable amount of freight.

**Routes:**

* Landquart–Chur–Reichenau-Tamins–Disentis-Mustér (72.9 km)
* Reichenau-Tamins–Filisur–Bever–Samedan–St. Moritz (79.4 km)
* Samedan–Pontresina (5.4 km)
* Landquart–Klosters–Davos Platz–Filisur (69.3 km)
* Klosters–Vereinatunnel–Sagliains (22 km)
* Scuol-Tarasp–Sagliains–Bever (39.4); maximum gradient 3.5%.
* Chur–Arosa (25.7 km); maximum gradient 6%.
* St. Moritz–Pontresina–Tirano (60.7 km); maximum gradient 7%. (1000 V DC)

**Depots:** 11 kV AC system: Landquart (depot and works), Chur, Samedan;
Berninabahn: Poschiavo.

# 3.2.1. BERNINABAHN STOCK (1000 V DC)
## CLASS ABe 4/4      (i)                      Bo-Bo

The survivors, all much rebuilt, of the original Berninabahn stock. Used on works duties and as reserve power. Fitted with track brakes for street running in Chur and Tirano. 36 and 37 were recently rebuilt as rescue units 9923 and 9924. At least 30 and 34 are in the old yellow livery.

**Built:** 1908–11; 35/6 rebilt 1951; rebuilt 1986/7.
**Builder–Mechanical Parts:** SIG/RhB.
**Builder–Electrical Parts:** SAAS (SAAS/MFO §).
**One Hour Rating:** 382 kW (426 kW §).
**Maximum Tractive Effort:** 55 kN (57 kN §).          **Wheel Diameter:** 850 mm.
**Weight:** 30 tonnes (31 tonnes †).                  **Length over Couplers:** 13.93 m (14.66 m †).
**Maximum Speed:** 55 km/h.                           **Accommodation:** 12/27 (12/29 †, 12/31 §).

| 30 † | 32 | 34 | 35 § |
|---|---|---|---|

## CLASS ABe 4/4      (ii)                     Bo-Bo

These railcars together with 51–56, haul most trains on the Berninabahn. Multiple and track brake fitted.

**Built:** 1964–5 (* 1972).
**Builder–Mechanical Parts:** SWS.
**Builder–Electrical Parts:** BBC/MFO/SAAS (*BBC/SAAS).
**One Hour Rating:** 680 kW.
**Maximum Tractive Effort:** 156 kN.                  **Wheel Diameter:** 920 mm.
**Weight:** 41 tonnes (43 tonnes *).                  **Length over Couplers:** 16.54 m (16.89 m *).
**Maximum Speed:** 65 km/h.                           **Accommodation:** 12/24.

| 41 | 43 | 45 | 47 * | 48 * | 49 * |
|---|---|---|---|---|---|
| 42 | 44 | 46 | | | |

*Still used Aug. 2010*   *To be withdrawn*   *47–49 to be recoiled*
*infavour of Allegra*   *for less prestigious runs*

# CLASS ABe 4/4[II]  (111)  **Bo-Bo**

Railcars with three-phase motors built to supplement 41–49. Multiple & track brake fitted.

**Built:** 1988 (51–53), 1990 (54–56).
**Builder–Mechanical Parts:** SWA.
**Builder–Electrical Parts:** ABB.
**One Hour Rating:** 1016 kW.
**Wheel Diameter:** 920 mm.
**Length over Couplers:** 16.90 m.
**Accommodation:** 12/16.

*k C2 R wkr*

**Maximum Tractive Effort:** 178 kN.
**Weight:** 47 tonnes.
**Maximum Speed:** 65 km/h.

| 51 | Poschiavo | 54 | Hakone |
| 52 | Brusio | 55 | Diavolezza |
| 53 | Tirano | 56 | Corviglia |

# CLASS De 2/2  *p.63 lower*  **Bo**

A former B-B motor luggage van, much rebuilt and used for shunting.

**Built:** 1909, rebuilt 1980.
**Builder–Mechanical Parts:** SIG.
**Builder–Electrical Parts:** Alioth.
**One Hour Rating:** 147 kW.
**Wheel Diameter:** 850 mm.
**Length over Couplers:** 7.15 m.

**Maximum Tractive Effort:** kN.
**Weight:** 13 tonnes.
**Maximum Speed:** 45 km/h.

151

# CLASS Ge 2/2  *p.63 lower*  **Bo**

Former B-B centre cab electric locos, normally used for shunting around Poschiavo and Tirano.

**Built:** 1911.
**Builder–Mechanical Parts:** SIG.
**Builder–Electrical Parts:** Alioth.
**Maximum Tractive Effort:** 35 kN.
**Weight:** 18 tonnes.
**Maximum Speed:** 45 km/h.

**One Hour Rating:** 242 kW.
**Wheel Diameter:** 975 mm.
**Length over Couplers:** 7.73 m.

161    | 162

# 3.2.2. 11 kV ELECTRIC & DIESEL LOCOMOTIVES

## CLASS Ge 2/4  **1B1**

Built as a mixed traffic loco at the time of electrification, 212 was rebuilt from loco 206 in 1943 as a shunter, with new off-centre-cab superstructure. Loco 211, which had an auxiliary diesel engine, has now been withdrawn.

**Built:** 1913, rebuilt 1943.
**Builder–Mechanical Parts:** SLM.
**Builder–Electrical Parts:** BBC/RhB.
**Traction Motor:** 1 single phase frame mounted with side rod drive.
**One Hour Rating:** 228 kW.
**Maximum Tractive Effort:** 60 kN.
**Wheel Diameter:** 1070 mm (powered); 750 mm (unpowered).
**Weight:** 33 tonnes.
**Length over Couplers:** 8.7 m.
**Maximum Speed:** 55 km/h.

212    |

# CLASS Ge 3/3                                            C

Modern shunting locos, a single motor drives all wheels through cardan shafts.

**Built:** 1984.
**Builder–Mechanical Parts:** RACO.
**Builder–Electrical Parts:** BBC.
**Traction Motor:** 1 single phase frame mounted with cardan shift drive.
**One Hour Rating:** 425 kW.                    **Maximum Tractive Effort:** 102 kN.
**Driving Wheel Diameter:** 920 mm.             **Weight:** 33 tonnes.
**Length over Couplers:** 8.64 m.               **Maximum Speed:** 40 km/h.

214            | 215            |

# CLASS Ge 2/4                                          1B1

Historic locomotive in old brown livery, based at Samedan. Originally part of the same class as 212, but when rebuilt from 204 for shunting in 1945/6 retained the original box cab.

**Built:** 1913, rebuilt 1945/6.
**Builder–Mechanical Parts:** SLM.
**Builder–Electrical Parts:** BBC/RhB.
**Traction Motor:** 1 single phase frame mounted with side rod drive.
**One Hour Rating:** 428 kW.                    **Maximum Tractive Effort:** 59 kN.
**Driving Wheel Diameter:** 1070 mm.            **Pony Wheel Diameter:** 710 mm.
**Weight:** 31.8 tonnes.                        **Length over Couplers:** 8.70 m.
**Maximum Speed:** 30 km/h.

222            |

# CLASS Gm 3/3                                            C

Diesel shunters used at Landquart and Chur, they have a two-speed transmission giving different characteristics for shunting and line operation.

**Built:** 1975–6.                              **Builder:** Moyse.
**Engine:** MTU of 396 kW.                      **Transmission:** Hydraulic.
**Maximum Tractive Effort:** 153 kN.            **Wheel Diameter:** 920 mm.
**Weight:** 34 tonnes.                          **Length over Couplers:** 7.96 m.
**Maximum Speed:** 35/55 km/h.

231            | 232            | 233            |

# CLASS Gm 4/4                                          B-B

A unique loco (although similar to DB V51 and V52 narrow gauge designs), originally built to 860 mm gauge for a cement works in Itzehoe, Germany, then had three other owners. Converted to metre gauge by Schöma in 1967 and purchased in 1988 from the Brohltalbahn in Germany (loco D4) for use on construction work on the Vereina Tunnel. Now used on ballast trains.

**Built:** 1958. Rebuilt by RhB Landquart works in 1999.
**Builder:** MaK (Type 400 BB, works number 400029).
**Engine:** Two Cummins KT 19-L of 136 kW.     **Transmission:** Hydraulic.
**Maximum Tractive Effort:** 86 kN.            **Wheel Diameter:** 850 mm.
**Weight:** 36 tonnes.                          **Length over Couplers:** 9.68 m.
**Maximum Speed:** 50 km/h.

241            |

# CLASS Gmf 4/4                                         B-B

First used on construction work on the Vereina Tunnel and now used on general ballast work.

**Built:** 1992.
**Builder:** Gmeinder/Kaelble/RhB (Gmeinder Type D75 BB).
**Engine:** Caterpillar of 560 kW.             **Transmission:** Hydraulic. Voith.
**Maximum Tractive Effort:** 165 kN.           **Wheel Diameter:**      mm.
**Weight:** 50 tonnes.                          **Length over Couplers:** 11.70 m.
**Maximum Speed:** 60 km/h.

242            | 243            |

# CLASS Ge 4/6                                    1D1

Historic locomotive in brown livery, based at Samedan.The last survivor of an assortment of locos of this wheel arrangement dating from the time of electrification. It has been retained as a historic loco. The body contains two traction motors geared to a single layshaft driving through an additional layshaft and coupling rods.

**Built:** 1914.
**Builder–Mechanical Parts:** SLM.
**Builder–Electrical Parts:** MFO.
**Traction Motors:** 2 single phase frame mounted with side rod drive.
**One Hour Rating:** 588 kW.               **Maximum Tractive Effort:** 106 kN.
**Driving Wheel Diameter:** 1070 mm.       **Pony Wheel Diameter:** 710 mm.
**Weight:** 56.3 tonnes.                   **Length over Couplers:** 11.10 m.
**Maximum Speed:** 55 km/h.

353            |

# CLASS Ge 6/6            ⟨62 lower⟩            C-C

The last survivors of "Baby Crocodiles" 401–415 built in the 1920s to the same configuration as their SBB counterparts. They no longer have any regular work, being retained at Samedan and Landquart as reserve locos and for specials. 402, 406, 407 and 411 are preserved, but none in operating order.

**Built:** 1929.
**Builder–Mechanical Parts:** SLM.         **Builder–Electrical Parts:** BBC/MFO.
**Traction Motors:** 2 single phase frame mounted with jackshaft/side rod drive.
**One Hour Rating:** 794 kW.               **Maximum Tractive Effort:** 172 kN.
**Wheel Diameter:** 1070 mm.               **Weight:** 66 tonnes.
**Length over Couplers:** 13.30 m.         **Maximum Speed:** 55 km/h.

414            | 415

# CLASS Ge 4/4$^I$            ⟨63 white⟩            Bo-Bo

Mixed traffic locos, extensively refurbished with new cabs. They see use in push-pull mode on Pontresina–Scuol-Tarasp trains. All equipped with regenerative brakes and for push-pull and multiple operation.

**Built:** 1947 (601–604), 1953 (605–610); rebuilt 1986–92.
**Builder–Mechanical Parts:** SLM.
**Builder–Electrical Parts:** BBC/MFO.
**Traction Motors:** 4 single phase fully suspended with BBC spring drive.
**One Hour Rating:** 1176 kW.              **Maximum Tractive Effort:** 142 kN.
**Wheel Diameter:** 1070 mm.               **Weight:** 48 tonnes.
**Length over Couplers:** 12.10 m.         **Maximum Speed:** 80 km/h.

| 601 | Albula | | 605 | SILVRETTA | | 608 | Madrisa |
| 602 | Bernina | | 606 | Kesch | | 609 | Linard |
| 603 | Badus *on loan to ...* | | 607 | Surselva | | 610 | Viamala |
| 604 | Calanda | | | | | | |

# CLASS Ge 4/4$^{II}$            ⟨front cover⟩            Bo-Bo

The standard RhB electric, used throughout the AC system, fitted with thyristor control and DC motors. Resembles a mini version of an SBB Re 4/4 II.

**Built:** 1973 (*1984–5).
**Builder–Mechanical Parts:** SLM.         **Builder–Electrical Parts:** BBC.
**Traction Motors:** 4 pulsating current fully suspended with BBC spring drive.
**One Hour Rating:** 1648 kW.              **Maximum Tractive Effort:** 179 kN.
**Wheel Diameter:** 1070 mm.               **Weight:** 50 tonnes.
**Length over Couplers:** 12.96 m.         **Maximum Speed:** 90 km/h.

All equipped with regenerative brakes and for push-pull operation.

| 611 | | Landquart | 623 | * | Bonaduz |
|---|---|---|---|---|---|
| 612 | | Thusis | 624 | * | Celerina/Schlarigna |
| 613 | | Domat/Ems | 625 | * | Küblis |
| 614 | | Schiers | 626 | * | Malans |
| 615 | | Klosters | 627 | * | Reichenau–Tamins |
| 616 | | Filisur | 628 | * | S-chanf |
| 617 | | Ilabz | 629 | * | Tiefencastel |
| 618 | | Bergün/Bravuogn | 630 | * | Trun |
| 619 | | Samedan | 631 | * | Untervaz |
| 620 | | Zernez | 632 | * | Zizers |
| 621 | * | Felsberg | 633 | * | Zuoz |
| 622 | * | Arosa | | | |

## CLASS Ge 4/4<sup>III</sup>    (h 61 uther)    Bo-Bo

A general purpose locomotive used mainly on Chur–St Moritz RE trains. 650–652 were added to operate car-carrying trains through the Vereina tunnel. Push-pull equipped. All are in advertising liveries.

**Built:** 1993–4/1997.
**Builder-Mechanical Parts:** SLM.
**Builder-Electrical Parts:** ABB.
**Traction Motors:** Four 3-phase.
**Maximum Tractive Effort:** 200 kN.
**Weight:** 61 tonnes.
**Maximum Speed:** 100 km/h.

**One Hour Rating:** 2500 kW.
**Wheel Diameter:** 1070 mm.
**Length over Couplers:** 16.00 m.

| 641 | | Maienfeld | 647 | | Grüsch |
|---|---|---|---|---|---|
| 642 | | Breil/Brigels | 648 | | Susch |
| 643 | | Vals | 649 | | Lavin |
| 644 | | Savognin | 650 | | Seewis im Prättigau |
| 645 | | Tujetsch | 651 | | Fideris |
| 646 | | Sta. Maria/Val Müstair | 652 | | Vaz/Obervaz Lenzerheide-Valbella |

## CLASS Ge 6/6    Bo-Bo-Bo

Articulated locos, mainly used on freight trains between Chur and St. Moritz, but with some passenger work. The two halves of the body are joined by a hinge with its axis horizontal; the centre bogie has some sideplay. 704 has its name in metal letters.

**Built:** 1958 *, 1965 †.
**Builder–Mechanical Parts:** SLM.
**Builder–Electrical Parts:** MFO/BBC.
**Traction Motors:** Six single-phase fully suspended with BBC spring drive.
**One Hour Rating:** 1764 kW.
**Wheel Diameter:** 1070 mm.
**Length over Couplers:** 14.50 m.

**Maximum Tractive Effort:** 214 kN.
**Weight:** 65 tonnes.
**Maximum Speed:** 80 km/h.

| 701 | * | Raetia | 705 | † | Pontresina/Puntrasch |
|---|---|---|---|---|---|
| 702 | * | Curia | 706 | † | Disentis/Mustér |
| 703 | † | St. Moritz | 707 | † | Scuol |
| 704 | † | Davos | | | |

# 3.2.3. ELECTRO-DIESEL LOCOMOTIVES

## CLASS Gem 4/4    Bo-Bo

These electro-diesels are the only main-line locos that can be used throughout the system. They operate as electrics on the Berninabahn and as diesel elsewhere. Used on the Bernina Express between Samedan and Tirano, on snowplough duties, and on works trains. The locos are known as "Steinbock" (ibex) and "Murmeltier" (marmot) but carry stylised images rather than names.

**Built:** 1968. Rebuilt 2001/3 by RhB.
**Builder–Mechanical Parts:** SLM.          **Builder–Electrical Parts:** BBC/MFO/SAAS.
**Diesel Engines:** Two Cummins VT12-825B1 of 463 kW each.
**Traction Motors:** 4 single phase axle hung nose suspended.
**One Hour Rating:** 680 kW (electric), 926 kW (diesel).
**Maximum Tractive Effort:** 192 kN.          **Wheel Diameter:** 920 mm.
**Weight:** 50 tonnes.          **Length over Couplers:** 13.54 m.
**Maximum Speed:** 65 km/h.

Fitted for mw operation; can also mw with ABe 4/4 41–9 and 51–56 under electric traction.

| 801 | | 802 | |

# 3.2.4. 11 kV AC ELECTRIC RAILCARS

## CLASS ABe 4/4                                    Bo-Bo

Operates with driving trailers BDt 1721–3. Now historic stock, based at Samedan.

**Built:** 1939; rebuilt by RhB in 1983/4.          **Builder–Mechanical Parts:** SWS.
**Builder–Electrical Parts:** BBC/MFO.          **One Hour Rating:** 440 kW.
**Maximum Tractive Effort:** 78 kN.          **Wheel Diameter:** 850 mm.
**Weight:** 39 tonnes.          **Length over Couplers:** 18.00 m.
**Maximum Speed:** 70 km/h.          **Accommodation:** 12/28 1T.

501

## CLASS Be 4/4                                    Bo-Bo

Single-ended motor coaches (gangwayed at the non-driving end), used on Klosters–Landquart–Chur–Filisur local services , operating as 2-, 3- or 4-car sets with driving trailers ABDt 1711–6 and intermediate trailers B 2411–2420. They have thyristor control, DC motors and electropneumatic brakes. To be replacded by "Allegra" EMUs from 2011.

**Built:** 1971 (* 1979).          **Builder–Mechanical Parts:** FFA/SIG.
**Builder–Electrical Parts:** SAAS.          **One Hour Rating:** 776 kW.
**Maximum Tractive Effort:** 112 kN.          **Wheel Diameter:** 750 mm.
**Weight:** 44.6 tonnes.          **Length over Couplers:** 18.70 m.
**Maximum Speed:** 90 km/h.          **Accommodation:** –/40 1T.

| 511 | 513 | 515 | * | 516 | * |
| 512 | 514 | | | | |

## CLASS ABe 8/12          "ALLEGRA"          3-CAR UNITS

These units will replace loco-hauled trains and existing EMUs on both the 11 kV AC system and the Berninabahn. The first 15 sets will be dual-voltage and will operate on the Bernina and Arosa lines plus Landquart–Davos from 2010. In a second stage, five single-voltage 4-car units will be ordered for a Chur area suburban service running Thusis–Chur–Landquart–Schiers. In the longer term RhB plans to buy ten similar single-voltage 5-car units for a service running Disentis-Mustér–Chur–Landquart–Klosters–Scuol-Tarasp.

**Built:** 2009–          **Builder:** Stadler.
**One hour rating:** 2600 kW (AC); 2400 kW (DC).
**Maximum Tractive Effort:** 260 kN          **Driving Wheel Diameter (new):** 685 mm.
**Weight:** 106 tonnes.
**Wheel Arrangement:** Bo-Bo + 2-2 + Bo-Bo.
**Length over Couplers:** 18.46 m + 16.12 m + 18.46 m.
**Accommodation:** 12/26 (2) + –/32 (8) 1T + 12/18 (4).
**Maximum Speed:** 100 km/h.

| 3501 | 3505 | 3509 | 3513 |
| 3502 | 3506 | 3510 | 3514 |
| 3503 | 3507 | 3511 | 3515 |
| 3504 | 3508 | 3512 | |

# 3.2.5. TRACTORS, SNOWPLOUGHS, ETC

As with other Swiss railways, the RhB owns a selection of tractors and snowploughs, plus an assortment of other departmental motive power. 9213 is a self-propelled steam rotary snowplough, still occasionally used at times of severe weather, but also used on specials!

| Class | Number | Builder | km/h | tonnes | kW | Built |
|-------|--------|---------|------|--------|-----|-------|
| Tm 2/2 | 15 § | RACO/SLM | 30 | 9 | 37 | 1957 |
| Tm 2/2 | 16 § | RACO/SLM | 30 | 9 | 37 | 1957 |
| Tm 2/2 | 20 § | RACO/SLM | 30 | 9 | 41 | 1962 |
| Tm 2/2 | 21 § | RACO/SLM | 30 | 9 | 41 | 1965 |
| Tm 2/2 | 22 § | RACO/SLM | 30 | 9 | 41 | 1965 |
| Tm 2/2 | 25 § | RACO/SLM | 30 | 9 | 41 | 1965 |
| Tm 2/2 | 26 § | RACO/SLM | 30 | 9 | 41 | 1969 |
| Te 2/2 | 71 | SLM/SAAS | 30 | 13 | 97 | 1946 |
| Te 2/2 | 72 | SLM/SAAS | 30 | 13 | 97 | 1946 |
| Te 2/2 | 73 | SLM/SAAS | 30 | 13 | 97 | 1946 |
| Te 2/2 | 74 | SE/GSEG | 50 | 24 | 216 | 1969 |
| Te 2/2 | 75 | SE/GSEG | 50 | 24 | 216 | 1969 |
| Ta 1/2 | 80 | WIND | 3.9 | 9.2 | 6 | 1980 |
| Tm 2/2 | 81 | RACO/RhB | 80 | 22 | 336 | 1987 |
| Tm 2/2 | 83 | RACO/RhB | 80 | 22 | 336 | 1987 |
| Tm 2/2 | 84 | RACO/RhB | 80 | 22 | 336 | 1987 |
| Tm 2/2 | 85 | RACO/RhB | 60 | 24 | 336 | 1990 |
| Tm 2/2 | 86 | RACO/RhB | 60 | 24 | 336 | 1990 |
| Tm 2/2 | 87 | RACO/RhB | 60 | 24 | 336 | 1990 |
| Tm 2/2 | 88 | RACO/RhB | 60 | 24 | 336 | 1990 |
| Tm 2/2 | 89 | RACO/RhB | 60 | 24 | 336 | 1990 |
| Tm 2/2 | 90 | RACO/RhB | 60 | 24 | 336 | 1994 |
| Tm 2/2 | 93 + | SCH/DZ | 35 | 21 | 172 | 1971 |
| Tm 2/2 | 95 | WIND | 50 | | | 1998 |
| Tm 2/2 | 96 | WIND | 50 | | | 1998 |
| Tm 2/2 | 97 | WIND | 50 | | | 1998 |
| Tm 2/2 | 98 | WIND | 50 | | | 1998 |
| Tmf 2/2 | 111 | SCH | 16/50 | 24 | 317 | 2001 |
| Tmf 2/2 | 112 | SCH | 16/50 | 24 | 317 | 2001 |
| Tmf 2/2 | 113 | SCH | 16/50 | 24 | 317 | 2001 |
| Tmf 2/2 | 114 | SCH | 16/50 | 24 | 317 | 2001 |
| Tmf 2/2 | 115 | SCH | 16/50 | 24 | 317 | 2006 |
| Tmf 2/2 | 116 | SCH | 16/50 | 24 | 317 | 2004 |
| Tmf 2/2 | 117 | SCH | 16/50 | 24 | 317 | 2004 |
| Tmf 2/2 | 118 | SCH | 16/50 | 24 | 317 | 2004 |
| Tmf 2/2 | 119 | SCH | 16/50 | 24 | 317 | 2004 |
| Tmf 2/2 | 120 | SCH | 16/50 | 24 | 317 | 2004 |
| Xm 2/2 | 9912 | RACO/SAU | 30 | 10 | 41 | 1962 |
| Xm 2/2 | 9915 | PFING/SAU/MFO | 55 | 20 | 112 | 1958 |
| Xm 2/2 | 9916 | RACO/NEN/DZ | 40 | 13 | 100 | 1963 |
| Xm 2/2 | 9917 | STAD/RhB/DZ | 55 | 27 | 224 | 1974 |
| Xm 4/4 | 9918 | WIND/CUMM | 90 | | 485 | 1994 |
| Xm 4/4 | 9919 | WIND/CUMM | 90 | | 485 | 1994 |
| Xe 4/4 | 9920 | SIG/Alioth | 45 | 31 | 298 | 1908 |
| Xmf 2/2 | 9921 | RACO | 50 | 25 | 283 | 1994 |
| Xe 4/4 | 9922* | SIG/SAAS | 55 | 55 | 426 | 1911 |
| Xe 4/4 | 9923 # | SIG/SAAS/MFO | 55 | 55 | 426 | 1911 |
| Xe 4/4 | 9924 # | SIG/SAAS/MFO | 55 | 55 | 429 | 1911 |

* ex BDe 4/4 38 in 1992.
§ 15–26 renumbered from, 64–7, 62/3, 57–61, 56 repectively.
+ 93 was former Tauern Scheiteltunnel no. DL 2.
# ex ABe 4/4 36 and 37 in 2008.

# 3.3. ZENTRALBAHN                                                    ZB

In 2005 the Interlaken–Luzern Brünig line, operated by SBB (which holds 66% of shares), merged with the LSE, which already used the Hergiswil–Luzern section of the Brünig line. Although both have the Riggenbach rack system and 15 kV AC electrification, there is still little interworking of former Brünig and LSE stock. Through trains on the Brünig line are operated by Class HGe 101 locos and Engelberg trains are operated by BDeh 140 units. Most "lowland" stopping services are now worked by Class ABe 130 EMUs. In October 2009 ZB ordered four 7-car rack EMUs plus six 3-car EMUs which will replace the long-distance trains hauled by Class HGe 101.

The LSE was once an isolated 3-phase electrified line connecting the lake steamers at Stansstad with the towns of Stans and Engelberg. The line was modernised and upgraded in the 1960s. A link was built from Stansstad to join the SBB Brunig line at Hergiswil. At the same time, the electrical system was changed to 15 kV AC. There is rack operation near the Engelberg end of the line, although a tunnel to avoid this will open in December 2010. Major changes to motive power will follow.

**Electrical System:** 15 kV 16.7 Hz AC
**Rack system:** Riggenbach.
**Routes:**
• Luzern SBB–Hergiswil–Meiringen–Interlaken Ost (74.0 km), maximum gradient 12.1%.
• Hergiswil–Engelberg (24.8 km), maximum gradient 24.6%.
**Depots:** Ex SBB: Meiringen; ex LSE: Stansstad, Engelberg.

# 3.3.1. ELECTRIC LOCOMOTIVES

## CLASS HGe 101                              ʌ⁶⁺                 Bo–Bo

These locos are based on prototypes 1951/2, now sold to the FO. All through Luzern–Interlaken trains are worked by this type. They are maintained at Meiringen.

**Built:** 1989–90.
**Builder–Mechanical Parts:** SLM.               **Builder-Electrical Parts:** ABB.
**One Hour Rating:** 1836 kW.                     **Continuous Tractive Effort:** 130 kN.
**Driving Wheel Diameter:** 965 mm.               **Weight:** 63 tonnes.
**Length over Couplers:** 14.80 m.                **Maximum Speed:** 100 km/h (40 km/h on rack).
**Former Class:** HGe 4/4.

| | | |
|---|---|---|
| 101 961-1 Horw | 101 964-5 Sachseln | 101 967-8 Brienz |
| 101 962-9 Hergiswil | 101 965-2 Lungern | 101 968-6 Ringgenberg |
| 101 963-7 Alpnach | 101 966-0 Brünig-Hasliberg | |

## CLASS De 110                                                    Bo–Bo

These motor luggage vans were rebuilt from Class Deh 4/4 (locos 901 to 916) dating from the electrification of the line (see Class Deh 120). The rack equipment has been removed and push-pull equipment fitted. They are still used on a few local trains on the adhesion sections Luzern–Stans, Luzern–Giswil and Interlaken–Meiringen although most of these services have been taken over by Class 130. Most of Class Deh 4/4 became Class 110 or 120 but 905 and 907 went to LSE (now part of ZB) and were renumbered 121 and 122, now officially 110 021 and 022.

**Built:** 1941–2, rebuilt 1986–94 by SBB and Stadler.
**Builder-Mechanical Parts:** SLM.               **Builder-Electrical Parts:** MFO †, SAAS *.
**One Hour Rating:** 894 kW.                      **Maximum Tractive Effort:** 102 kN.
**Driving Wheel Diameter:** 900 mm.               **Weight:** 42 tonnes.
**Length over Couplers:** 14.60 m.                **Maximum Speed:** 75 km/h.
**Former Class:** Deh 4/4.

| | | |
|---|---|---|
| 110 001-5  * | 110 002-3  † | 110 003-1  †* |
| 121  (110 021) | 122  (110 022) | |

## CLASS Deh 4/6                                                   Bo–2–Bo

This loco is as Class 110 but in its original state. The outer bogies are used during adhesion working, while on the rack sections the central rack-fitted bogie provides most of the power. The loco is now used at Meiringen for testing stock on the rack and in autumn 2009 was repainted in its original green livery, with its origonal number, for use on historic trains.

Details as Class 110 except:

**Maximum Tractive Effort:** 102 kN (adhesion), 216 kN (rack).
**Maximum Speed:** 75 km/h (adhesion), 30 km/h (rack).

**Pony Wheel Diameter:** 710 mm
**Weight:** 54 tonnes.

914 (120 011-2)

# 3.3.2. ELECTRIC RAILCARS

## CLASS ABe 130                           3-CAR UNITS

Recent adhesion-only "SPATZ" (*Schmalspur Panorama Triebzug*) EMUs with panoramic windows used mainly on the Luzern–Stans and Giswil services together with similar trailers. 130 001/010 are dedicated to Meiringen–Interlaken as they have track circuit brushes due to kerosene deposited on the rails by local military aircraft!

**Built:** 2004/5.
**Length:** 51.93 m.
**Power Rating:** 1150 kW.
**Maximum Speed:** 100 km/h.
**Wheel Arrangement:** 2-Bo-Bo-2.

**Builder:** Stadler.
**Weight:** 66 tonnes.
**Maximum Tractive Effort:** 100 kN.
**Accommodation:** 19/– (9) 1T + –/76 + –/39 (5).

| | | |
|---|---|---|
| 130 001 Haslital | 130 005 | 130 008 Mörlialp |
| 130 002 | 130 006 | 130 009 |
| 130 003 | 130 007 | 130 010 Brienzer Rothorn |
| 130 004 Stanserhorn | | |

## CLASS BDeh 140                     SINGLE RAILCARS

These units were inherited from LSE and still operate only on the Engelberg line, with up to six trailers. They are still numbered 1 to 8 although number 6 also carries 140 006 on the side.

**Built:** 1964 (1–5); 1970 6/7; 1980 8.
**Accommodation:** –/32 (2) 1T.
**Maximum speed:** 75 km/h (adhesion); 20 km/h (rack).
**Weight:** 48 tonnes.
**Wheel Arrangement:** Bo-Bo.

**Builders:** SWP/SLM/BBC.

**One Hour Rating:** 736 kW.
**Length over Couplers:** 17.84 m.

| | | | | | |
|---|---|---|---|---|---|
| 140 001 | 140 003 | 140 005 | 140 006 | 140 007 | 140 008 |
| 140 002 | 140 004 | | | | |

# 3.3.3. OTHER STOCK

171 201 to 203 are the narrow gauge equivalent of SBB's 139–179 electric tractors. Tm$^{II}$ 172 101, 102, 597, 598, 982 and 983 are all similar track trolleys – the narrow gauge equivalent of the SBB 601–853 series. 980 (rebuilt from SBB 709 in 1987) was sold to the MIB. 985 and 986 were sold to the FO. ZB ordered another Class 104 tractor, to be numbered 104 002, in 2009.

| Class | No. | Name | Builder | km/h | tonnes | kW | Built |
|---|---|---|---|---|---|---|---|
| HGm | 104 001-3 | | STAD/MTU/TSA | 60/25 | 23 | 550 | 2005 |
| Te | 171 201-7 | | SLM/MFO | 60 | 26 | 260 | 1962 |
| Te | 171 202-5 | | SLM/MFO | 60 | 26 | 260 | 1962 |
| Te | 171 203-3 | MEIRINGEN | SLM/MFO | 60 | 26 | 260 | 1962 |
| Tm$^{II}$ | 172 101-8 | † | RACO/SAU | 45 | 10 | 70 | 1964 |
| Tm$^{II}$ | 172 102-6 | | RACO/DZ/VR | 45 | 10.4 | 80 | 1961 |
| Tm$^{II}$ | 172 103-4 | | RACO/DZ/VOITH | 50 | 16 | 115 | 1967 |
| Tm$^{II}$ | 172 597-7 | | RACO/SAU | 45 | 10 | 70 | 1959 |
| Tm$^{II}$ | 172 598-5 | | RACO/SAU | 45 | 10 | 70 | 1959 |
| Tm$^{III}$ | 172 599-3 | § | Gmeinder | 60 | 24 | 165 | 1957 |
| Tm$^{II}$ | 172 982-1 | | RACO/SAU | 45 | 10 | 70 | 1964 |
| Tm$^{II}$ | 172 983-9 | | RACO/SAU | 45 | 10 | 70 | 1967 |
| Xtm | 691 101-0 | | - | 25 | 17 | - | 1972 |
| Xrotm | 791 051-6 | | Beilhack | 60 | 24 | - | 1986 |

† Ex SBB 734 in 1994 (rebuilt from standard gauge by SBB's Olten works).
§ Ex SWEG V22.02, Germany in 1981.

# 4. OTHER PRIVATE RAILWAYS

Switerland has many "private" railways ranging from short branch lines such as the Orbe-Charvornay to BLS Lötschbergbahn which owns one of the two main lines across the Alps and now operates most of the Bern S-Bahn network. Under an open access regime, there is an increasing tendency for stock from the standard gauge railways to work on SBB main lines. The term "private" is used, although most railways are majority-owned by local authorities, particularly the cantons.

## OWNING GROUPS

Many Swiss railways have now been grouped together as follows:

### AAR bus + Bahn

This group includes the WSB and bus services around Aarau.

### APPENZELLERBAHNEN

This was once only the name of the metre gauge network south of St. Gallen but since the merger in 2006 is also applied to the RHB, the RhW and the TB. AB also manages the FW.

### BERNER OBERLAND BAHNEN

The Berner Oberland Bahnen group is mainly owned by the Canton of Bern and operates the Berner Oberland Bahn plus the Schynige Platte Bahn. These railways are marketed jointly with the Jungfraubahnen group as "Jungfraubahnen"

### JUNGFRAUBAHNEN

This private group owns the Jungfraubahn, the Wengernalpbahn, the BLM plus various cable cars.

### MONTREUX OBERLAND BERNOIS

This group comprises the Montreux Oberland Bernois (MOB) itself plus the Montreux–Territet–Glion–Naye (MTGN) and the Chemins de Fer Electriques Vevysans (CEV)

### TRANSPORTS DE MARTIGNY ET REGIONS (TMR)

The former MC and MO had a common management since 1990 and merged as TMR in 2000. The MC and MO names have slowly been phased out in favour of tourist brandings Mont-Blanc Express and Saint-Bernard Express. TMR and SBB have now set up a joint venture known as RégionAlps which will operate revamped local services on all standard gauge lines around Martigny. This should see SBB EMUs running on MO lines and MO trains on SBB lines.

### TRANSPORTS PUBLICS DU CHABLAIS (TPC)

TPC was formed in 1999 from the merger of four metre gauge lines around Aigle and Bex – the AL, AOMC, ASD and BVB. TPC also operates 21 bus routes. A common station in Aigle was completed in 2008. The AOMC line was rebuilt parallel to the SBB main line and a common depot for the three railways built at En Châlex, south of Aigle on the AOMC line. The AL and ASD units work to the depot at reduced power. All the old depots except Les Diablerets have been demolished or downgraded.

**Works/depot** for AL, AOMC, ASD: En Châlex.

### TRANSPORTS RÉGIONAUX NEUCHÂTELOIS ( TRN)

This company was formed in 1999 to group local rail and bus companies in the Neuchâtel area.

### TRAVYS

This group in western Switzerland includes the OC, PBr and YStCM.

# CHANGES IN OPERATOR NAMES & GROUPING

There have been a very large number of changes in operator names since the last edition of SWISS RAILWAYS. We therefore include this table to help the reader.

| Former name | New name or group |
|---|---|
| Aigle-Leysin (AL) | Now part of TPC |
| Aigle-Ollon-Monthey-Champéry (AOMC) | Now part of TPC |
| Aigle-Sépey-Diablerets (ASD) | Now part of TPC |
| Bremgarten-Dietikon | Now BDWM |
| Brünig line (SBB) | Merged with LSE to form Zentralbahn (ZB) |
| Bodensee Toggenburg (BT) | Now part of SOB |
| Bex-Villars-Bretaye (BVB) | Now part of TPC |
| Brig-Visp-Zermatt (BVZ) | Merged with FO to form MGB |
| Chemins de Fer des Montagnes Neuchâteloises (CMN) | Now part of TRN. |
| Emmenthal-Burgdorf-Thun (EBT) | Now part of BLS after being part of RM. |
| Furka Oberalp (FO) | Merged with BVZ to form MGB. |
| Gruyère-Fribourg-Morat (GFM) | Renamed TPF. |
| Lausanne-Gare (LG) | Rebuilt as part of metro Line 2, run by TL. |
| Lausanne-Ouchy (LO) | Rebuilt as part of metro Line 2, run by TL. |
| Lokoop | Bankrupt, all locos sold. |
| Luzern-Stans-Engelberg (LSE) | Merged with Brünig line to form ZB. |
| Martigny-Châtelard (MC) | Now known as Mont-Blanc Express. |
| Martigny-Orsières (MO) | Now known as Saint-Bernard Express. |
| Mittel Thurgau Bahn (MThB) | Bankrupt. Stock sold or part of Thurbo. |
| Orbe-Chavornay (OC) | Now part of Travys. |
| Oberaargau Solothurn Seeland Transport (OSST) | Renamed ASm. |
| Chemin de Fer de Pont-Brassus (PBr) | Now part of Travys. |
| Rorschach Heiden Bergbahn (RHB) | Now part of Appenzellerbahnen. |
| Rheineck Walzenhausen (RhW) | Now part of Appenzellerbahnen. |
| Regionalverkehr Mittelland (RM) | Merger of EBT, SMB and VHB, now in BLS. |
| Régional de Val de Travers (RVT) | Now part of TRN. |
| Solothurn-Münster Bahn (SMB) | Now part of BLS after being part of RM. |
| Trogenerbahn (TB) | Now part of Appenzellerbahnen. |
| Vereinigte Huttwil Bahnen (VHB) | Now part of BLS after being part of RM. |
| Wohlen-Meisterschwanden (WM) | Closed. |
| Wynental und Suhrentalbahn (WSB) | Now part of AAR bus+bahn. |
| Yverdon-St. Croix (YStC) | Now part of Travys. |

**Notes:**

(1)  Railways are presented in alphabetical order of title. An index by abbrevaiation is given on the following page.

(2)  Numbers in brackets after the railway name are table numbers in the SBB Timetable.

(3)  In the details given for each railway, the main depot(s) are shown in bold. The other places mentioned are "sheds" for overnight/winter stabling and can be very small.

# EISENBAHN AMATEUR MAGAZINE

**EISENBAHN AMATEUR** is a monthly magazine containing a wide range of information mostly about Swiss railways with a section on model railway items. It is produced to a very high standard and contains many colour and black/white photographs. Although written mostly in German, the captions are in German and French. It is not essential to read these languages to enjoy the magazine. A4 size typically about 64 pages.

## SPECIAL SUBSCRIPTION RATES FOR SRS MEMBERS

Once again the SRS is pleased to offer its members the opportunity to obtain a copy of this leading Swiss railway magazine direct from the publishers to your doormat at **substantial** savings from the cover price and direct subscription. Although regrettably increased again for 2011, the rate still represents value for money.

Calculations for the subscription rate to **EISENBAHN AMATEUR** were made in July. Forecasting the rate of exchange so far in advance of the bulk order being placed in December is difficult and caution has to be exercised because exchange rates fluctuations. As subscribers will be aware the exchange rate for the pound against the Swiss Franc has continued to be at a low level for the last twelve months. Because **NO costs** must fall on the members of the **SRS** who DO NOT subscribe to **EISENBAHN AMATEUR**, the subscriber rate (overleaf) includes all costs associated.

Please note that this is not an application form for the renewal of your membership of the Swiss Railways Society. A separate form for this will be sent out with the December issue of "Swiss Express".

Please note the closing date for applications together with the address shown overleaf to which subscriptions must be sent.

**Don't wait - act now - send in your subscription today**

# EISENBAHN AMATEUR MAGAZINE 2011

## APPLICATION FORM

*This is <u>NOT</u> the SRS membership renewal form*

PLEASE USE BLOCK CAPITALS

Name: .............................................................................

Address: ..........................................................................

..........................................................................

..........................................................................

Post Code: ...................................................

SRS No: ........................................................ (membership number)

Tele No: ........................................................ (in case of queries)

Email: ........................................................... (in case of queries)

Payment should be made in sterling by cheque or draft and must be made out to "Swiss Railways Society" payable in the U.K. and drawn on a U.K. bank.

Payment and this form must be sent to:

**Mr. I. S. Athey, Craigwood, Lanton, Jedburgh, TD8 6SU**

Amount enclosed:  £.........................
Mail (outside Europe)                    Surface/Air Mail (please cross out which does not apply)

## SUBSCRIPTION RATES

UK & Europe
> Existing and past subscribers      £60.00
> NEW subscribers                          £65.00

| REST OF THE WORLD | Surface | Airmail |
|---|---|---|
| Existing and past subscribers | £60.00 | £81.00 |
| NEW subscribers | £65.00 | £85.00 |

(Note: We are exceptionally able to accept, US Dollar currency cheques, payable through a UK bank however any such payment requires an extra £10.00 to cover bank charges.)

**Applications must be received by Saturday 4th DECEMBER 2010**

# INDEX TO PRIVATE RAILWAYS BY ABBREVIATION

# 4.1 AARE SEELAND mobil                    ASm

Previously known as Oberaargau Solothurn Seeland Transport (OSST), this is the group name for the bus company OAK and three light railways to the north and west of Bern. The BTI is completely separate from the other two in the area south of Biel known as Seeland. The RVO was known as the OJB (Oberaargau Jura Bahn) until July 1990. There is now a common numbering system. BTI stock is in the 500 series although units from the other network can be used there. In 2009, 101 was in use there. Some of the operation of the Solothurn–Niederbipp–Langenthal line is on street. Reopening of the line from Niederbipp to Oensingen is planned. There is significant freight around Langenthal hauled by ASm with standard gauge wagons on metre gauge "skates". BTI carries stone between a quarry at Siselen and a cement plant at Sutz, usually returning with infill material. Trains are formed of three tipping hoppers topped-and-tailed by electric railcars. The standard gauge shunter works tanks from Niederbipp to Oberbipp.

**Gauge:** 1000 mm.
**Electrical System:** 1200 V DC
**Routes:**
• Solothurn–Niederbipp (14.5 km)
• Niederbipp–Langenthal (11.0 km)
• Langenthal–St. Urban Ziegelei (7.0 km)
• Biel–Täuffelen–Ins (20.2 km).
**Depots: Langenthal** (former RVO), **Täuffelen** (BTI), **Wiedlisbach** (SNB).

## REGIONALVERKEHR OBERAARGAU (413)                    RVO

## SOLOTHURN–NIEDERBIPP BAHN (413)                    SNB

# CLASS Be 4/8                    3-CAR UNITS

ASm received three 3-car low-floor EMUs nicknamed STAR (*Schmalspur Triebzug für Attraktiven Regionalverkehr*) in 2008. The units work the Solothurn–Niederbipp–Langenthal and Langenthal–St. Urban lines. Three more units were on order in 2009.

**Built:** 2008.
**Builder:** Stadler/Bombardier.
**Wheel Arrangement:** Bo-2-2-Bo.
**Length over Couplers:** 39 m.
**Power Rating:** 660 kW.

**Accommodation:** –/26 (5) + –/48 (6) + –/27 (5).
**Weight:** 50 t.
**Maximum Speed:** 80 km/h.

| 110 | JUPITER | | 111 | MERKUR | | 112 | VENUS |

# OTHER FORMER RVO/SNB STOCK

| Class | No. | Name | Builder | Seats | km/h | tonnes | kW | Built |
|-------|-----|------|---------|-------|------|--------|----|-------|
| Be 4/4 | 101 | | SWS/MFO/BBC | 40 (8) | 65 | 32 | 368 | 1966 |
| Be 4/4 | 102 | Bipperlisi | SWS/MFO/BBC | 40 (8) | 65 | 32 | 368 | 1966 |
| Be 4/4 | 103* | | SWS/MFO | 48 | 65 | 33.7 | 368 | 1970 |
| Be 4/4 | 104* | | SWS/MFO | 48 | 65 | 33.7 | 368 | 1970 |
| Be 4/4 | 107* | | SWS/SAAS/MFO/BBC/OJB | 40 (8) | 60 | 32 | 368 | 1973 (86) |
| BRe 4/4 | 116 h | | RING/ALIOTH/MFO | 40 | 40 | 23.2 | 216 | 1907 |
| De 4/4 | 121 | | STAD/SIG/BBC | - | 65 | 45 | 620 | 1987 |
| Ge 4/4 | 126 | | SIG/BBC | - | 35 | 20 | 206 | 1917 (72) |
| Tm 2/2 | 141 | | RACO/Deutz | - | 60 | 19 | 177 | 1985 |
| Tm 2/2 | 142 | | RACO/PER | - | 28 | 5.3 | 41 | 1933 |
| Be 4/4 | 301 | | SWS/MFO | 40 | 65 | 32 | 368 | 1966 |
| Be 4/4 | 302 | | SWS/MFO | 40 | 65 | 32 | 368 | 1966 |
| Be 4/4 | 303 | SOLOTHURN | SWS/MFO | 40 | 65 | 32 | 368 | 1971 |
| Be 4/4 | 304 | WIEDLISBACH | SWS/MFO | 40 | 65 | 32 | 368 | 1978 |
| De 4/4 | 321 | | SZB/MFO | - | 50 | 30.1 | 264 | 1957 (69) |

## STANDARD GAUGE

| | | | | | | | | |
|-------|-----|------|---------|-------|------|--------|----|-------|
| Em 837 826-7 | | | HEN/Voith/Volvo | - | 60 | 60 | 383 | 1965 |

\* 103 and 104 are ex BTI 502 and 501 respectively. Be 4/4 107 was formerly RVO Be 4/4 103.
h Historic railcar "Buffetwagen".

# CLASS Be 2/6    3-SECTION UNITS

These are early Stadler GTW 2/6 EMUs formed of a short central power unit with a driving trailer either side. They operate all passenger services between Biel/Bienne and Ins. Numbering is a little confusing – sets in normal formation are numbered 501 upwards with the power unit numbered 5010 and the trailers 5011 and  5012, the latter numbers being shown on the ends. However, there is no "set" 508 as 5080 is a spare power unit. 509 and 510 were added to the fleet recently to allow the Biel/Bienne–Täuffelen peak service to be raised to quarter-hourly. The name is carried on the power unit. Confusion was rife in 2009 as power units were swapped during their overhaul.

**Built:** 501–508 1997; 509/510 2007.
**Builder:** 501–508 Stadler/SLM/Adtranz; 509/510 Stadler.
**Wheel Arrangement:** 2-Bo-2.
**Accommodation:** –/36 (8) + –/36 (8).
**Length over Couplers:** 30.00 m.
**Power Rating:** 320 kW.
**Weight:** 33.5 tonnes.
**Maximum Speed:** 80 km/h

| | | | | | | | |
|---|---|---|---|---|---|---|---|
| 5011 | 5010 | Mörigen | 5012 | 5061 | 5060 | | 5062 |
| 5021 | 5020 | Täuffelen - Gerolfingen | 5022 | 5071 | 5070 | | 5072 |
| 5031 | 5030 | Nidau | 5032 | | 5080 | Ipsach | |
| 5041 | 5040 | Ins | 5042 | 5091 | 5099 | | 5092 |
| 5051 | 5050 | Sutz - Lattringen | 5052 | 5101 | 5100 | | 5102 |

## OTHER BTI STOCK

| Class | No. | Name | Builder | Seats | km/h | tonnes | kW | Built |
|---|---|---|---|---|---|---|---|---|
| BRe 4/4 | 516§ | SEELAND | SWS/MFO | 40 | 60 | 26 | 282 | 1947 |
| Be 4/4 | 523 | | SWS/MFO | 48 | 65 | 33.7 | 368 | 1965 |
| Be 4/4 | 525 | | SWS/MFO | 48 | 65 | 33.7 | 368 | 1970 |
| Tm | 541 | | RACO/DZ | - | 75 | 19 | 177 | 1985 |
| Tm | 542 | | RJ/RACO/ZÜR | - | 45 | 4.8 | 22 | 1929 (92) |

§  Restaurant railcar, nicknamed "Ankerstube". Originally BTI BDe 4/4 6. Stored at Biel/Bienne.


# 4.2. AIGLE–LEYSIN (125)    AL

**Group:** TPC.

This  line has street running in Aigle and then, after reversal, climbs steeply from Leysin dépôt with rack assistance.

**Gauge:** 1000 mm.
**Electrical System:** 1500 V DC
**Rack System:** Abt. Maximum gradient 23%.
**Route:** Aigle–Leysin Grand Hotel (6.2 km)

| Class | No. | Name | Builder | Seats | km/h | tonnes | kW | Built |
|---|---|---|---|---|---|---|---|---|
| He 2/2 | 12 * | | SLM/MFO/SIG | - | 7.5 | 20.3 | 264 | 1915 |
| Te 2/2 | 101 | | ACMV/BBC/AL | | 20 | 11.6 | 82 | 1949 |
| ARseh 2/4 | 201 * | | SLM/BBC/AL | 32 | 25/15 | 24.5 | 250 | 1946 |
| BDeh 2/4 | 202 | | SLM/BBC | 48 | 25/15 | 24.5 | 250 | 1946 |
| BDeh 2/4 | 203 | | SLM/BBC | 48 | 25/15 | 24.5 | 250 | 1946 |
| BDeh 4/4 | 301 | | SIG/SAAS | 48 | 40/24 | 33 | 596 | 1966 |
| BDeh 4/4 | 302 | | SIG/SAAS | 48 | 40/24 | 33 | 596 | 1966 |
| BDeh 4/4 | 311 § | YVORNE | ACMV/SLM/BBC | 32 | 40/25 | 36 | 836 | 1987 |
| BDeh 4/4 | 312 § | OLLON | ACMV/SLM/BBC | 32 | 40/25 | 36 | 836 | 1987 |
| BDeh 4/4 | 313 § | LA BERNEUSE | ACMV/SLM/ABB | 32 | 40/25 | 36 | 836 | 1993 |

§  Formerly numbered 303–305
*  Historic stock. Loco no. 12 is to be restored as a monument. 201 is a dining railcar ex BDeh.

# 4.3. AIGLE–OLLON–MONTHEY–CHAMPÉRY (126) AOMC

**Group:** TPC.

The AOMC was formed by the merger of the Aigle-Ollon-Monthey and Monthey-Champéry-Morgins in 1946. Only the line to Champéry has rack sections so the former BLT railcars only work Aigle–Monthey shuttles. 501–503, 511–514 were previously 1–3 and 11–14.

**Gauge:** 1000 mm.
**Electrical System:** 850 V DC.
**Rack System:** Strub. Maximum gradient 13%.
**Routes:**

- Aigle–Monthey Ville (11.2 km)
- Monthey Ville–Champéry (13.0 km).

| Class | No. | Name | Builder | Seats | km/h | tonnes | kW | Built |
|---|---|---|---|---|---|---|---|---|
| BDeh 4/4 | 501 | VAUD | ACMV/SLM/BBC | 32 (6) | 65/30 | 40 | 656 | 1987 |
| BDeh 4/4 | 502 | VALAIS | ACMV/SLM/BBC | 32 (6) | 65/30 | 40 | 656 | 1987 |
| BDeh 4/4 | 503 | EUROPE | ACMV/SLM/ABB | 32 (6) | 65/30 | 40 | 656 | 1992 |
| BDeh 4/4 | 511 | CHAMPÉRY | SWP/BBC | 40 | 50/18 | 30.4 | 368 | 1954 |
| BDeh 4/4 | 512 | VAL D'ILLIEZ | SWP/BBC | 40 | 50/18 | 30.4 | 368 | 1954 |
| BDeh 4/4 | 513 | MONTHEY | SWP/BBC | 40 | 50/18 | 30.4 | 368 | 1954 |
| BDeh 4/4 | 514 | TROISTORRENTS | SWP/BBC | 40 | 50/18 | 30.4 | 368 | 1954 |
| Be 4/4 | 101* | YVORNE | SWP/BBC | 44 | 65 | 27 | 382 | 1966 |
| Be 4/4 | 102* | CHABLAIS | SWP/BBC | 44 | 65 | 27 | 382 | 1966 |
| Be 4/4 | 103* | COLLOMBEY-MURAZ | SWP/BBC | 44 | 65 | 27 | 382 | 1966 |
| Be 4/4 | 105* | AIGLE | SWP/BBC | 44 | 65 | 27 | 382 | 1966 |
| Beh 4/8 | 591 | | STAD/BOMB | 48+48 | 70/30 | 53 | 1000 | 2001 |
| Beh 4/8 | 592 | Portes du Soleil | STAD/BOMB | 48+48 | 70/30 | 53 | 1000 | 2001 |

* ex BLT (Birsigtalbahn) 14, 12, 13, 16, 11 respectively in 1985/6.

# 4.4. AIGLE–SÉPEY–DIABLERETS (124) ASD

**Group:** TPC.

The least used of the four lines in the group, serving a sparsely populated area.

**Gauge:** 1000 mm.
**Electrical System:** 1500 V DC.
**Routes:**

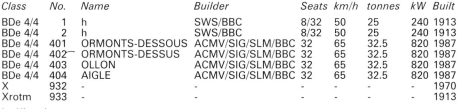

- Aigle–Les Planches–Le Sepey (13.8 km)
- Les Planches–Les Diablerets 8.5 km). Maximum gradient 6%.

**Depot:** Les Diablerets.

| Class | No. | Name | Builder | Seats | km/h | tonnes | kW | Built |
|---|---|---|---|---|---|---|---|---|
| BDe 4/4 | 1 | h | SWS/BBC | 8/32 | 50 | 25 | 240 | 1913 |
| BDe 4/4 | 2 | h | SWS/BBC | 8/32 | 50 | 25 | 240 | 1913 |
| BDe 4/4 | 401 | ORMONTS-DESSOUS | ACMV/SIG/SLM/BBC | 32 | 65 | 32.5 | 820 | 1987 |
| BDe 4/4 | 402 | ORMONTS-DESSUS | ACMV/SIG/SLM/BBC | 32 | 65 | 32.5 | 820 | 1987 |
| BDe 4/4 | 403 | OLLON | ACMV/SIG/SLM/BBC | 32 | 65 | 32.5 | 820 | 1987 |
| BDe 4/4 | 404 | AIGLE | ACMV/SIG/SLM/BBC | 32 | 65 | 32.5 | 820 | 1987 |
| X | 932 | - | - | - | - | - | - | 1970 |
| Xrotm | 933 | - | - | - | - | - | - | 1913 |

h Historic car.

# 4.5. APPENZELLERBAHNEN (854, 855, 856)
## AB

**Group:** Appenzellerbahnen

The Appenzellerbahn (AB) and St. Gallen–Gais–Appenzell (SGA) merged in 1989 to form the Appenzellerbahnen. Power cars 11–15, working in 3-car sets, have the Riggenbach system and work St. Gallen–Gais–Appenzell. Units 16/17 have Strub rack and work Gais–Alstätten Stadt in 2-car sets. 41–45 are adhesion only and work Gossau–Appenzell–Wasserauen in 3-car sets.

A new line is to be built by 2013 to avoid the rack section on the St. Gallen–Appenzell line then the latter will be connected with the TB to form a cross-St. Gallen S-Bahn suburban line with a 15-minute service.

**Gauge:** 1000 mm.
**Electrical System:** 1500 V DC.
**Rack Systems:** St. Gallen–Riethüsli Riggenbach; Stoss–Alstätten Strub.
**Routes:**
• St. Gallen–Gais–Appenzell (20.1 km). Maximum gradient 10%.
• Wasserauen–Appenzell–Herisau–Gossau SG (32.1 km)
• Gais–Alstätten Stadt (7.7 km). Maximum gradient 16%.
**Depots:** Gais (main works), Herisau, Wasserauen, Appenzell.

| Class | No. | Name | Builder | Seats | km/h | tonnes | kW | Built |
|---|---|---|---|---|---|---|---|---|
| Ge 4/4 | 1 | | STAD/SLM/ABB | - | 75 | 43 | 1000 | 1994 |
| BCFeh 4/4 | 5 | h | SLM/SIG/BBC | 6/39 | 40/24 | 40 | 440 | 1931 |
| ABDeh | 6 | ALTSTÄTTEN | SLM/BBC | 6/32 | 55/30 | 36 | 470 | 1953 |
| BDeh 4/4 | 11 | ST. GALLEN | FFA/SLM/BBC | 40 | 65/40 | 44 | 820 | 1981 |
| BDeh 4/4 | 12 | TEUFEN | FFA/SLM/BBC | 40 | 65/40 | 44 | 820 | 1981 |
| BDeh 4/4 | 13 | BÜHLER | FFA/SLM/BBC | 40 | 65/40 | 44 | 820 | 1981 |
| BDeh 4/4 | 14 | GAIS | FFA/SLM/BBC | 40 | 65/40 | 44 | 820 | 1981 |
| BDeh 4/4 | 15 | APPENZELL | FFA/SLM/BBC | 40 | 65/40 | 44 | 820 | 1981 |
| BDeh 4/4 | 16 | | SWA/SLM/ABB | 40 | 65/40 | 45 | 820 | 1993 |
| BDeh 4/4 | 17— | | SWA/SLM/ABB | 40 | 65/40 | 45 | 820 | 1993 |
| BCe 4/4 | 30 h § | | SIG/MFO | 12/40 | 65 | 34.2 | 450 | 1933 |
| BDe 4/4 | 41 † | GOSSAU | FFA/SIG/BBC | 39 | 75 | 36 | 820 | 1986 |
| BDe 4/4 | 42 † | HERISAU | FFA/SIG/BBC | 39 | 75 | 36 | 820 | 1986 |
| BDe 4/4 | 43 † | GONTEN | FFA/SIG/BBC | 39 | 75 | 36 | 820 | 1986 |
| BDe 4/4 | 44 † | | SWA/SIG/ABB | 39 | 75 | 37 | 820 | 1993 |
| BDe 4/4 | 45 † | | SWA/SIG/ABB | 39 | 75 | 37 | 820 | 1993 |
| BDe 4/4 | 46 | WALDSTATT | FFA/SIG/MFO | 32 | 65 | 43 | 510 | 1968(96) |
| BDe 4/4 | 47 | URNÄSCH | FFA/SIG/MFO | 32 | 65 | 43 | 510 | 1968(98) |
| Te 2/2 | 49 [4] | | SWS/MFO/AB | - | 45 | 12 | 100 | 1912(55) |
| De 4/4 | 50 | | FFA/MFO/AB | - | 65 | 30 | 455 | 1966(88) |
| BCFm 2/4 | 56 h | | SIG/SZ/MFO | 6/24 | 45 | 32 | 136 | 1929 |
| Xm 1/2 | 89 [4] | | SWS/SIG/SAU/AB | - | 45 | 15 | 75 | 1912(62) |
| Tm 2/2 | 91 | | - | - | - | - | - | - |
| Tm 2/2 | 97 [1] | | O&K | - | 30 | 23 | 150 | 1959 |
| Tm 2/2 | 98 [2] | Schorsch | SCHÖMA | - | - | - | - | 1972 |
| Xrotm 2/2 | 99 | | RACO/BEIL/DZ | - | 30 | 18 | 150 | 1974 |
| Tm 2/2 | 501 [3] | | OK/SAU | - | 18 | 18.5 | 105 | 1957 |

h  Historic cars.
§  Formerly ABe 4/4 43.
†  Formerly numbered 31–35.
[1]  Ex RAG 159, then RBW, CGS, RhB, LSB, DFB.
[2]  Acquired in 1998. Built for 900 mm gauge as DL16 for Arlberg road tunnel project, Austria. Works No. 3325.
[3]  Acquired in 1969. Ex Wandsbeker Industriebahn 2, ex Steinhuder Meer Bahn 101 in 1969.
[4]  49 and 89 (formerly 51) were converted from SB/AWW CFe 2/2 1 and 2 respectively.

# 4.6. BDWM TRANSPORT (654)　　BDWM

Since the last edition of this book the standard gauge WM has closed and standard gauge freight from Wohlen to Bremgarten stopped in 2007, meaning loco 103 will probably be sold. The standard gauge depot is at Bremgarten West This leaves just the Bremgarten–Dietikon metre gauge line, a light railway with mostly roadside running. The company has ordered 14 Type ABe 4/8 3-car EMUs with first class accommodation from Stadler for delivery from December 2009. This will lead to the withdrawal of the unusual articulated B-B-B-B BDe 8/8 units. Type Be 4/8 are very similar to modern sets in service with AAR and RBS but with just two cars. They are to be sold to AAR when the Stadler sets are in service. Set 25 has a bistro counter, reducing seating by 16.

**Gauge:** 1000 mm. Bremgarten West–Wohlen is standard/metre gauge.
**Electrical System:** 1200 V DC.
**Route:** Dietikon–Bremgarten–Wohlen (18.9 km). Maximum gradient 5.4%.
**Depot:** Bremgarten.

## CLASS ABe 4/8　　　　　　　　　　3-CAR UNITS

These new EMUs will replace all of the current EMUs.

**Built:** 2009–
**Builder:** Stadler.
**Overall Length:** 37.50 m.
**Driving Wheel Diameter:** 750 mm.
**Maximum Tractive Effort:** 120 kN.
**Accommodation:** 20/70 (14).
**Weight:** 52 tonnes.
**One Hour Rating:** 1200 kW.
**Wheel Arrangement:** Bo-2-2-2-Bo.
**Maximum Speed:** 80 km/h.

| | | | | | |
|---|---|---|---|---|---|
| 5001 | 5004 | 5007 | 5009 | 5011 | 5013 |
| 5002 | 5005 | 5008 | 5010 | 5012 | 5014 |
| 5003 | 5006 | | | | |

# OTHER ROLLING STOCK

| Class | No. | Name | Builder | Seats | km/h | tonnes | kW | Built |
|---|---|---|---|---|---|---|---|---|
| BDe 8/8 | 1 | AARGAU | SWS/MFO | 93 | 70 | 50 | 588 | 1969 |
| BDe 8/8 | 2 | KANTON ZÜRICH | SWS/MFO | 93 | 70 | 50 | 588 | 1969 |
| BDe 8/8 | 3 | WOHLEN | SWS/MFO | 93 | 70 | 50 | 588 | 1969 |
| BDe 8/8 | 4 | BREMGARTEN | SWS/MFO | 93 | 70 | 50 | 588 | 1969 |
| BDe 8/8 | 5 | ZUFIKON | SWS/MFO | 93 | 70 | 50 | 588 | 1969 |
| BDe 8/8 | 6 | BERIKON | SWS/MFO | 93 | 70 | 50 | 588 | 1969 |
| BDe 8/8 | 7 | WIDEN | SWS/MFO | 93 | 70 | 50 | 588 | 1969 |
| BDe 8/8 | 8 | RUDOLFSTETTEN | SWS/MFO | 93 | 70 | 50 | 588 | 1969 |
| BDe 8/8 | 9 | DIETIKON | SWS/MFO | 93 | 70 | 50 | 588 | 1969 |
| BDe 4/4 | 10 h | Mutschellen-Zähni | SWS/MFO/BD | 40 | 45 | 32 | 216 | 1932 |
| Be 4/8 | 21 | | SWA/SIG/ABB | 50+54 | 80 | 54 | 640 | 1993 |
| Be 4/8 | 22 | | SWA/SIG/ABB | 50+54 | 80 | 54 | 640 | 1993 |
| Be 4/8 | 23 | | SWA/SIG/ABB | 50+54 | 80 | 54 | 640 | 1993 |
| Be 4/8 | 24 | | SWA/SIG/ABB | 50+54 | 80 | 54 | 640 | 1993 |
| Be 4/8 | 25 | | SWA/SIG/ABB | 50+54 | 80 | 54 | 640 | 1993 |
| Tm 2/2 | 51 | | STAD/BBC/SAU | - | 50 | 13 | 88 | 1967 |
| Tm 2/2 | 52 | | STAD/BBC/SAU | - | 50 | 13 | 88 | 1968 |

### STANDARD GAUGE STOCK

| Class | No. | Name | Builder | Seats | km/h | tonnes | kW | Built |
|---|---|---|---|---|---|---|---|---|
| Em 2/2 | 103 | | STAD/BBC/MB | - | 80 | 38 | 350 | 1984 |

h   historic stock.

# 4.7. BERGBAHN LAUTERBRUNNEN–MÜRREN (313)     BLM

**Group:** Jungfraubahnen.

The BLM runs from Grütschalp (where there is a cable car from Lauterbrunnen – the funicular was recently replaced) along a mountain ledge, to Mürren where road vehicles are banned.

**Gauge:** 1000 mm.
**Electrical System:** 550 V DC.
**Route:** Grütschalp–Mürren (4.3 km). Maximum gradient 5%.
**Depot:** Grütschalp.

| Class | No. | Name | Builder | Seats | km/h | tonnes | kW | Built |
|---|---|---|---|---|---|---|---|---|
| CFe 2/4 | 11 h | | SIG/MFO | 40 | 25 | 17.5 | 100 | 1913 |
| Be 4/4 | 21 | | SIG/BBC/SAAS | 48 | 30 | 25 | 200 | 1967 |
| Be 4/4 | 22 | | SIG/BBC/SAAS | 48 | 30 | 25 | 200 | 1967 |
| Be 4/4 | 23 | | SIG/BBC/SAAS | 48 | 30 | 25 | 200 | 1967 |
| Xrotm | 25 | | PETER/FORD | – | 25 | 5 | 125 | 1956 |

h   Historic car.

# 4.8. BERNER OBERLAND BAHN (311, 312)     BOB

**Group:** Berner Oberland Bahnen

This line runs from Interlaken to Lauterbrunnen and Grindelwald, at both of which connections are made with the WAB. At Wilderswil, the line also connects with the Schynige Platte Bahn. There are rack sections south of Zweilütschinen on both routes. 309 was sold to the BZB in Germany. The BOB being the "main line" out of Interlaken, trains are often formed of 12 cars as far as Zweilütschinen where trains divide and join. Shunters 1 and 31 are nicknamed Chrigel and Ferdinand respectively but the names are not carried.

**Gauge:** 1000 mm.
**Electrical System:** 1500 V DC.
**Rack System:** Riggenbach.
**Routes:**
• Interlaken Ost–Wilderswil–Zweilütschinen–Lauterbrunnen (12.3 km). Maximum gradient 9%.
• Zweilütschinen–Grindelwald (11.2 km). Maximum gradient 12%.
**Depots:** Zweilütschinen (2).

| Class | No. Name | Builder | Seats | km/h | tonnes | kW | Built |
|---|---|---|---|---|---|---|---|
| Tm 2/2 | 1 | STAD/SAU/BBC/MFO/SIG | - | 30 | 15 | 120 | 1946 |
| Xrote | 5 | SIG/BBC/Peter/BOB | - | 30 | 13 | 170 | 1954 |
| HGe 3/3 | 24 h | SLM/BBC/MFO | - | 40/15 | 35.6 | 294 | 1914 |
| HGe 3/3 | 29 h | SLM/MFO/BBC | - | 40/15 | 36.5 | 300 | 1926 |
| HGm 2/2 | 31 | STECK/SLM/DZ | - | 60/30 | 19.5 | 296 | 1985 |
| Deh 4/4 | 302 w | SLM/BBC | - | 60/40 | 40 | 632 | 1949 |
| Deh 4/4 | 303 s | SLM/BBC | - | 60/40 | 40 | 632 | 1949 |
| ABeh 4/4 | 304 | SLM/SIG/BBC | 12/32 1T | 70/30 | 44 | 1000 | 1965 |
| ABeh 4/4 | 305 GUNDLISCHWAND | SLM/SIG/BBC | 12/32 1T | 70/40 | 44 | 1000 | 1965 |
| ABeh 4/4 | 306 LÜTSCHENTAL | SLM/SIG/BBC | 12/32 1T | 70/40 | 44 | 1000 | 1965 |
| ABeh 4/4 | 307 WILDERSWIL | SLM/SIG/BBC | 12/32 1T | 70/40 | 44 | 1000 | 1965 |
| ABeh 4/4 | 308 GSTEIGWILER | SLM/SIG/BBC | 12/32 1T | 70/40 | 44 | 1000 | 1979 |
| ABeh 4/4 | 310 MATTEN b. INTERLAKEN | SLM/SIG/BBC | 12/32 1T | 70/40 | 44 | 1000 | 1979 |
| ABeh 4/4¹¹ | 311 GRINDELWALD | SLM/BBC | 12/24 1T | 70/40 | 44.5 | 1256 | 1986 |
| ABeh 4/4¹¹ | 312 INTERLAKEN | SLM/BBC | 12/24 1T | 70/40 | 44.5 | 1256 | 1986 |
| ABeh 4/4¹¹ | 313 LAUTERBRUNNEN | SLM/BBC | 12/24 1T | 70/40 | 44.5 | 1256 | 1986 |

h   Historic stock.
s   Used as a snowplough.
w   Used for works trains.

# 4.9. BEX–VILLARS–BRETAYE (127, 128) BVB

**Group:** TPC.

This rack and adhesion line is run in two sections, Bex–Villars and Villars–Bretaye. The upper section is very heavily used by skiers in winter and operates up to quarter-hourly but in the low season is only three returns per day. The local "tram" service from Bex to Bévieux has been cut to one return per day with railcar 16 whilst 15 operates a couple of Villars–Glyon runs.

**Gauge:** 1000 mm.
**Electrical System:** 700 V DC.
**Rack System:** Abt. Maximum gradient 20%.
**Route:** Bex–Villars-sur-Ollon (12.4 km), Villars-sur-Ollon–Col-de-Bretaye (4.7 km).
**Depots:** Bévieux, Villars.

| Class | No. | Name | Builder | Seats | km/h | tonnes | kW | Built |
|---|---|---|---|---|---|---|---|---|
| Be 2/2 | 9 | * h | SWS/MFO | 20 | 37 | 15 | 108 | 1915 |
| Be 2/3 | 15 | | SWS/SLM/MFO | 28 | 40 | 15 | 96 | 1948 |
| Be 2/3 | 16 | | SWS/SLM/MFO | 28 | 40 | 15 | 96 | 1948 |
| BDeh 2/4 | 22 | | SLM/MFO | 53 | 35/18 | 19 | 96 | 1940 |
| BDeh 2/4 | 23 | | SLM/MFO | 53 | 35/18 | 19 | 96 | 1941 |
| BDeh 2/4 | 24 | | SLM/MFO | 53 | 35/18 | 19 | 96 | 1941 |
| BDeh 2/4 | 25 | | SLM/MFO | 53 | 35/18 | 19 | 96 | 1944 |
| BDeh 2/4 | 26 | | SLM/MFO | 53 | 35/18 | 19 | 96 | 1945 |
| HGe 4/4 | 31 | LAVEY-MORCLES | SIG/MFO | - | 35 | 24.4 | 368 | 1953 |
| HGe 4/4 | 32 | VILLARS | SIG/MFO | - | 35 | 24.4 | 368 | 1964 |
| Te 2/2 | 42 | | SIG/BVB/ACEC/MFO | - | 35 | 8.5 | 108 | 1898 |
| BDeh 4/4 | 81 | GRYON | SLM/SWP/SAAS | 24 | 40/16 | 36.5 | 720 | 1977 |
| BDeh 4/4 | 82 | OLLON | SLM/SWP/SAAS | 24 | 40/16 | 36.5 | 720 | 1977 |
| BDeh 4/4 | 83 | BEX | ACMV/SLM/BBC | 24 | 40/25 | 36.1 | 720 | 1988 |
| Beh 4/8 | 91 | Bretaye | STAD/BOMB | 40+40 | 45/30 | 54 | 1000 | 2000 |
| Beh 4/8 | 92 | LA BARBOLEUSE | STAD/BOMB | 40+40 | 45/30 | 54 | 1000 | 2001 |
| Beh 4/8 | 93 | TUTTLINGEN | STAD/BOMB | 40+40 | 45/30 | 54 | 1000 | 2001 |
| Xrote | 913 | | Rolba/Oehler/BVB/MFO | - | - | 5.5 | 60 | 1952 |
| Xrotm | 920 | | Rolba/FFA | - | | 16.5 | 220 | 1971 |
| Xe 4/4 | 1501 ‡ | | SWS/BBC | - | 55 | 15 | 148 | 1948 |

\* ex VBZ 1225 in 1958.
‡ ex VBZ Be 4/4 501, later 1501 in 1980.
h Historic car.

# 4.10. BIÈRE–APPLES–MORGES (156)   BAM

BAM is part of Transports de la Région Morges-Bière-Cossonay (MBC) which also includes bus companies TPM and MBC which carry the same green and white livery. One of the few narrow gauge lines in Switzerland electrified at high voltage AC. Car 14 was originally 13, renumbered for superstitious reasons! 11, 12 and 14 usually operate with driving trailers Bt 51, 52 and 53 respectively. This is the only narrow gauge line in Switzerland where freight receipts can exceed those from passengers – the line serves an important army base near Bière as well as autumn sugar beet traffic. The two electric locos are basically the same as RhB Class Ge 4/4 III but also have standard gauge buffer beams. BAM has bought the two standard gauge tractors from SBB as the latter pulled out of shunting at Morges.

**Gauge:** 1000 mm.
**Electrical System:** 15 kV 16.7 Hz AC.
**Routes:**
• Morges–Apples–Bière (19.1 km. Maximum gradient 3.5%.
• Apples–L'Isle-Mont-la-Ville (10.7 km), junction–Bière Casernes (1.9 km).
**Depots:** Bière, L'Isle.

| Class | No. | Name | Builder | Seats | km/h | tonnes | kW | Built |
|-------|-----|------|---------|-------|------|--------|-----|-------|
| BDe 4/4 | 2 | h | SWS/SAAS | 40 | 65 | 36 | 500 | 1943 |
| BDe 4/4 | 5 | h | SWS/SAAS | 40 | 65 | 36 | 500 | 1949 |
| Be 4/4 | 11 | | ACMV/SIG/SAAS | 40 (5) | 75 | 46 | 780 | 1981 |
| Be 4/4 | 12 | | ACMV/SIG/SAAS | 40 (5) | 75 | 46 | 780 | 1981 |
| Be 4/4 | 14 | | ACMV/SIG//SAAS | 40 (5) | 75 | 46 | 780 | 1981 |
| Be 4/4 | 15 | § | ACMV/HESS/BBC | 40 (5) | 75 | 44.5 | 780 | 1981 |
| Ge 4/4 | 21 | LA MORGES | SLM/ABB | - | 100 | 62.2 | 2400 | 1994 |
| Ge 4/4 | 22 | LA VENOGE | SLM/ABB | - | 100 | 62.2 | 2400 | 1994 |
| Tm 2/2 | 41 | BOUBOU | RACO/Cummins | - | 50/75 | 22 | 336 | 1990 |

h  Historic unit.
§  Former YStC no. 3.

## STANDARD GAUGE SHUNTERS
For full details see SBB Class Te$^{\text{III}}$

| Class | No. | Builder | | km/h | tonnes | kW | Built |
|-------|-----|---------|---|------|--------|-----|-------|
| Te$^{\text{III}}$ | 147 | SLM/MFO | - | 60 | 28 | 245 | 1965 |
| Te$^{\text{III}}$ | 155 | SLM/MFO | - | 60 | 28 | 245 | 1965 |

# 4.11. BRIENZ-ROTHORN BAHN (475)   BRB

One of the few non-electrified lines in Switzerland, the BRB was entirely steam operated until diesels were introduced to augment the fleet in the 1970s. However, most trains remain steam, and the railway purchased a new oil-fired steam loco from SLM in 1992 then two more in 1996! These usually operate together with just two of the other, coal-fired locos. The line is pure rack, and boasts the greatest height difference between lowest (566 m) and highest (2244 m) stations of any Swiss railway.

**Gauge:** 800 mm.
**Rack System:** Abt.
**Route:** Brienz–Rothorn Kulm (7.6 km). Maximum gradient 25%.
**Depot:** Brienz.

| Class | No. | Name | Builder | Seats | km/h | tonnes | kW | Built |
|-------|-----|------|---------|-------|------|--------|-----|-------|
| H 2/3 | 1 * | | SLM | - | 9.5 | 17 | 175 | 1891 |
| H 2/3 | 2 | | SLM | - | 9.5 | 17 | 175 | 1891 |
| H 2/3 | 3 | | SLM | - | 9.5 | 17 | 175 | 1892 |
| H 2/3 | 4 | | SLM | - | 9.5 | 17 | 175 | 1892 |
| H 2/3 | 5 † | | SLM | - | 9.5 | 17 | 175 | 1891 |
| H 2/3 | 6 | | SLM | - | 9.5 | 20 | 225 | 1933 |
| H 2/3 | 7 | | SLM | - | 9.5 | 20 | 225 | 1936 |
| Hm 2/2 | 9 | | STECK/MTU | - | 14 | 13.5 | 485 | 1975 |
| Hm 2/2 | 10 | | STECK/MTU | - | 14 | 13.5 | 485 | 1975 |
| Hm 2/2 | 11 | | STECK/MTU | - | 14 | 13.5 | 485 | 1987 |
| H 2/3 | 12 | BERN | SLM | - | 14 | 15.7 | 300 | 1992 |
| H 2/3 | 14 | | SLM | - | 14 | 15.7 | 300 | 1996 |
| H 2/3 | 15 | | SLM | - | 14 | 15.7 | 300 | 1996 |
| H 2/3 | 16 § ▬ | | SLM | - | 14 | 16 | 300 | 1992 |

* ex FMG 7, 1962.                § ex MTGN 1.
† ex WAB 1, 1911.

# 4.12. CHEMINS DE FER DU JURA (236, 237, 238) CJ

The CJ comprises two separate systems, a short standard gauge branch linking Porrentruy and Bonfol, and a lengthy metre gauge system meeting the SBB at La Chaux de Fonds, Tavannes and Glovelier. The metre gauge will be extended by 2020 from Glovelier to Delémont by adding an additional rail to the existing SBB line. The metre gauge network still hauls standard gauge freight stock on transporter wagons.

**Gauge:** 1435/1000 mm.
**Electrical System:** 15 kV 16.7 Hz AC (1435 mm), 1500 V DC (1000 mm).
**Routes:**
**1435 m gauge:**
• Porrentruy–Bonfol (10.9 km).
**1000 mm gauge:**
• Tavannes–Le Noirmoint–La Chaux de Fonds (44.0 km.) Maximum gradient 5%.
• Le Noirmont–Glovelier (30.3 km).
**Depots:** Bonfol (1435 mm), **Tramelan, Saignelégier**, Le Noirmont (1000 mm).

## STANDARD GAUGE STOCK:

| No. | Old No. | Name | Builder | Seats | km/h | tonnes | kW | Built |
|---|---|---|---|---|---|---|---|---|
| Xm | 182 | | ROBEL/DZ | - | 50 | 7.3 | 62 | 1961 |
| Tm 232 181-8 | 181 a | | SLM/MAN | - | 60 | 30 | 280 | 1971 |
| Tm 232 182-6 | 182 | | RACO/SAU | - | 60 | 24 | 155 | 1981 |
| Tem 232 183-4 | † | | MFO/BBC/SAAS/BLS | - | 65 | 30 | 258 | 1967 |
| Tm 237 480-9 | - | | SLM/BBC | - | 30 | 27 | 100 | 1962 |
| BDe 577 101-9 | 101 | BONFOL | SWS/MFO/BBC | –/68 | 70 | 50.5 | 640 | 1968 |
| BDe 577 102-7 | 102 | ALLE | SWS/MFO/BBC | –/60 | 70 | 51 | 640 | 1980 |
| De 587 111-6 | 111 | VENDLINCOURT | SWS/BBC/SAAS/CJ | - | 100 | 48 | 1064 | 1980 |
| RBDe 560 141-4 § | | | FFA/SIG/SWP/ABB | –/56 | 140 | 70 | 1650 | 1984 |

§ Ex SBB 560 002-8 in 2008.          a Ex EBT in 1969.
† ex BLS 225 058-0 in 2009.

## METRE GAUGE STOCK:

*h 132 wheels*

| Class | No. | | Builder | Seats | km/h | tonnes | kW | Built |
|---|---|---|---|---|---|---|---|---|
| BCe 2/4 | 70 h | | SWS/BBC | 4/32 | 45 | 22 | 124 | 1913 |
| De 4/4ᴵ | 401 | | SIG/SAAS | - | 60 | 36 | 544 | 1952 |
| De 4/4ᴵ | 402 | | SIG/SAAS | - | 60 | 36 | 544 | 1953 |
| De 4/4ᴵᴵ | 411 | | SIG/BBC/FFA | - | 90 | 41 | 820 | 1953 |
| Tm 2/2 | 501 | | Moyse/Deutz | - | 34 | 24 | 120 | 1967 |
| Te 2/2 | 504 | | BBC | - | 45 | 15 | 126 | 1913 |
| Xm | 509 | | Beilhack/Deutz | - | 60 | 26 | 263 | 1985 |
| ABDe 4/4ᴵ | 603 | | SIG/SAAS | 9/16 | 70 | 26.5 | 332 | 1953 |
| BDe 4/4ᴵ | 608 | | SIG/SAAS | 32 | 70 | 26.5 | 332 | 1953 |
| BDe 4/4ᴵᴵ | 611 | | FFA/BBC/SIG | 32 | 90 | 36 | 820 | 1985 |
| BDe 4/4ᴵᴵ | 612 | | FFA/BBC/SIG | 32 | 90 | 36 | 820 | 1985 |
| BDe 4/4ᴵᴵ | 613 | | FFA/BBC/SIG | 32 | 90 | 36 | 820 | 1985 |
| BDe 4/4ᴵᴵ | 614 | | FFA/BBC/SIG | 32 | 90 | 36 | 820 | 1985 |
| BDe 4/4 | 621 ‡ | | SWS/SIG/SAAS/CJ | 16 | 60 | 35 | 528 | 1947 |
| ABe 2/6 | 631 | Pouillerel | STAD/AD | 9/68 (5) 1T | 90 | 43 | 320 | 2001 |
| ABe 2/6 | 632 | Mont-Soleil | STAD/AD | 9/68 (5) 1T | 90 | 43 | 320 | 2001 |
| ABe 2/6 | 633 | La Gruère | STAD/AD | 9/68 (5) 1T | 90 | 43 | 320 | 2001 |
| ABe 2/6 | 634 | Le Tabeillon | STAD/AD | 9/68 (5) 1T | 90 | 43 | 320 | 2001 |
| Bef 4/4 | 641 § | | SWS/BBC/SAAS/CJ | 24 | 65 | 45 | 720 | 1973 |
| Bef 4/4 | 642 § | | SWS/BBC/SAAS/CJ | 24 | 65 | 45 | 720 | 1973 |

h Restored as museum car from Xe 2/4 no. 503.
‡ ex FW 207 in 1991. Previously BTI no. 5.
§ ex RhB ABe 4/4 487 and 488 respectively. Used for freight.

# 4.13. CHEMINS DE FER ÉLECTRIQUES VEVYSANS (112) CEV

**Group:** MOB.

Once a much larger system, two sections remain in operation – the adhesion line from Vevey to Blonay and the rack line from Blonay to Les Pléiades. These are usually worked separately although railcars 71–75 can operate throughout. 71 was rebuilt in 2000 with a modern body and only one cab and works as a 2-car set with Bt 224. 72 had a similar rebuild in 2002 but is still a single car with two cabs. 73 and 75 operate with driving trailers Bt 221 and 222. The Blonay–Chamby museum line was once part of the CEV and is still used to move stock between CEV and the MOB. Class 7000 units also work on the MOB.

**Gauge:** 1000 mm.
**Electrical System:** 850 V DC.
**Rack System:** Strub. Maximum gradient 20%.
**Route:** Vevey–Blonay–Les Pléaides (10.5 km).
**Depots:** **Vevey**, Blonay.

| Class | No. | Name | Builder | Seats | km/h | tonnes | kW | Built |
|-------|-----|------|---------|-------|------|--------|-----|-------|
| He 2/2 | 1 | | SLM/MFO/SIG | - | 20 | 17.4 | 390 | 1911(51) |
| BDeh 2/8 | 71 + Bt 224 | | SWP/SAAS/MOB | 50+46 (4) | 50/16 | 33.8 | 428 | 1969 |
| BDeh 2/4 | 72 | | SWP/SAAS/MOB | 48 | 50/16 | 33.8 | 428 | 1970 |
| BDeh 2/4 | 73 | | SWP/SAAS | 48 | 50/16 | 33.8 | 428 | 1970 |
| BDeh 2/4 | 75 | | SWP/SAAS | 48 | 50/16 | 33.8 | 428 | 1983 |
| Te 2/2 | 81 | | SWS/MFO/CEV | - | 30 | 12 | 62 | 1921 |
| Te 2/2 | 82 | | CEV/MFO | - | 25 | 9.3 | 60 | 1938 |
| Xrot | 91 | | - | - | - | - | - | - |
| BDe 4/4 | 103 | | SWS/MFO | - | 45 | 23.4 | 208 | 1903(51) |
| Be 2/6 | 7001 | VEVEY | STAD/SLM/AD | 38 (4)+38 (4) | 80 | 33.5 | 592 | 1997 |
| Be 2/6 | 7002 | * | STAD/SLM/AD | 38 (4)+38 (4) | 80 | 33.5 | 592 | 1997 |
| Be 2/6 | 7003 | BLONAY | STAD/SLM/AD | 38 (4)+38 (4) | 80 | 33.5 | 592 | 1998 |
| Be 2/6 | 7004 | MONTREUX | STAD/SLM/AD | 38 (4)+38 (4) | 80 | 33.5 | 592 | 1998 |

* SAINT LÉGIER-LA CHIESAZ

# 4.14. CHEMIN DE FER PONT BRASSUS (201)
## PBr

**Group**: Travys

A somewhat remote 13.3 km line in the west of the country, the PBr was for many years operated by the SBB and its predecessors. The PBr never owned any motive power until tractor 101 was purchased from the SBB in 1982. Services have always run through to Vallorbe, but from 1989 these have been extended to Lausanne using railcars 2184–5, numbered in the SBB list and operated by them, but financed by the local canton and lettered for the PBr (Vallée de Joux) – these were numbered into PBr stock in 1996. Class 568 are to be rebuilt in the same "Domino" style as SBB Class 560 and renumbered as Class 560.

**Gauge**: 1435 mm.
**Electrical System**: 15 kV 16.7 Hz AC
**Route**: Le Pont–Le Brassus (13.0 km).
**Depot**: Le Brassus.

| Class | No. | Old Class | Old No. | Builder | Seats | km/h | tonnes | kW | Built |
|---|---|---|---|---|---|---|---|---|---|
| Te | 219 306-8 | Te II | - | - | | 60 | 22 | 175 | 1962 |
| Tm | 238 303-2 | Tm 2/2 | 103 | RACO/DZ | - | 60 | 21 | 204 | 1993 |
| Tm | 238 304-0 | Tm 2/2 | § | - | - | 45 | 9 | 75 | 1968 |
| ABDe | 538 316-1 | ABDe 4/4 | 16 | * | 12/31 (2) | 100 | 64 | 1110 | 1965 |
| RBDe | 568 384-2 | RBDe 4/4 | 2184 | FFA/SIG/SWP/ABB | –/56 | 140 | 70 | 1790 | 1989 |
| RBDe | 568 385-9 | RBDe 4/4 | 2185 | FFA/SIG/SWP/ABB | –/56 | 140 | 70 | 1790 | 1989 |

\* Former MThB 16 (536 616) built by SIG/SWS/SAAS/BBC/MFO.
§ Ex BLS 64.

# 4.15. DOLDERBAHN (732)  **Db**

Managed by Zürich tramway operator VBZ. Converted from a funicular in 1973, this rack railway connects with the Zürich tram routes 3, 8 and 15 at Römerhof. The only two points are for a loop in the middle of the line.

**Gauge**: 1000 mm.
**Electrical System**: 600 V DC .
**Route**: Römerhof–Bergstation (1.328 km). Maximum gradient 19%.
**Depot**: Both upper and lower stations have closing doors and pits for stabling and maintenance, with room for one set at the top and one at the bottom!

| Class | No. | Name | Builder | Seats | km/h | tonnes | kW | Built |
|---|---|---|---|---|---|---|---|---|
| Bhe 1/2 | 1 | | SLM/GANG/BBC | 26 | 25 | 22.2 | 150 | 1973 |
| Bhe 1/2 | 2 | | SLM/GANG/BBC | 26 | 25 | 22.2 | 150 | 1973 |

# 4.16. FERROVIE AUTOLINEE REGIONALI TICINESE (620) FART
# SOCIETÀ SUBALPINA DI IMPRESE FERROVIARIE   SSIF

This international light railway links Locarno in Switzerland with Domodossola in Italy, traversing spectacular scenery, which gives the line its nickname "Centovalli" – a hundred valleys. It is also known as the "Vigezzina" in Italy. The SSIF is an Italian company operating the western half of the line. Through services, using mainly panoramis units 81–87 but also 21–24, are jointly operated and the stock is numbered in a common series. Local services at each end are operated by units 51–64. The route into Lugano was rebuilt on a new underground alignment in 1990.

**Gauge:** 1000 mm.
**Electrical System:** 1200 V DC
**Routes:**
- Domodossola–Camedo (SSIF 32.2 km)
- Camedo–Locarno (FART 18.3 km). Maximum gradient 6%.

**Depots: Ponte Brolla** (works), **Locarno (FART); Domodossola Vigezzina**, Re (SSIF).

| Class | No. | Co. | Name | Builder | Seats | km/h | tonnes | kW | Built |
|-------|-----|-----|------|---------|-------|------|--------|-----|-------|
| Be 2/2 | 7 | FART | h | MAN/BBC | 18 | 40 | 11 | 60 | 1908 |
| Tm 2/2 | 9 | FART | | RACO/DZ | | | 21 | - | 1989 |
| ABDe 4/4 | 16 | SSIF | h | CET/BBC/SSIF | ⁻6/30 | 45 | 33 | 310 | 1923 (75) |
| ABFe 4/4 | 17 | SSIF | h | CET/BBC | 6/30 | 45 | 33 | 310 | 1923 |
| ABDe 4/4 | 18 | SSIF | | CET/BBC | - | 45 | 33 | 310 | 1923 |
| ABe 8/8 | 21 | SSIF | ROMA | SWP/TIBB | 24/80 | 60 | 60 | 725 | 1959 |
| ABe 8/8 | 22 | SSIF | TICINO | SWP/TIBB | 24/80 | 60 | 60 | 725 | 1959 |
| ABe 8/8 | 23 | SSIF | OSSOLA | SWP/TIBB | 24/80 | 60 | 60 | 725 | 1959 |
| ABe 8/8 | 24 p | SSIF | VIGEZZO | SWP/TIBB | 24/80 | 60 | 60 | 725 | 1959 |
| ADe 6/6 | 31 | FART | TICINO | SWP/TIBB | 53/– | 60 | 45 | 540 | 1963 |
| ABDe 6/6 | 32 | FART | VALLESE | SWP/TIBB | 18/48 | 60 | 45 | 540 | 1963 |
| ABe 6/6 | 33 | SSIF | SEMPIONE | SWP/TIBB | 10/72 | 60 | 45.5 | 545 | 1968 |
| ABe 6/6 | 34 | SSIF | PIEMONTE | SWP/TIBB | 10/72 | 60 | 45.5 | 545 | 1968 |
| ABe 6/6 | 35 | SSIF | VERBANO | SWP/TIBB | 10/72 | 60 | 45.5 | 545 | 1968 |
| ABe 4/6 | 52 | FART | MURALTO | ACMV/SIG/ABB | 18/64 | 80 | 45.9 | 640 | 1992 |
| ABe 4/6 | 53 | FART | ASCONA | ACMV/SIG/ABB | 18/64 | 80 | 45.9 | 640 | 1993 |
| ABe 4/6 | 54 | FART | INTRAGNA | ACMV/SIG/ABB | 18/64 | 80 | 45.9 | 640 | 1993 |
| ABe 4/6 | 55 | FART | VALLEMAGGIA | ACMV/SIG/ABB | 18/64 | 80 | 45.9 | 640 | 1993 |
| ABe 4/6 | 56 | FART | LAGO MAGGIORE | ACMV/SIG/ABB | 18/64 | 80 | 45.9 | 640 | 1993 |
| ABe 4/6 | 57 | FART | CITTÀ DI BERNA | ACMV/SIG/ABB | 20/59 | 80 | 45.9 | 640 | 1993 |
| ABe 4/6 | 58 | FART | LOSANNA | ACMV/SIG/ABB | 20/59 | 80 | 45.9 | 640 | 1993 |
| ABe 4/6 | 61 | SSIF | S. MARIA MAGGIORE | ACMV/SIG/ABB | 18/64 | 80 | 45.9 | 640 | 1992 |
| ABe 4/6 | 62 | SSIF | RE | ACMV/SIG/ABB | 18/64 | 80 | 45.9 | 640 | 1992 |
| ABe 4/6 | 63 | SSIF | MALESCO | ACMV/SIG/ABB | 18/64 | 80 | 45.9 | 640 | 1992 |
| ABe 4/6 | 64 | SSIF | DRUOGNO | ACMV/SIG/ABB | 18/64 | 80 | 45.9 | 640 | 1992 |

h  Historic cars.
p  rebuilt in 2007 as panorama train.

## CLASS ABe 12/16 (SSIF)     4-CAR UNITS

These are panoramic EMUs which operate most end-to-end services and incur a small supplement. ABe 4/4 Pp 81–86 are driving power cars, Be 4/4 Pp 87–89 intermediate power cars and Rimorchiata P 810–812 intermediate trailers. Formations may not be permanent and are as at July 2009. A fourth unit i son order.

**Built:** 2007     **Builders:** OFV/CORIFER
**Length:** 16.25 + 15.55 + 15.55 + 16.25 m.     **Power Rating:** 1020 kW.
**Accommodation:** 17/19 1T + –/51 1T + –/51 1T + –/54. 1T
**Weight:** 31.8 + 30.2 + 30.2 + 31.8 tonnes.     **Maximum Speed:** 70 km/h.

| | | | |
|---|---|---|---|
| 81 Domodossola | 811 | 88 | 84 Craveggia |
| 82 Toceno | 810 | 87 | 83 Masera |
| 85 Trantano | 812 | 89 | 86 Villette |

OFV = Officine Ferroviarie Veronesi

# 4.17. FERROVIA LUGANESI (635)  FLP

Formerly known as Ferrovia Lugano-Ponte Tresa. The only survivor of several light railways in the Lugano area, the FLP has been modernised and new cars purchased. Be 4/12 units were delivered as Be 4/8 but received low floor centre cars from Stadler in 2002/3.

**Gauge:** 1000 mm.
**Electrical System:** 1000 V DC
**Route:** Lugano–Ponte Tresa (12.2 km)
**Depot:** Agno.

*132*

| Class | No. | Name | Builder | Seats | km/h | tonnes | kW | Built |
|-------|-----|------|---------|-------|------|--------|-----|-------|
| Tm 2/2 | 1 | | GLEIS/IVECO | - | 60 | 20 | 200 | 1994 |
| Be 4/12 | 21 | Lema | SIG/BBC | 184 | 60 | 62.9 | 330 | 1978 |
| Be 4/12 | 22 | Malcantone | SIG/BBC | 184 | 60 | 62.9 | 330 | 1979 |
| Be 4/12 | 23 | Vedeggio | SIG/BBC | 184 | 60 | 62.9 | 330 | 1979 |
| Be 4/12 | 24 | Magliasena | SIG/BBC | 184 | 60 | 62.9 | 330 | 1979 |
| Be 4/12 | 25 | Ceresio | SIG/BBC | 184 | 60 | 62.9 | 330 | 1979 |
| Be 4/8 | 41* | | SIG/BBC | 112 | 60 | 46 | 335 | 1979 |
| Be 4/8 | 42* | Melezza | SIG/BBC | 112 | 60 | 46 | 335 | 1979 |

\*   Ex FART 41/2 in 1993.

# 4.18. FORCHBAHN (731)  FB

Run by Zürich tramway operator VBZ. Once a tramway basically operated as a rural extension of the Zürich system, this light railway over the Forch Pass has been upgraded mostly to roadside running, but with some sections of private right-of-way and the section through Zumikon in tunnel. The cars run (limited stop) over the Zürich tram tracks from the terminus at Stadelhofen (adjacent to the SBB station) to Rehalp. When the Stadler sets were introduced, BDe 4/4 11–16 were sold to Madagascar! Units 21–32 and 51–58 are tramway-style vehicles. The Stadler "Tango" units are 2-car low-floor articulated Bo-Bo-2 half trains (very similar to those on the Trogenerbahn) with a cab at one end. These usually operate in back-to-back pairs 61+62 and so on, although half trains are added in the peaks, making trains too long for the Zürich tram stations. This line passes the Zürich tram museum at Burgwies. CFe 2/2 is a vintage tram in VBZ blue and white livery which operates with trailer 11 (former 111). Xe 4/4 is for works trains and snow cleaning. BDe 4/4 10 is for charters.

**Gauge:** 1000 mm.
**Electrical System:** 1200 V DC (600 V over VBZ tram tracks).
**Route:** Zürich Rehalp–Forch–Esslingen (13.0 km). Maximum gradient 6.7%.
**Depot:** Forch.

| Class | No. | Name | Builder | Seats | km/h | tonnes | kW | Built |
|-------|-----|------|---------|-------|------|--------|-----|-------|
| CFe 2/2 | 4 | h | SWS/MFO | 24 | 36 | 20.2 | 150 | 1912 (35) |
| Xe 4/4 | 9 | | SWS/MFO/VBZ | - | 70 | 26 | 300 | 1948 (82) |
| BDe 4/4 | 10 | h | SWS/MFO | 40 | 65 | 26.5 | 300 | 1948 (67) |
| Be 8/8 | 21+22 | | SWS/SWP/BBC | 86 | 65 | 42 | 610 | 1976 |
| Be 8/8 | 23+24 | | SWS/SWP/BBC | 86 | 65 | 42 | 610 | 1976 |
| Be 8/8 | 25+26 | | SWS/SWP/BBC | 86 | 65 | 42 | 610 | 1976 |
| Be 8/8 | 27+28 | | SWS/SWP/BBC | 86 | 65 | 42 | 610 | 1981 |
| Be 8/8 | 29+30 | | SWS/SWP/BBC | 86 | 65 | 42 | 610 | 1981 |
| Be 8/8 | 31+32 | | SWS/SWP/BBC | 86 | 65 | 42 | 610 | 1986 |

| | | | | | | | |
|---|---|---|---|---|---|---|---|
| Be 4/4 | 51 | SWP/SIG/ABB | 46 | 65 | 24.5 | 500 | 1993 |
| Be 4/4 | 52 | SWP/SIG/ABB | 46 | 65 | 24.5 | 500 | 1993 |
| Be 4/4 | 53 | SWP/SIG/ABB | 46 | 65 | 24.5 | 500 | 1993 |
| Be 4/4 | 54 | SWP/SIG/ABB | 46 | 65 | 24.5 | 500 | 1993 |
| Be 4/4 | 55 | SWP/SIG/ABB | 46 | 65 | 24.5 | 500 | 1993 |
| Be 4/4 | 56 | SWP/SIG/ABB | 46 | 65 | 24.5 | 500 | 1993 |
| Be 4/4 | 57 | SWP/SIG/ABB | 46 | 65 | 24.5 | 500 | 1993 |
| Be 4/4 | 58 | SWP/SIG/ABB | 46 | 65 | 24.5 | 500 | 1993 |
| Be 4/6 | 61 | STAD/BOMB | 34+25(3) | 80 | 33.3 | 400 | 2003 |
| Be 4/6 | 62 | STAD/BOMB | 34+25(3) | 80 | 33.3 | 400 | 2003 |
| Be 4/6 | 63 | STAD/BOMB | 34+25(3) | 80 | 33.3 | 400 | 2003 |
| Be 4/6 | 64 | STAD/BOMB | 34+25(3) | 80 | 33.3 | 400 | 2003 |
| Be 4/6 | 65 | STAD/BOMB | 34+25(3) | 80 | 33.3 | 400 | 2003 |
| Be 4/6 | 66 | STAD/BOMB | 34+25(3) | 80 | 33.3 | 400 | 2004 |
| Be 4/6 | 67 | STAD/BOMB | 34+25(3) | 80 | 33.3 | 400 | 2004 |
| Be 4/6 | 68 | STAD/BOMB | 34+25(3) | 80 | 33.3 | 400 | 2004 |
| Be 4/6 | 69 | STAD/BOMB | 34+25(3) | 80 | 33.3 | 400 | 2004 |
| Be 4/6 | 70 | STAD/BOMB | 34+25(3) | 80 | 33.3 | 400 | 2004 |
| Be 4/6 | 71 | STAD/BOMB | 34+25(3) | 80 | 33.3 | 400 | 2004 |
| Be 4/6 | 72 | STAD/BOMB | 34+25(3) | 80 | 33.3 | 400 | 2004 |
| Be 4/6 | 73 | STAD/BOMB | 34+25(3) | 80 | 33.3 | 400 | 2004 |

h  Historic cars.

# 4.19. FRAUENFELD–WIL BAHN (841)    FW

This light railway has mostly roadside running, with street running in Frauenfeld. Now managed by the Appenzellerbahnen.

**Gauge:** 1000 mm.
**Electrical System:** 1200 V DC.
**Route:** Frauenfeld–Wil (16.9 km).
**Depot:** Wil.

| Class | No. | Name | Builder | Seats | km/h | tonnes | kW | Built |
|---|---|---|---|---|---|---|---|---|
| Be 4/4 | 11 | FRAUENFELD | FFA/BBC | 40(7) | 75 | 35 | 620 | 1985 |
| Be 4/4 | 12 | MATZINGEN | FFA/BBC | 40(7) | 75 | 35 | 620 | 1985 |
| Be 4/4 | 13 | WÄNGI | FFA/BBC | 40(7) | 75 | 35 | 620 | 1985 |
| Be 4/4 | 14 | MÜNCHWILEN | FFA/BBC | 40(7) | 75 | 35 | 620 | 1985 |
| Be 4/4 | 15 | STADT WIL | FFA/BBC | 40(7) | 75 | 35 | 620 | 1985 |
| Be 4/4 | 16 | KUFSTEIN IM TIROL | STAD/ABB/SIG | 40(7) | 75 | 35 | 620 | 1992 |
| Be 4/4 | 17 | TUTTWIL | STAD/ABB/SIG | 40(7) | 75 | 35 | 620 | 1992 |

# 4.20. GORNERGRAT BAHN (142)     GGB

Managed by the MGB with a short connection with the latter at Zermatt. A pure rack mountain railway climbing 1484 metres in 9.4 km, finishing at the highest open air station in Europe, at 3089 metres a.s.l. Views at the summit, especially of the Matterhorn, are astonishing.This line and the Jungfraubahn are the only Swiss railways electrified on the three-phase system which requires two overhead wires. 3061/62 are mainly used for freight.

**Gauge:** 1000 mm.
**Electrical System:** 725 V 50 Hz three-phase.
**Rack System:** Abt.
**Route:** Zermatt–Gornergrat (9.4 km). Maximum gradient 20%.
**Depot:** Zermatt. Some stock is stabled in a tunnel around 1500 metres out of Zermatt.

| Class | No. | Notes | Builder | Seats | km/h | tonnes | kW | Built |
|---|---|---|---|---|---|---|---|---|
| He 2/2 | 3001 | | SLM/SIG/BBC | - | 9 | 13.3 | 184 | 1898 (1966) |
| He 2/2 | 3002 | h | SLM/SIG/BBC | - | 9 | 13.3 | 184 | 1898 (1966) |
| He 2/2 | 3003 | | SLM/SIG/BBC | - | 9 | 11.4 | 184 | 1898 (1975) |
| Dhe 2/4 | 3015 | f | SLM/BBC/MFO/GGB | - | 15 | 17.5 | 190 | 1954 (2004) |
| Dhe 2/4 | 3017 | * | SLM/BBC/SIG/GGB | - | 15 | 18 | 190 | 1958 |
| Bhe 2/4 | 3019 | | SLM/BBC/SIG | 56 | 15 | 18 | 190 | 1961 |
| Bhe 2/4 | 3020 | | SLM/BBC/SIG | 56 | 15 | 18 | 190 | 1961 |
| Bhe 2/4 | 3021 | | SLM/BBC/SIG | 56 | 15 | 18 | 190 | 1961 |
| Bhe 2/4 | 3022 | | SLM/BBC/SIG | 56 | 15 | 18 | 190 | 1961 |
| Bhe 4/8 | 3041 | | SLM/BBC | 120 | 15 | 35.7 | 380 | 1965 |
| Bhe 4/8 | 3042 | | SLM/BBC | 120 | 15 | 35.7 | 380 | 1965 |
| Bhe 4/8 | 3043 | | SLM/BBC | 120 | 15 | 35.7 | 380 | 1967 |
| Bhe 4/8 | 3044 | | SLM/BBC | 120 | 15 | 35.7 | 380 | 1967 |
| Bhe 4/8 | 3051 | | SLM/ABB | 128 | 28 | 49.5 | 804 | 1993 |
| Bhe 4/8 | 3052 | | SLM/ABB | 128 | 28 | 49.5 | 804 | 1993 |
| Bhe 4/8 | 3053 | | SLM/ABB | 128 | 28 | 49.5 | 804 | 1993 |
| Bhe 4/8 | 3054 | | SLM/ABB | 128 | 28 | 49.5 | 804 | 1993 |
| Bhe 4/4 | 3061 | | SLM/BBC | 28 | 15.3 | 27.2 | 380 | 1981 |
| Bhe 4/4 | 3062 | | SLM/BBC | 28 | 15.3 | 27.2 | 380 | 1981 |
| Bhe 4/6 | 3081 | | STAD | 116 | 30 | 48 | 1000 | 2006 |
| Bhe 4/6 | 3082 | | STAD | 116 | 30 | 48 | 1000 | 2006 |
| Bhe 4/6 | 3083 | | STAD | 116 | 30 | 48 | 1000 | 2006 |
| Bhe 4/6 | 3084 | | STAD | 116 | 30 | 48 | 1000 | 2006 |
| Xrote | 3931 | | SLM/MFO | - | - | 14.2 | - | 1943 |
| Xrote | 3932 | | SLM/BEIL/MFO | - | - | 14.2 | - | 1970 |

f Converted to carry supplies to hotels on line.
s Historic train. On display at Stalden in 2009.
* Converted to breakdown train.

## RIFFELALP TRAM

There is a 675 m-long 800 mm gauge tram line which connects Riffelalp station on the Gornergrat Bahn to the 5-star Riffelalp Hotel. It was opened in 1899, but closed in 1959 when tne hotel was closed after a fire. It reopened in June 2001. The two four-wheeled trams of Class Ce2/2 were built in 1899 as overhead electric and rebuilt as battery vehicles in 2001. It is thought that there is very little of the original vehicles remaining.

## CLASS Ce 2/2

**Built:** 1899 as overhead electric. Rebuilt 2001 as battery electric.
**Battery:** 80 V 320 Ah.
**Traction Motors:** 2 x 10 kW.
**Length:** 5.3 m.
**Width:** 1.5 m.
**Seats:** 12

# 4.21. JUNGFRAUBAHN (311, 312)　　JB

**Group:** Jungfraubahnen.

This rack line starting at Kleine Scheidegg, where it connects with the WAB, climbs in tunnel from Eigergletscher through the Eiger and Mönch to Jungfraujoch, the highest railway station in Europe (3454 m), below the summit of the Jungfrau (4158 m). There are superb views here but the trip is very expensive, even with the 25% reduction given with the Swiss Pass.

**Gauge:** 1000 mm.
**Electrical System:** 1125 V 50 Hz three-phase AC.
**Rack System:** Strub.
**Route:** Kleine Scheidegg–Jungfraujoch (9.3 km). Maximum gradient 25%.
**Depots:** Eigergletscher, Kleine Scheidegg (2).

## CLASS BDhe 2/4　　　　　　　　　SINGLE UNITS

**Built:** 1955–1966.
**Builder:** SLM/BBC (SLM/BBC/JB*).
**Wheel Arrangement:** Bo-2.　　　　　　**Length over Couplers:**
**Traction Motors:** 2 x 220 kW.　　　　　**Weight:** 24 (25*) tonnes.
**Accommodation:** –/41 (4).　　　　　　**Maximum Speed:** 24 km/h.

| 201 | 203 | 205 | 207 | 209  * | 210 |
| 202 | 204 | 206 | 208 | | |

\* Named EUROTUNNEL

## CLASS BDhe 4/8　　　　　　　　　2-CAR UNITS

**Built:** 1992/2002.
**Builder:** SLM/ABB (211–214); Stadler/Bombardier (215–218).
**Wheel Arrangement:** Bo-2 + 2-Bo.　　　**Length over Couplers:** 15.675 + 15.675 m.
**Traction Motors:** 4 x 201 kW.　　　　　**Weight:** 22.4 + 22.4 tonnes.
**Accommodation:** 48 + 56.　　　　　　**Maximum Speed:** 27 km/h.

| 211  * | 213 | 215 | 216 | 217 | 218 |
| 212 | 214 | | | | |

\* Named Adolf Guyer-Zeller.

## OTHER STOCK

| Class | No. | Name | Builder | Seats | km/h | tonnes | kW | Built |
|-------|-----|------|---------|-------|------|--------|-----|-------|
| He 2/2 | 8 | | SLM/BBC | - | 18.5 | 16 | 280 | 1912 |
| He 2/2 | 9 | | SLM/BBC | - | 18.5 | 15 | 280 | 1912 |
| He 2/2 | 10 | | SLM/BBC | - | 18.5 | 15 | 280 | 1912 |
| He 2/2 | 11 | h | SLM/BBC | - | 18.5 | 15 | 280 | 1912 |
| X rote | 51 | | SLM/MFO/BEIL | - | 12 | 14 | 376 | 1937 |

h  Historic locomotive.

# 4.22. LAUSANNE–ECHALLENS–BERCHER (101) LEB

A light railway serving the area to the north of Lausanne. The railway was extended in 2000 from the inconveniently located terminus at Lausanne Chauderon to a new terminus at Flon, nearer the town centre and with an interchange with Lausanne's two "metro" lines (see TL). The company also has two preserved steam locos for heritage trains.

**Gauge:** 1000 mm.
**Electrical System:** 1500 V DC.
**Route:** Lausanne Flon–Echallens–Bercher (22.8 km). Maximum gradient 6%.
**Depots:** Echallens.

| Class | No. | Name | Builder | Seats | km/h | tonnes | kW | Built |
|-------|-----|------|---------|-------|------|--------|-----|-------|
| Tm 2/2 | 1 | DIEMA/DEUTZ | - | 40 | 4 | | | 1985 |
| Tm 2/2 | 2 | RACO/CUMM | - | 50/80 | 22 | | | 1988 |
| BDe 4/4 | 21 h | ROPRAZ | SWS/SAAS | 40 | 60 | 30 | 324 | 1935 |
| Are 4/4 | 25 h | GROS-DE-VAUD | SWS/SAAS | 32 | 60 | 30 | 324 | 1947 |
| Be 4/4 | 26 | JOUXTENS-MÉZERY | SWS/SAAS | 40 | 80 | 35 | 588 | 1966 |
| Be 4/4 | 27 | ETAGNIÈRES | SWS/SAAS | 40 | 80 | 35 | 588 | 1966 |
| Be 4/8 | 31 | LAUSANNE | ACMV/SIG/BBC | 56+64 | 80 | 33.5 + 21 | 808 | 1985 |
| Be 4/8 | 32 | ECHALLENS | ACMV/SIG/BBC | 56+64 | 80 | 33.5 + 21 | 808 | 1985 |
| Be 4/8 | 33 | BERCHER | ACMV/SIG/BBC | 56+64 | 80 | 33.5 + 21 | 808 | 1985 |
| Be 4/8 | 34 | PRILLY | ACMV/SIG/ABB | 48+64 | 80 | 33.5 + 21 | 808 | 1991 |
| Be 4/8 | 35 | ROMANEL | ACMV/SIG/ABB | 48+64 | 80 | 33.5 + 21 | 808 | 1991 |
| Be 4/8 | 36 | CHESEAUX | ACMV/SIG/ABB | 48+64 | 80 | 33.5 + 21 | 808 | 1991 |

h   Historic cars (22 is now with NStCM).

# 4.23. MEIRINGEN–INNERTKIRCHEN BAHN (474) MIB

Originally built in 1926 as a construction railway for a hydro-electric scheme, this line was opened to the public in 1946. Initially the line was battery operated, and was only electrified in 1977, sadly not at 15 kV AC which means interchange with ZB at Meiringen is awkward. The line is still owned by the local electricity generator KWO and the terminus is surrounded by power station buildings.

**Gauge:** 1000 mm.
**Electrical System:** 1200 V DC.
**Route:** Meiringen–Innertkirchen KWO (4.8 km)
**Depot:** Innertkirchen KWO.

| Class | No. | Names | Builder | Seats | km/h | tonnes | kW | Built |
|-------|-----|-------|---------|-------|------|--------|-----|-------|
| Be 4/4 | 8 | Oberhasli/Innertkirchen | STAD/SIG/ABB | 40 | 75 | 24.5 | 360 | 1996 |
| Tm | 10 * | | RACO/SAU | - | 45 | 10 | 70 | 1962 |
| BDe 4/4 | 11 † | | SIG/SAAS | 32 | 70 | 26.5 | 332 | 1953 |

*   Ex Brünigbahn Tm 980. Ex SBB 709 in 2000.
†   Ex CJ BDe 4/4 604 in 2005.

# 4.24. MONT-BLANC EXPRESS (132)

**Group:** TMR

## FORMER MARTIGNY–CHÂTELARD (132)        MC

This rack and adhesion line possesses a number of unusual features. From Martigny to Vernayez overhead current collection is used, but the remainder of the line to Châtelard, which includes the rack sections, has third rail. The third rail is being gradually converted to overhead. At Châtelard, the MC links with the metre gauge SNCF line from St. Gervais, which uses a similar third rail system. The MC and the SNCF have purchased five EMUs to enable a joint through service to be operated. SNCF sets are numbered Z 801+802 to Z 805+806. The MC units 21 and 22 are Z 821+822 and 823+824. They are maintained jointly with SNCF. These work through services to France whilst other units work Swiss-only trains.

**Gauge:** 1000 mm.
**Electrical System:** 800 V DC overhead and third rail.
**Rack System:** Riggenbach. Maximum gradient 20%.
**Route:** Martigny–Le Châtelard (18.1 km).
**Depots:** **Vernayaz**, Finhaut, Le Châtelard.

| Class | No. | | Builder | Seats | km/h | tonnes | kW | Built |
|---|---|---|---|---|---|---|---|---|
| BDeh 4/4 | 4 | | SWP/SAAS | 52 | 50/25 | 40 | 560 | 1957 |
| BDeh 4/4 | 5 | | SWP/SAAS | 52 | 50/25 | 40 | 560 | 1957 |
| Xemh 4/4 | 6 | | SWP/SAAS | 52 | 50/25 | 40 | 560 | 1957 |
| BDeh 4/4 | 7 | | SWP/SAAS | 52 | 50/25 | 40 | 560 | 1964 |
| BDeh 4/4 | 8 | | SWP/SAAS | 52 | 50/25 | 40 | 560 | 1964 |
| BDeh 4/8 | 21 | | ACMV/SLM/AD | 48+48 | 70/16 | 72 | 1000 | 1997 |
| BDeh 4/8 | 22 | | ACMV/SLM/AD | 48+48 | 70/16 | 72 | 1000 | 1997 |
| Te 2/2 | 91 | † | SWS/MFO/MC | - | 40 | 16.6 | 108 | 1962(81) |
| Tmx 2/2 | 204 | * | BEIL | - | 50 | 16 | 149 | 1982 |
| BDeh 4/4 | 501 | | SWP/SLM/BBC | 44 | 65/24 | 41.1 | 716 | 1979 |

\*   Can be fitted with rotary snowplough.
†   ex VBZ 1906 in 1974.

# 4.25. MONTE GENEROSO (636)    MG

The only mountain rack line south of the Gotthard pass, the MG was electrified as late as 1982. For many years prior to this, the line was diesel operated. Some of the old diesel stock still remains on the line, either stored or for works or reserve use.

**Gauge:** 800 mm.
**Electrical System:** 800 V DC.
**Rack System:** Abt.
**Route:** Capolago–Generoso Vetta (9.0 km). Maximum gradient 22%.
**Depot:** Capolago.

| Class | No. | Name | Builder | Seats | km/h | tonnes | kW | Built |
|---|---|---|---|---|---|---|---|---|
| Thm 2/3 | 1 | * | SLM/MG/VM | - | 14 | 13 | 400 | 1953 (93) |
| Thm 2/2 | 7 | | BÜH/CAT/MG | - | 14 | 10.2 | 300 | 1975 (89) |
| Bhe 4/8 | 11 | MENDRISIO | SLM/SE | 48+48 | 22 | 34.1 | 810 | 1982 |
| Bhe 4/8 | 12 | MENDRISIO | SLM/SE | 48+48 | 22 | 34.1 | 810 | 1982 |
| Bhe 4/8 | 13 | SALORINO | SLM/SE | 48+48 | 22 | 34.1 | 810 | 1982 |
| Bhe 4/8 | 14 | SAN GALLO | SLM/SE | 48+48 | 22 | 34.1 | 810 | 1982 |

\*   Built on the frames of steam locos 5/6 (new 1890).

# 4.26. MONTREUX OBERLAND BERNOIS (120) MOB

**Group:** MOB.

The MOB is a lengthy metre gauge railway linking Montreux with Zweisimmen, where connections can be made with BLS for Interlaken, plus a branch from Zweisimmen to Lenk. There are connections with the Blonay–Chamby (BC) preserved line at Chamby and with the TPF at Montbovon. The climb out of Montreux is one of the world's steepest adhesion-worked lines, and excellent views can be had over Lac Léman (Lake Geneva). The company also manages CEV and MTGN and owns the Vevey–Chexbres standard gauge line whose operation is subcontracted to SBB. Exchanges of stock between the MOB and CEV are made over the BC.

Most of the company's trains are now marketed as Golden Pass and most trains on the regular Montreux–Zweisimmen service are formed of luxury panoramic or heritage coaches. A project to convert the line from Zweisimmen to Interlaken (BLS owned) to mixed gauge to enable through trains to operate to Luzern over the Brünig line was dropped in 2008. The plan is now to fit stock with gauge-changing bogies.

Class 3000 are now used on works trains; 3004–3006 are in dark blue livery. Class 4000 are 2-car EMUs which haul other coaches on the less prestigious Montreux–Zweisimmen trains. Class 5000 are now centre cars with a driving trailer on each side. They were completely rebuilt in 2004/5 and work only services from Zweisimmen to Lenk and Gstaad. CEV's Class 7000 units are used on the Montreux suburban service. Class 8000 are identical to RhB 641–652 and are all in advertising liveries.

**Gauge:** 1000 mm.
**Electrical System:** 850 V DC.
**Routes:**
- Montreux–Chamby–Montbovon–Zweisimmen (62.4 km)
- Zweisimmen–Lenk (12.9 km). Maximum gradient 7%.

**Depots: Chernex**, Montreux, Zweisimmen.

λ 131

| Class | No. | Name | Builder | Seats | km/h | tonnes | kW | Built |
|---|---|---|---|---|---|---|---|---|
| Tm 2/2 | 2 | a | Deutz | – | 30 | 17.5 | 92 | 1953 |
| Tm 2/2 | 3 | * | Deutz | – | 30 | 16 | 88 | 1954 |
| Tm 2/2 | 4 | b | DMG/PUCH/SAU | – | 35 | 10.4 | 48 | 1934 |
| Tmf 2/2 | 5 | c | Gmeinder | – | – | 29 | 220 | 1977 |
| Tmf 2/2 | 6 | c | Gmeinder | – | – | 29 | 220 | 1977 |
| Tm 2/2 | 7 | b | RhB/SAU/MFO | – | 55 | 19 | 112 | 1950 |
| De 4/4 | 28 | | SIG/BBC | – | 50 | 36.2 | 388 | 1924 |
| BDe 4/4 | 37 | d | SIG/MFO/SWS/VBW | 36 | 60 | 25 | 218 | 1913 |
| Be 4/4 | 1001 | e | ACMV/BBC/SWS/MFO | 64 | 45 | 30.4 | 308 | 1955 |
| Be 4/4 | 1002 | e SAANEN | SWS/SAAS | 56 | 60 | 29 | 176 | 1951 |
| Gm 4/4 | 2003 | MONTBOVON | MOY/CFD/POY | – | 80 | 44 | 485 | 1976 |
| Gm 4/4 | 2004 | ALBEUVE | MOY/CFD/Scania | – | 80 | 44 | 632 | 1982 |
| BDe 4/4 | 3001 | ROUGEMONT | SIG/BBC | – | 75 | 35.7 | 440 | 1944 |
| BDe 4/4 | 3002 | CHÂTEAU D'OEX | SIG/BBC | – | 75 | 35.7 | 440 | 1944 |
| BDe 4/4 | 3004 | | SIG/BBC | – | 75 | 35.7 | 440 | 1944 |
| BDe 4/4 | 3005 | | SIG/BBC | – | 75 | 36 | 440 | 1946 |
| BDe 4/4 | 3006 | | SIG/BBC | – | 75 | 36 | 440 | 1946 |
| ABDe 8/8 | 4001 | | SIG/BBC/SAAS | 22/68 | 70 | 60 | 880 | 1968 |
| ABDe 8/8 | 4002 | VAUD | SIG/BBC/SAAS | 22/68 | 70 | 60 | 880 | 1968 |
| ABDe 8/8 | 4003 | BERN | SIG/BBC/SAAS | 22/68 | 70 | 60 | 880 | 1968 |
| ABDe 8/8 | 4004 | FRIBOURG | SIG/BBC/SAAS | 22/69 | 70 | 60 | 880 | 1968 |
| Be 4/4 | 5001 | | SIG/SAAS | 48 | 80 | 32 | 448 | 1976 |
| Be 4/4 | 5002 | | SIG/SAAS | 48 | 80 | 32 | 448 | 1976 |
| Be 4/4 | 5003 | | SIG/SAAS | 48 | 80 | 32 | 448 | 1979 |
| Be 4/4 | 5004 | | SIG/SAAS | 48 | 80 | 32 | 448 | 1979 |
| GDe 4/4 | 6001 | VEVEY | SLM/BBC | – | 90 | 48.2 | 1053 | 1983 |
| GDe 4/4 | 6002 | ROSSINIÈRE | SLM/BBC | – | 90 | 48.2 | 1053 | 1983 |
| GDe 4/4 | 6003 | SAANEN | SLM/BBC | – | 90 | 48.2 | 1053 | 1983 |
| GDe 4/4 | 6004 | INTERLAKEN | SLM/BBC | – | 90 | 48.2 | 1053 | 1983 |
| GDe 4/4 | 6005 | VILLE DE BULLE § | SLM/BBC | – | 90 | 48.2 | 1053 | 1983 |

| | | | | | | | | |
|---|---|---|---|---|---|---|---|---|
| GDe 4/4 | 6006 | NEIRIVUE § | SLM/BBC | - | 90 | 48.2 | 1053 | 1983 |
| Ge 4/4 | 8001 | | SLM/ABB | - | 120 | 62 | 2000 | 1995 |
| Ge 4/4 | 8002 | | SLM/ABB | - | 120 | 62 | 2000 | 1995 |
| Ge 4/4 | 8003 | | SLM/ABB | - | 120 | 62 | 2000 | 1995 |
| Ge 4/4 | 8004 | | SLM/ABB | - | 120 | 62 | 2000 | 1995 |

a   No. 2 ex Inselbahn Juist (Germany) in 1982. Ex Herforder Kleinbahn no. 14.
b   No. 4 and 7 ex RhB Xm 2/2 9913 and 9914 in 1995 and 2008.
c   5 and 6 Gmeinder Type 300B ex Halberger Hütte, Brebach (Germany) 25 and 26 in 2008.
d   No. 37 ex VBW 37 in 1988.
e   1001 ex LCD 9 in 1972. 1002 ex BA 4 in 1973.
§   Ex TPF 101 and 102 in 2007. Identical to 6001–6004.
*   No. 3 ex Verkehrsbetriebe Grafschaft Hoya (Germany) V121 in 1984. Still carried in 2009!

# 4.27. MONTREUX–TERRITET–GLION–NAYE (121) MTGN

**Group:** MOB.

The MTGN was formed in 1992 by the merger of the Montreux Glion Naye (MGN) rack line with the Territet–Glion funicular. The MGN itself was the result of a 1987 merger between the Montreux–Glion (MGI) and Glion–Naye (GN) railways which had been operated as a single entity for almost 50 years. A pure rack line giving fantastic views over Lac Léman.

**Gauge:** 800 mm.
**Electrical System:** 850 V DC.
**Rack System:** Abt. Maximum gradient 22%.
**Route:** Montreux–Glion–Rochers-de-Naye (10.3 km).
**Depot:** Glion.

| Class | No. | Name | Builder | Seats | km/h | tonnes | kW | Built |
|---|---|---|---|---|---|---|---|---|
| HGe 2/2 | 2 | | SLM/MFO | - | 13 | 14.2 | 162 | 1909 |
| HGe 2/2 | 3 § | VEYTAUX | SLM/MFO/MOB | - | 13 | 14.5 | 162 | 1909 (76) |
| Xrote | 3 | | RACO/Beil/MFO | - | - | 7.5 | - | 1954 |
| Hm 2/2 | 4 | BRIENZ ‡ | RC/BÜH/CAT/PLEI/MG | - | 14 | 12.3 | 415 | 1973 |
| Bhe 2/4 | 201 (S) | | SLM/BBC | 52 | 18 | 15.5 | 150 | 1938 |
| Bhe 2/4 | 203 | | SLM/BBC | 52 | 18 | 15.5 | 150 | 1938 |
| Bhe 2/4 | 204 | | SLM/BBC | 52 | 18 | 15.5 | 150 | 1938 |
| Bhe 2/4 | 207 | | SLM/BBC | 52 | 18 | 15.5 | 150 | 1949 |
| Bhe 4/8 | 301 | MONTREUX | SLM/SE | 48+48 | 25 | 34 | 800 | 1983 |
| Bhe 4/8 | 302 | VEYTAUX | SLM/SE | 48+48 | 25 | 34 | 800 | 1983 |
| Bhe 4/8 | 303 | VILLENEUVE | SLM/SE | 48+48 | 25 | 34 | 800 | 1983 |
| Bhe 4/8 | 304 | LA TOUR DE PEILZ | SLM/SE | 48+48 | 25 | 34 | 800 | 1992 |

‡   ex BRB No. 8 in 1996.
§   Formerly numbered 101. Rebuilt and used with Xrote 3.

# 4.28. NYON–ST. CERGUE–MOREZ (155) NStCM

Once an international line linking Nyon on Lac Leman (Lake Geneva) with Morez in France, the French section was closed as long ago as 1958. Now part of Transport Publics de la region Nyonnaise (TPN). The more modern units 201 to 211 are used on the hourly service whilst the older stock runs on the Nyon–St. Cergue peak extras.

**Gauge:** 1000 mm.
**Electrical System:** 1500 V DC.
**Route:** Nyon–St. Cergue–La Cure (27.0 km). Maximum gradient 6.0%.
**Depots: Nyon Les Plantaz,** St. Cergue.

| Class | No. | Builder | Seats | km/h | tonnes | kW | Built |
|---|---|---|---|---|---|---|---|
| Be 4/4 | 201 | ACMV/BBC/SAAS | 40 | 65 | 33 | 752 | 1985 |
| Be 4/4 | 202 | ACMV/BBC/SAAS | 40 | 65 | 33 | 752 | 1985 |
| Be 4/4 | 203 | ACMV/BBC/SAAS | 40 | 65 | 33 | 752 | 1985 |
| Be 4/4 | 204 | ACMV/BBC/SAAS | 40 | 65 | 33 | 752 | 1985 |
| Be 4/4 | 205 | ACMV/BBC/SAAS | 40 | 65 | 33 | 752 | 1986 |
| BDe 4/4 | 211 | ACMV/ABB | 24 | 65 | 33 | 752 | 1991 |
| BDe 4/4 | 221 ‡ | SWS/SAAS | 40 | 60 | 30 | 324 | 1935 |
| BDe 4/4 | 231 § | SIG/SAAS | 40 | 70 | 26.5 | 332 | 1952 |
| BDe 4/4 | 232 § | SIG/SAAS | 40 | 70 | 26.5 | 332 | 1952 |
| Xtm 2/2 | 251 * | Beilhack | - | 50 | 22.1 | 149 | 1984 |
| Tm 2/2 | 261 + | O&K | - | 15 | 16 | 35 | 1958 |

‡   ex LEB 22 in 1991. Departmental use.
§   ex CJ 606 in 2003 and 607 in 2007 respectively.
*   Can be fitted with rotary snowplough in winter.
+   O&K Type MV4A, works number 25845. Originally built to standard gauge for Nieuwe Matex, Rotterdam. Converted to metre gauge by Metrag and sold to NStCM in 1996.

# 4.29. OENSINGEN BALSTHAL BAHN (412) OeBB

A short branch line connecting with the SBB Olten–Solothurn line at Oensingen and using a motley selection of second-hand stock. The company has close links with the Seetalbahn and runs its preserved stock there – 15301 is known as the "Seetalkrokodil". Also owns 0-6-0T steam locos E 3/3 1 (ex KLB) and E 3/3 2.

**Gauge:** 1435 mm.
**Electrical System:** 15 kV AC 16.7 Hz.
**Route:** Oensingen–Balsthal (4 km).
**Depot:** Balsthal.

| Class | Old SBB No. | OeBB No. | Builder | Seats | km/h | tonnes | kW | Built |
|---|---|---|---|---|---|---|---|---|
| Köf | | 3 x | - | - | - | - | - | - - |
| Em 4/4 | | 20 a | LEW | - | 30/60 | 60 | 478 | 1982 |
| Em 4/4 | | 22 b | LEW | - | 30/60 | 60 | 478 | - |
| Ce 2/2 | | 102 | SLM/SAAS | - | 60 | 28 | 257 | 1944 |
| RBe 2/4 | 1007 | 202 c | SLM/BBC/MFO/SAAS | -/67 | 125 | 38 | 394 | 1938 |
| RBe 4/4 | 540 019-7 | 205 | SIG/SWS | -/60 | 125 | 72 | 1988 | 1964 |
| RBe 4/4 | 540 074-2 | 206 | SIG/SWS | -/60 | 125 | 72 | 1988 | 1965 |
| RBde 4/4 | 560 000-2 | 207 | FFA/SIG/SWP/ABB | -/56 | 140 | 70 | 1650 | 1984 |
| BDe 4/4 | 1641 | 641 d | SLM/SWP | -/40 | 110 | 57 | 1200 | 1955 |
| BDe 4/4 | 1651 | 651 d | SLM/SWP | -/40 | 110 | 57 | 1200 | 1954 |
| De 6/6 | 15301 "Krokodil" | 15301 | SLM/BBC | - | 50 | 73 | 862 | 1926 |

a   ex DB 345 164-8, ex BLS Em 845 001-7.
b   V60D ex Konservenfabrik Estavayer.
c   ex SBB in 1974. "Roter Pfeil", similar to RAe 2/4 1001 in SBB Historic fleet.
e   ex SBB in 1997. OeBB also has 1632 for spares.

x   Named "FULLINA".

# 4.30. ORBE CHAVORNAY (211)     OC

**Group:** Travys.

A 4 km branch line north of Lausanne which is the only Swiss private standard gauge adhesion line with DC electrification. As a consequence, it has been used for testing stock built for export. Passenger trains are operated by unit 14 at weekends and in holidays and by 15 plus driving trailer 51 in the school term. The line generates significant freight around Les Granges et Cossonay including daily vans of Nespresso coffee to Payerne.

**Gauge:** 1435 mm.
**Electrical System:** 750 V DC
**Route:** Cossonay–Orbe (3.9 km).
**Depots:** Orbe, Les Granges.

| New number | Class | Old No. | Name | Builder | Seats | km/h | tonnes | kW | Built |
|---|---|---|---|---|---|---|---|---|---|
| - | Ee 2/2 | 1 | | SIG/MFO | - | 50 | 40 | 455 | 1970 |
| - | Ee 2/2 | 2 | | SIG/MFO | - | 50 | 40 | 455 | 1970 |
| - | Em 3/3 | 3 | | HEN/MTU | - | 47 | 60 | 550 | 1985 |
| - | BDe 4/4 | 13 h | | SWS/MFO | 70 | 50 | 29.5 | 130 | 1920 |
| - | Be 2/2 | 14 | Orbe/Chavornay | STAD/ABB | 40 | 80 | 20.2 | 360 | 1990 |
| - | BDe 4/4 | 15 * | La Sihl | SWS/MFO | 46 | 60 | 28.3 | 330 | 1960 |
| - | De 2/2 | 32 | | SWS/MFO | - | 45 | 15.4 | 106 | 1902 |
| Tm 238 305-7 | Tm I | § | | RACO | - | 45 | 10 | 66 | 1962 |

h  Historic unit.
*  Ex SZU BDe 4/4 513. Accompanying Bt 51 named L'Orbe.
§  Ex PBr. Ex SBB 479.

# 4.31. PILATUS BAHN (473)     PB

The world's steepest rack railway, requiring the "Locher" rack system, comprising a double-sided horizontal rack rail, the railcars having two pinions, one on each side of the rack. Although there is a published timetable, many extras run and trains arrive from Pilatus at Alpnachstad in short succession. There is a traverser here as the single platform can only hold two trains.

**Gauge:** 800 mm.
**Electrical System:** 1550 V DC
**Rack System:** Locher.
**Route:** Alpnachstad–Pilatus Kulm (4.8 km). Maximum gradient 48%.
**Depot:** Alpnachstad.

| Class | No. | Builder | Seats | km/h | tonnes | kW | Built |
|---|---|---|---|---|---|---|---|
| Bhe 1/2 | 21 | SLM/MFO | 40 | 12 | 9.65 | 155 | 1937 |
| Bhe 1/2 | 22 | SLM/MFO | 40 | 12 | 9.65 | 155 | 1937 |
| Bhe 1/2 | 23 | SLM/MFO | 40 | 12 | 9.65 | 155 | 1937 |
| Bhe 1/2 | 24 | SLM/MFO | 40 | 12 | 9.65 | 155 | 1937 |
| Bhe 1/2 | 25 | SLM/MFO | 40 | 12 | 9.65 | 155 | 1937 |
| Bhe 1/2 | 26 | SLM/MFO | 40 | 12 | 9.65 | 155 | 1937 |
| Bhe 1/2 | 27 | SLM/MFO | 40 | 12 | 9.65 | 155 | 1937 |
| Bhe 1/2 | 28 | SLM/MFO | 40 | 12 | 9.65 | 155 | 1937 |
| Bhe 1/2 | 29 | SLM/MFO | 40 | 12 | 9.6 | 155 | 1962 |
| Bhe 1/2 | 30 | SLM/MFO | 40 | 12 | 10.5 | 175 | 1968 |
| Ohe 1/2 | 31 | SLM/MFO | - | 12 | 8.3 | 155 | 1954 |
| Xhm 1/2 | 32 | SLM/STAD/BBC | - | 12 | 11.3 | 320 | 1981 |

Note: Only one underframe exists for cars 29 & 31, the bodies being exchanged as required. Hence, only one of these two cars can be in use at any one time.

# 4.32. POST TELEPHON TELEGRAPH PTT

Not a private railway, the Swiss Post Office is included since it uses shunting locos at a number of locations, often involving operation into SBB stations. Em 3/3 6 has moved to Eurovapor as 837 814-3 and Tm 2/2 12 to Swisscom as 237 937-8. 9, 11 and 14 were stored at BLS's Oberburg depot in early 2009. This type is identical to BLS locos Ee 936 132–135.

| Class | No. | Builder | km/h | tonnes | kW | Built | Location |
|---|---|---|---|---|---|---|---|
| Em 2/2 | 1 | - | - | - | - | 1934 | - |
| Te<sup>III</sup> | 3 | SLM/SAAS | 60 | 28 | 250 | 1954 | Lausanne |
| Ee 3/3 | 4 | SLM/BBC/MFO/SAAS | 45 | 45 | 502 | 1962 | Luzern |
| Te<sup>III</sup> | 5 | SLM/MFO | 60 | 28 | 245 | 1965 | Lausanne |
| Tm | P06 | - | - | - | - | - | Härkingen |
| Ee 3/3 | 7 | SLM/BBC | 40 | 45 | 428 | 1928 | Zürich Mülligen |
| Ee 3/3 | 8 | SLM/BBC | 60 | 48 | 660 | 1985 | Bern Schanze |
| Ee 3/3 | 9 (S) | SLM/BBC | 60 | 48 | 660 | 1985 | Zürich Mülligen |
| Ee 3/3 | 10 | SLM/BBC | 60 | 48 | 660 | 1985 | Bern Schanze |
| Ee 3/3 | 11 (S) | SLM/BBC | 60 | 48 | 660 | 1985 | Bern |
| Tm | 13 | UNIMOG/MERC | 20 | 6.8 | 92 | 1978 | Kriens |
| Ee 3/3 | 14 (S) | SLM/ABB | 60 | 48 | 660 | 1992 | Luzern |
| Tm 2/2 | P15 § | Henschel | - | - | - | 1958 | - |
| Tm 2/2 | P16 * | Stadler | 35 | 40 | 330 | - | Daillens |
| Tm 2/2 | P17 * | Stadler | 35 | 40 | 330 | - | Härkingen |
| Tm 2/2 | P18 * | Stadler | 35 | 40 | 330 | - | Frauenfeld |

§ Henschel Type DH 240 B. Named Gusti. Ex SERSA Tm 237 951-9.
* Also numbered 237 916-2, 237 917-0 and 237 918-8. These are of the same type as SBB 233 910/911

# 4.33. REGIONALVERKEHR BERN–SOLOTHURN (295, 307, 308) RBS

After running under common management for many years, the former SZB (Solothurn Zollikofen Bern) and VBW (Vereinigte Bern Worb Bahnen) merged as the RBS in 1985. The railway provides frequent suburban services from Bern, at one time all routes entering the town over the urban tram tracks. This explains the right-hand running on most sections. A new line, terminating in an underground station below Bern HB was opened in 1965, and is used by all Solothurn line trains, plus those on the ex VBW route from Worb via Bolligen. The other ex VBW route to Worb via Muri still enters Bern over the urban tram tracks, and for many years terminated at the inconveniently-located Helvetiaplatz. Due to the width and weight of the existing rolling stock, the cars could not continue further. Therefore, new tramway type cars were purchased for this route which was extended to Bern Zytglogge in 1997. The voltage of this line was lowered from 800 to 600 V DC to be fully compatible with the tramways. The voltage on the Solothurn line is eventually expected to be boosted to 1500 V DC.

The RBS network represents 13% of Bern's S-Bahn in length but carries 17 million passengers a year – 50% of traffic. Six new low-floor sets are being delivered by Stadler in 2009. Tmf 2/2 tractors 167 and 168 are also on order.

**Gauge:** 1000 mm.
**Electrical System:** 1250 V DC (Line G 600 V DC).
**Routes:**
• Line G Worb Dorf–Gümlingen–Bern Egghölzli (9.7 km;
• Line J Bern HB–Worblaufen–Solothurn (33.6 km);
• Line W Worblaufen–Boll-Utzigen–Worb Dorf (1.2 km);
• Line Z Worblaufen–Unterzollikofen (1.4 km).
**Depots:** Solothurn, Worblaufen, Worbboden; Worb Dorf (Line G).

# 1250 V DC STOCK

## CLASS RABe 4/12                    3-CAR UNITS

Six new low-floor units being delivered. They are known as NExT (*Niederflur Express Triebzug*) by Stadler by the *"Orangen"* being all orange, by the locals. They will operate on the Solothurn–Bern service, allowing a half-hourly service to be introduced. The fastest narrow gauge trains in Switzerland.

**Built:** 2009
**Wheel Arrangement:** 2-2 + Bo-Bo + 2-2
**Accommodation:** 18/136 (3).
**Power rating:** 1400 kW.

**Builder:** Stadler, Altenrhein.
**Length:** 19.835 + 20.330 + 19.835 m.
**Weight:** 79 tonnes.
**Maximum Speed:** 120 km/h.

| 21 | 22 | 23 | 24 | 25 | 26 |

## CLASS Be 4/8 & Be 4/12             3-CAR UNITS

These units were delivered as 2-car but extended by the addition of a Stadler/Bombardier low-floor car from 2001 to 2009. They operate all trains on S-Bahn Lines S7 (Line W) and S9 (Line Z) plus short workings to Urtenen and Jegenstorf on S8 (Line J).

**Built:** 1974 (units 41–52); 1978 (53–61).
**Wheel Arrangement:** Bo-Bo + 2-2 + 2-2.
**Accommodation:** –/64 (+ –/56) + –/64.
**Power Rating:** 326 kW.

**Builders:** SIG/BBC.     *Mandarinli*
**Length:** 59.50 m (*40 m 2-car)
**Weight:** 62.7 tonnes (*48.7 tonnes 2-car).
**Maximum Speed:** 75 km/h.

| 41 | 45 | 49 | 53 Lugano | 56 * | 59 |
| 42 | 46 | 50 | 54 * | 57 | 60 |
| 43 | 47 | 51 | 55 * | 58 | 61 * |
| ~~44~~ | 48 | 52 | | | |

## CLASS ABe 4/12                     3-CAR UNITS

These modern light rail vehicles are very similar to those used on the BDWM and WSB. Built as 2-car sets they have received a low-floor centre car with a central first class section labelled "Prima" in 1994–2001. They are used only on the fast Bern–Solothurn service on S-Bahn Line S8.

**Built:** 1992/93.
**Builders:** SWA/SAG/ABB.
**Wheel Arrangement:** Bo-2+2-2+2-Bo.
**Accommodation:** –/60 + 18/36 + –/60.
**Power Rating:** 640 kW.

*'La Prima'*
**Length:** 59.73 m.
**Weight:** 80 tonnes.
**Maximum Speed:** 90 km/h.

62 Bolligen/Ittigen
63 Worb/Vechigen
64 Stettlen/Ostermundingen
65 Solothurn/Bern
66 Urtenen/Mooseedorf
67 Lohn Ammansegg/Lüterkofen Ichertswil

68 Bätterkinden/Schalunen
69 Büren zum Hof/Fraubrunnen
70 Grafenried/Jegenstorf — *Seconda*
71 Biberist/Zuchwil
72 Münchenbuchsee/Zollikofen — *Seconda*

# 600 V DC STOCK

## CLASS Be 4/8                       3-SECTION TRAM

These are the only vehicles which work on Line G. They were being repainted from the older white, blue and orange livery into a less attractive all-over blue in 2009. Sets will receive an additional section built by Stadler in 2009/10.

**Built:** 1987/88.
**Builders:** SWP/SIG/ABB.
**Wheel Arrangement:** B-2-2-B.
**Accommodation:** –/74.
**Power Rating:** 300 kW.

**Length:** 31.20 m.
**Weight:** 36.5 tonnes.
**Maximum Speed:** 65 km/h.

| 81 | 84 Muri / Gümlingen | 87 |
| 82 | 85 | 88 |
| 83 | 86 | 89 |

## OTHER STOCK

| Class | No. | Builder | Seats | km/h | tonnes | kW | Built |
|---|---|---|---|---|---|---|---|
| Bre 4/4 | 1 h | SWS/MFO/SZB | 44 | 75 | 40 | 512 | 1916 (87) |
| CFe 4/4 | 11 h § | SWS/MFO/SZB | 36 | 75 | 34 | 256 | 1916 (91) |
| De 4/4 | 101 | SZB/MFO | - | 50 | 36 | 256 | 1961 |
| Ge 4/4 | 111 † | AEG/VBW | - | 40 | 32 | 470 | 1927 (57) |
| Ge 4/4 | 112 † | AEG/VBW | - | 40 | 34 | 470 | 1927 (67) |
| Gem 4/4 | 121 | SIG/MFO/DZ/SZB | - | 45 | 24 | 132 | 1912 (60) |
| Tm 2/2 | 161 | - | - | 40 | 13 | 70 | 1966 (02) |
| Tm 2/2 | 162 | RACO/DZ | - | 30 | 3.2 | 37 | 1932 (67) |
| Tmf 2/2 | 165 | SCHÖMA | - | 60 | 25 | 336 | 1996 |
| Tmf 2/2 | 166 | SCHÖMA | - | 60 | 25 | 336 | 1996 |

† Dual voltage stock.
h Historic car.
§ renumbered ex BDe 4/4 24.

# 4.34. RHEINECK WALZENHAUSEN (858)
## RhW

**Group:** Appenzellerbahnen

Once a tramway with a connecting funicular, the whole line was converted to rack and adhesion operation in 1958. This is one of the smallest Swiss railways, less than 2 km long with just one item of motive power.

**Gauge:** 1200 mm.
**Electrical System:** 600 V DC.
**Rack System:** Riggenbach.
**Route:** Rheineck–Walzenhausen (1.9 km)
**Depot:** Ruderbach (but car normally stables overnight in Walzenhausen station).

| Class | No. | Builder | Seats | km/h | tonnes | kW | Built |
|---|---|---|---|---|---|---|---|
| BDeh1/2 | 1 | SLM/FFA/BBC | 28 | 30/20 | 14.7 | 215 | 1958 |

# 4.35. RIGIBAHNEN (602, 603)          RB

The RB was formed in 1992 by the merger of the Arth Rigi Bahn (ARB) and Vitznau Rigi Bahn (VRB). The VRB was the very first Swiss mountain rack line, pioneering the Riggenbach system, opened in 1871. It connects with the steamers on the Vierwaldstättersee (Lake Lucerne) at Vitznau, while the former ARB connects with the Gotthard main line at Arth Goldau. The two lines run side by side at the summit of the Rigi. Both lines are pure rack. Since the merger, the two lines have retained their separate liveries of red for the VRB and blue for the ARB. Numbers did not change with the merger. Readers should be warned that three items of stock carry number 1 and most numbers here are duplicated by non-powered historic stock. The AB also has three steam locos – vertical boilered no. 7 (SLM works number 1, 1873) plus 16 and 17 built in 1923 and 1925. 11–15 are usually used on the ARB and are paired with driving trailers 21–25 in order. 1–5 plus 21 and 22 (plus trailers 31 and 32) are used on the VRB. It is possible to sit next to the driver on most units. The VRB still carries milk churns on a small wagon.

**Gauge:** 1435 mm.
**Electrical System:** 1500 V DC.
**Rack System:** Riggenbach.
**Routes:**
• Arth-Goldau–Rigi Kulm (8.6 km).
• Rigi Kulm–Vitznau (6.9 km).
**Depots: Arth Goldau, Vitznau**, Rigi Kulm.

| Class | No. | | Builder | Seats | km/h | tonnes | kW | Built |
|-------|-----|---|---------|-------|------|--------|----|-------|
| Ta 2/2 | 1 | †§ a | RACO/STAD/MFO/BBC | - | 8 | 7.5 | 7 | 1982 |
| Xm | 1 | †§ | RACO | - | - | 17 | - | 1974 |
| Bhe 2/4 | 1 | †§ | SLM/BBC | 64 (4) | 18 | 18.7 | 335 | 1937 |
| Bhe 2/4 | 2 | † | SLM/BBC | 64 (4) | 18 | 18.7 | 335 | 1937 |
| Bhe 2/4 | 3 | † | SLM/BBC | 64 (4) | 18 | 18.7 | 335 | 1937 |
| Bhe 2/4 | 4 | † | SLM/BBC | 64 (4) | 18 | 18.7 | 335 | 1953 |
| Bhe 4/4 | 5 | † | SLM/SIG/BBC | 62 | 30 | 36.3 | 870 | 1965 |
| CFhe 2/3 | 6 | * h | SLM/SWS/MFO | 60 | 15 | 23.5 | 395 | 1911 (39) |
| BDhe 2/4 | 7 | * h | SLM/SIG/MFO | 60 | 15 | 25.5 | 455 | 1925 (39) |
| He 2/3 | 8 | * | SLM/MFO | - | 15 | 33.6 | 455 | 1930 (39) |
| BDhe 2/4 | 11 | * | SLM/SAAS | 60 (2) | 21 | 29 | 485 | 1949 |
| BDhe 2/4 | 12 | * | SLM/SAAS | 60 (2) | 21 | 27.3 | 485 | 1949 |
| BDhe 2/4 | 13 | * | SLM/SAAS | 60 (2) | 21 | 26.5 | 485 | 1954 |
| BDhe 2/4 | 14 | * | SLM/SAAS | 60 (2) | 21 | 26.5 | 485 | 1967 |
| BDhe 4/4 | 15 | * | SLM/BBC | 60 (2) | 18.6 | 30.3 | 835 | 1982 |
| He 2/2 | 18 | † | SLM/BBC | - | 18 | 14.9 | 335 | 1938 |
| Bhe 4/4 | 21 | † | SLM/BBC | 74 | 30 | 30.5 | 824 | 1986 |
| Bhe 4/4 | 22 | † | SLM/BBC | 74 | 30 | 30.5 | 824 | 1986 |

* ex ARB.
† ex VRB
h Historic car.
§ Number duplicated.
a Battery shunter used at Vitznau, built from parts of SBB Tm 540 (new 1949).

# 4.36. RORSCHACH HEIDEN BERGBAHN (857)                                      RHB

**Group:** Appenzellerbahnen

A short rack and adhesion line running into the hills above Rorschach, with through running over SBB tracks from Rorscach to Rorschach Hafen. Good views over the Bodensee (Lake Constance) from the top. Stadler 2-car unit No. 25 works most services, and often has open vehicles coupled to it in good weather. The new numbers are not carried by the electric stock.

**Gauge:** 1435 mm.
**Electrical System:** 15 kV 16.7 Hz AC.
**Rack System:** Riggenbach.
**Route:** Rorschach–Heiden (5.5 km). Maximum gradient 9%.
**Depots:** Heiden, Rorschach.

| No. | Class | Old No. | Builder | Seats | km/h | tonnes | kW | Built |
|-----|-------|---------|---------|-------|------|--------|----|-------|
| DZeh 588 721-1 | DZeh 2/4 | 21 | SLM/MFO | - | 25 | 42.8 | 420 | 1930 |
| DZeh 588 722-9 | DZeh 2/4 | 22 | SLM/MFO | - | 25 | 42.8 | 420 | 1930 |
| BDeh 538 723-8 | ABDeh 2/4 | 23 | SLM/BBC/FFA | 8/49 | 25 | 42.3 | 550 | 1953 |
| BDeh 578 724-6 | ABDeh 2/4 | 24 | SLM/BBC/FFA | 8/49 | 25 | 42.3 | 550 | 1966 |
| - | BDeh 3/6 | 25 § | STAD/SLM/AD | 86 | - | 57.3 | 700 | 1998 |
| Thm 237 916-2 | - | - | * | - | - | - | - | - |

§ Named Rorschach and Heiden on one side plus Lutzenberg and Rorschacherberg on the other!
* 237 916 is ex Maschinenfabrik Rüti, which had a branch off the RHB line.

# 4.37. SAINT-BERNARD EXPRESS

**Group:** TMR

## FORMER MARTIGNY ORSIÈRES (133)                                    MO

A standard gauge line serving an area to the south of the Rhône Valley. Buses connect at Orsières for the Grand St. Bernard pass, of large rescue dog fame. The NINA Class 527 3-car EMUs operate some services on the SBB main line. Most details for these are the same as BLS Class 525.

**Gauge:** 1435 mm.
**Electrical System:** 15 kV 16.7 Hz AC
**Routes:**
• Martigny–Sembrancher–Orsières 19.3 km.
• Sembrancher–Le Chable (6.2 km). Maximum gradient 3.7%.
**Depot:** Orsières.

| No. | Old No. | Name | Builder | Seats | km/h | tonnes | kW | Built |
|-----|---------|------|---------|-------|------|--------|-----|-------|
| Tm 237 554-1 | - | Barry | - | - | - | - | - | - |
| RABe 527 511-0 | - | ENTREMONT | BOMB/AT | 16/136 | - | 80 | - | - |
| RABe 527 512-8 | - | MARTIGNY | BOMB/AT | 16/136 | - | 80 | - | - |
| RABe 527 513-6 | - | SAINT-MAURICE | BOMB/AT | 16/136 | - | 80 | - | - |
| ABDe 537 505-0 | 5 | | ACMV/BBC | 24 | 60 | 52 | 736 | 1955 |
| ABDe 537 506-8 | 6 | ORSIÈRES | § | 6/47 | 100 | 64 | 1076 | 1965 |
| ABDe 537 507-6 | 7 | MARTIGNY | § | 6/47 | 100 | 64 | 1076 | 1965 |
| ABDe 537 509-2 | 9 | SEMBRANCHER | § | 6/47 | 100 | 64 | 1076 | 1965 |
| § | | SIG/SWS/SAAS/BBC/MFO | | | | | | |

# 4.38. SCHYNIGE PLATTE BAHN (314)   SPB

**Group:** Berner Oberland Bahnen

This pure rack mountain line connects with the BOB at Wilderswil near Interlaken. Trains are still operated with open sided stock hauled by 4-wheel electric locomotives dating from the time of electrification. The line also has steam loco H5 built in 1894. Name plates seem to be added, removed and swapped between locos.

**Gauge:** 800 mm.
**Electrical System:** 1500 V DC
**Rack System:** Riggenbach.
**Route:** Wilderswil–Schynige Platte (7.3 km), Maximum gradient 25%.
**Depot:** Wilderswil.

## CLASS He 2/2                                    LOCOMOTIVES

**Built:** 1910–1912 (1914 *).
**Builder:** SLM/ALIOTH (SLM/BBC*).
**Wheel Arrangement:** B
**Traction Motors:** 2 x 110 kW.
**Maximum Speed:** 12 km/h.

**Length over Couplers:**
**Weight:** 16 (16.3*) tonnes.

| | | |
|---|---|---|
| 11 * WILDERSWIL | 16 ANEMONE | 61 ENZIAN |
| 12 * | 18 KROKUS | 62 ALPENROSE |
| 13 * MATTEN | 19 FLUHBLUME | 63 SILBERDISTEL |
| 14 * | 20 GSTEIGWILER | |

Note: SPB 16–20, 61–3 were originally WAB 56–63.

▲ Appenzellerbahnen EMU BDeh 4/4 no. 17 is one of only two units with the Strub rack system to operate the Gais to Altstätten line and is seen at Gais on 13 May 2009. **David Haydock**

▼ AOMC EMU 592 "Portes du Soleil" is seen next to ASD railcar 402 "ORMONT-DESSUS" at Aigle in May 2005 – before the station was rebuilt and the AOMC diverted over a new section of track. Units 91 to 93 on the BVB are very similar to AOMC 592. **David Cable**

▲ Aare Seeland Mobil (ex OJB, ex RVO, ex OSST) loco De 4/4 121 hauls two standard gauge wagons on skates out of Langenthal yard en route for the town's industrial estate on 17 March 2009.
**David Haydock**

▼ BOB 309 leads a typically long train into Zweilütschinen station on 18 June 2009. The train will split with six coaches continuing to Lauterbrunnen and six to Grindelwald.          **David Haydock**

▲ BRB steam loco H 2/3 16 (formerly MTGN no. 1) runs onto the depot at Brienz after working the last train of the day on 17 June 2009. This loco was built as recently as 1992.    **David Haydock**

▼ A busy scene on the CEV at Blonay on 14 April 2009. On the left is MOB diesel loco Gm 4/4 2003 "MONTBOVON" moving a new panoramic car from Vevey to Chernex via the Blonay–Chamby line. Behind the loco is EMU Be 2/6 "VEVEY" with a train from Vevey and on the right is CEV unit BDeh 2/8 71 with a service to Les Pléiades.    **David Haydock**

▲ CJ Stadler EMUs 632 "Mont-Soleil" and 633 "La Gruère" form connecting services to Glovelier and Tavannes at Le Noirmont on 18 March 2009. **David Haydock**

▼ FLP EMU Be 4/12 25 "Ceresio" arrives at Molinazzo station on 7 July 2009 with a train from Ponte Tresa to Lugano. These units are very similar to the older sets used by RBS in Bern. **Brian Denton**

▲ On 13 June 2009, GGB EMU Bhe 4/8 3052 crawls up the Abt rack into Gornergrat, the highest open air station in Europe at 3089 metres a.s.l. **Brian Denton**

▼ Jungfraubahn EMUs BDhe 4/8 213 and 212 stand at Kleine Scheidegg station on 18 June 2009 with set BDhe 2/4 207 on the left. **David Haydock**

▲ Monte Generoso EMU Bhe 4/6 11 "MENDRISIO" stands half out of the shed at Capolago on 7 July 2009. These units are very similar to those used on the MTGN from Montreux. **Brian Denton**

▼ MIB unit Be 4/4 no. 8, named "Oberhasli" and "Innertkirchen" arrives at the latter station on 17 July 2009. The terminus is between hydroelectric power buildings. **David Haydock**

▲ MOB unit Be 4/4 5002 – subject to radical rebuilding in 2004 – is seen at Zweisimmen on 16 April 2009 with a train for Lenk whilst ABDe 8/8 4001 waits to depart for Montreux with one of the few trains not branded "Golden Pass". **David Haydock**

▼ NStCM unit BDe 4/4 231 climbs out of Nyon with a train for St. Cergue on 20 March 2009, with Lac Léman just visible in the background. **David Haydock**

▲ Orbe Chavornay electric locos Ee 2/2 no. 2 (right) and 1 (left) are seen at Orbe on 18 March 2009 on either side of BDe 4/4 15 "La Sihl" and driving trailer Bt 51 "L'Orbe" forming the passenger service to Chavornay.                                                                                        **David Haydock**

▼ Rigibahnen Bhe 2/5 no. 3 forming a train to Vitznau and BDhe 2/4 no. 12 with a train to Arth Goldau stand at Rigi Kulm summit station on a cloudy 16 June 2009.                   **David Haydock**

▲ Regionalverkehr Bern-Solothurn EMU ABe 4/12 no. 69 named both "Büren zum Hof" and "Fraubrunnen" passes non-stop through Worblaufen on 19 March 2009 with a fast train from Solothurn to Bern. BDWM and WSB have similar units. **David Haydock**

▼ Rorschach Heiden Bahn's unique Stadler EMU BDeh 3/6 25 is seen at Rorschach Hafen on 10 June 2006. Note the open coaches attached to the rear. **Brian Denton**

▲ Saint Bernard Express (former Martigny-Orsières) "NINA" EMU RABe 527 511 "ENTREMONT" stands at Martigny with a train for Orsières on 15 April 2009. The striking livery includes many Saint Bernard dogs as decoration.     **David Haydock**

▼ SPB loco He 2/2 no. 16 "ANEMONE" stands with its train at Schynige Platte on 14 June 2009. The loco will celebrate its centenary in 2010. In the background is sister loco 63 "SILBERDISTEL".     **Brian Denton**

▲ SZU shunter 236 507 "MUTZ" shunts EMU (556) 522 at Zürich Giesshübel depot on 14 May 2009. Unit (556) 531 is visible on the right. **David Haydock**

▼ 750 mm gauge Waldenburgerbahn unit 15 "Bubendorf" plus two trailers approaches Liestal with a train from Waldenburg on 19 April 2009. Behind are the standard gauge tracks of the Basel-Olten main line. **Matthias Müller**

▲ No less than four Crossrail Class 185 locos, two from CB Rail and two from Beacon Rail, headed by 185 580, power a southbound intermodal service through Liestal on 13 February 2009.

**Brian Denton**

▼ Sersa G1700 diesel 843 151 "TRUDY" stands at Biasca on 16 July 2009.          **Philip Wormald**

▲ Bernmobil Vevey/ABB tram Be 4/8 737 has just left Zytglogge on 19 March 2009 with a Line 3 service to Saali and is crossing the river Aare, as Siemens Combino tram 753 heads in the opposite direction to Weissenbühl. **David Haydock**

▼ Like other operators, BVB in Basel has had problems with its Siemens Combino trams but all have now been rebuilt. This is 304 in Barfüsseplatz with Line 6 to Allschwil on 20 June 2009. **Brian Denton**

▲ Neuchâtel (TN) power cars 506 "Neuchâtel" and 503 "Colombier" sandwich driving trailer 552 at Place Pury in Neuchâtel with a service to Boudry on 26 April 2005.          **Mario Stefani**

▼ Thunersee 1906-vintage paddle steamer "BLÜMLISALP" leaves Spiez on 19 June 2009.
                                                                              **Brian Denton**

▲ Re 4/4 I no. 10034 in TEE livery, which is preserved at Koblenz in Germany, pilots ex DB 103 184 on a special train at Aadorf on 18 April 2009.                                    **Matthias Müller**

▼ SBB Historic electric loco Be 4/7 12504 and Club San Gottardo's 0-6-0T E 3/3 8501 are seen at Biasca on 8 September 2007.                                    **Brian Garvin**

▲ The Rhätische Bahn's 2-8-0 G 4/5 no. 107 is seen at Filisur with a special train on 12 September
2009.                                                                                    **Mario Stefani**

▼ Former Furka Oberalp Abt rack-fitted HG 3/4 2-6-0T no. 1 is now owned by Dampfbahn Furka
Bergstrecke and is seen at Gletsch on 3 July 2008.                                        **Les Nixon**

# 4.39. SIHLTAL ZÜRICH UETLIBERG (712, 713)
## SZU

Two lines whose management merged in 1973. The Sihltalbahn, which follows the river Sihl, provides a suburban service from Zürich to Langnau-Gattikon, with some trains continuing to Sihlwald (the line beyond to Sihlbrugg is no longer served) and is electrified on the same system as SBB. The shed at Sihlwald is now only used to house a steam loco and stock is stabled at Langnau-Gattikon. The Uetlibergbahn climbs the hills above Zürich to a terminus at Uetliberg (814 m above sea level) and is electrified at 1200 V DC. To enable trains from both lines to use the common section from Zürich HB to Giesshübel, the DC wires are offset, resulting in the tracks on this section having two sets of overhead wires, and giving the DC stock an odd appearance with off-centre pantographs. From May 1990, both lines were extended from the inconveniently-located Selnau terminus to a new underground terminus at the Hauptbahnhof using platforms built for the never constructed U-Bahn. Traffic quickly quadrupled!

In December 2008, Sunday services were boosted on the Sihltalbahn meaning that Ce 2/2 no. 2 can no longer be used on regular historic trains. SZU is sometimes known as the "Schnaagi-Schaagi" or "Langsamer Jakob"! SZU took over two SBB Class 450 locos plus their double-deck trailers in 2008 and is to receive more. These allowed the withdrawal of the 1968–71 BDe 576 sets.

All trains carry their short numbers (in bold) prominently, the longer numbers being less conspicuous. Trains on the Sihltalbahn are Class 450 sets or loco-powered with a mix of double-deck trailers and single-deck driving trailers. Uetlibergbahn power cars 521–528 are used in pairs – 521+522 and so on, with a trailer between.

**Gauge:** 1435 mm.
**Electrical Systems:** Sihltalbahn 15 kV 16.7 Hz AC; Uetlibergbahn 1200 V DC.
**Routes:**

- Zürich HB–Uetliberg (9.1 km), Maximum gradient 7.9%.
- Zürich HB–Sihlbrugg (17.4 km).

**Depot:** Giesshübel.

### SIHLTALBAHN STOCK (15 kV AC)

| No. | Name | | Builder | Seats | km/h | tonnes | kW | Built |
|-----|------|--|---------|-------|------|--------|----|----|
| Re | 456 **542**-0 | | SLM/SGP/ABB | - | 130 | 68 | 3200 | 1992 |
| Re | 456 **543**-8 | | SLM/SGP/ABB | - | 130 | 68 | 3200 | 1993 |
| Re | 456 **544**-6 | | SLM/SGP/ABB | - | 130 | 68 | 3200 | 1993 |
| Re | 456 **545**-3 | | SLM/SGP/ABB | - | 130 | 68 | 3200 | 1993 |
| Re | 456 **546**-1 | | SLM/ABB | - | 130 | 68 | 3200 | 1987 |
| Re | 456 **547**-9 | | SLM/ABB | - | 130 | 68 | 3200 | 1987 |
| Re | 456 **551**-1 | § | SLM/ABB | | 130 | 74 | 3200 | 1993 |
| Re | 456 **552**-9 | § | SLM/ABB | | 130 | 74 | 3200 | 1993 |

### UETLIBERGBAHN STOCK (1200 V DC)

| | No. | Name | Builder | Seats | km/h | tonnes | kW | Built |
|--|-----|------|---------|-------|------|--------|----|----|
| Be | 556 **521**-3 | | SLM/Siemens | 40 (12) | 70 | 44 | 800 | 1992 |
| Be | 556 **522**-1 | | SWS/Siemens | 40 (12) | 70 | 44 | 800 | 1992 |
| Be | 556 **523**-9 | | SLM/Siemens | 40 (12) | 70 | 44 | 800 | 1992 |
| Be | 556 **524**-7 | | SLM/Siemens | 40 (12) | 70 | 44 | 800 | 1993 |
| Be | 556 **525**-4 | | SLM/Siemens | 40 (12) | 70 | 44 | 800 | 1993 |
| Be | 556 **526**-2 | | SLM/Siemens | 40 (12) | 70 | 44 | 800 | 1993 |
| Be | 556 **527**-0 | | SLM/Siemens | 40 (12) | 70 | 44 | 800 | 1993 |
| Be | 556 **528**-8 | | SLM/Siemens | 40 (12) | 70 | 44 | 800 | 1992 |
| Be | 556 **531**-2 | | SWS/Siemens | 65+65 | 60 | 30+30 | 640 | 1978 |
| Be | 556 **532**-0 | UITIKON | SWS/Siemens | 65+65 | 60 | 30+30 | 640 | 1978 |

### OTHER STOCK

| | No. | Name | Builder | Seats | km/h | tonnes | kW | Built |
|--|-----|------|---------|-------|------|--------|----|----|
| Ce | 026 **502** * | HÄDE | SWS/MFO | 24 | 35 | 18.3 | 145 | 1923 |
| Tm | 236 **507**-0 | MUTZ | SIG/BBC/SAU | - | 55 | 39 | 240 | 1961 |
| Tm | 236 **508**-8 | ROBEL | Robel | 7 | 80 | 26 | 320 | 1994 |

\* ex Be 2/2 22 restored to its original condition as Uetliburgbahn Ce 2/2 2.
§ ex SBB 450 067 and 070 plus trailers respectively.

# 4.40. TRANSPORTS PUBLICS FRIBOURGEOIS TPF

This system was formerly known as the Gruyere-Fribourg-Morat (GFM). There are two separate standard gauge branches, Fribourg–Murten–Ins and Bulle–Romont, plus an extensive metre gauge system centred on Bulle. The metre gauge connects with the SBB at Palézieux and with the MOB at Montbovon. The Bulle–Romont service is infrequent and standard gauge EMUs are mainly employed on the through Fribourg–Ins–Neuchâtel service. The branch to Broc serves the Cailler (Nestlé) chocolate factory and generates significant freight traffic with standard gauge wagons carried on skates. 567 171 to 173 are the old design with a communicating door in the front end. 567 181/182 are very similar to BLS Class 565. In 2009, TPF had 567 316 on loan from TRN.

**Gauges:** 1435 mm, 1000 mm.
**Electrical System:** 15 kV 16.7 Hz AC (1435 mm), 800 V DC (1000 mm).
**Routes:**
*Standard gauge:*
• Fribourg–Ins (32.2 km).
• Bulle–Romont (18.2 km).
*Metre gauge:*
• Palézieux–Châtel St. Denis–Bulle–Montbovon (43.5 km)
• Bulle–Broc Fabrique (5.4 km). Maximum gradient 3.2%.
**Depots: Bulle, Fribourg** (1435 mm), Châtel St. Denis, Montbovon (1000 mm).
**Works:** Planchy.

## Metre Gauge Stock:

| Class | No. | Name | Builder | Seats | km/h | tonnes | kW | Built |
|---|---|---|---|---|---|---|---|---|
| Te 2/2 | 11 | | MFO | - | 30 | 16.5 | 88 | 1912 |
| Te 2/2 | 12 | | CEG/ALIOTH | - | 50 | 9 | 774 | 1913 |
| Te 4/4 | 13 | | CEG/ALIOTH | - | 45 | 25 | 148 | 1901 (27) |
| Te 4/4 | 14 | | CEG/ALIOTH | - | 50 | 21.5 | 264 | 1901 (33) |
| Tm 2/2 | 15 | b | SCH/DZ | - | 35 | 24 | 168 | 1971 |
| Tm 2/2 | 16 | | CFD | - | - | - | - | - |
| Be 4/4 | 115 | | SWS/ALIOTH | 44 | 60 | 29.5 | 296 | 1905 |
| Be 4/4 | 116 | | SWS/MFO | 58 | 75 | 35 | 486 | 1922 |
| BDe 4/4 | 121 | REMAUFENS | ACMV/ABB | | 90 | | 640 | 1992 |
| BDe 4/4 | 122 | LA TOUR DE TRÊME | ACMV/ABB | | 90 | | 640 | 1992 |
| BDe 4/4 | 123 | BROC | ACMV/ABB | | 90 | | 640 | 1995 |
| BDe 4/4 | 124 | VAUDENS | ACMV/ABB | | 90 | | 640 | 1995 |
| Be 4/4 | 131 | | SWS/BBC | 48 | 75 | 33 | 408 | 1943 |
| BDe 4/4 | 141 | GRUYERES | SWP/SAAS | 40 | 70 | 38 | 648 | 1972 |
| BDe 4/4 | 142 | SEMSALES | SWP/SAAS | 40 | 70 | 38 | 648 | 1972 |
| Be 4/4 | 151 | LA GRUYÈRE | SIG/SAAS | 48 | 80 | 32 | 448 | 1977 |
| Be 4/4 | 152 | CHÂTEL-ST.-DENIS | SIG/SAAS | 48 | 80 | 32 | 448 | 1977 |

## Standard Gauge Stock:

| No. | Class | Name | Builder | Seats | km/h | tonnes | kW | Built |
|---|---|---|---|---|---|---|---|---|
| Tm 82 | Tm 2/2 | | RACO/VR/MB | - | 45 | 33 | 236 | 1964 |
| Tm 837 084-3 | a Tm 3/3 | | KRUPP/MAN | - | 40 | 45.5 | 324 | 1963 |
| Tm 85 | § Tm 2/2 | | Moyse | - | 22 | 24 | 110 | 1977 |
| Tm 237 087-2 | † - | | Adtranz | - | 80 | 36.5 | 550 | 2000 |
| Ee 91 | Ee 2/2 | | SIG/BBC | - | 75 | 30 | 242 | 1960 |
| ABDe 537 161-2 | h ABDe 4/4 | | SIG/BBC | 18/34 | 100 | 56 | 736 | 1946 |
| RABDe 537 176-0 | = RABDe 4/4 | | SIG/SWS/SAAS | 12/39 | 100 | 64 | 1076 | 1965 |
| RABDe 567 171-4 | RABDe 4/4 | LA SARINE | SIG/SWS/BBC | 12/31 | 125 | 70 | 1700 | 1983 |
| RABDe 567 172-2 | RABDe 4/4 | VULLY | SIG/SWS/BBC | 12/31 | 125 | 70 | 1700 | 1983 |
| RABDe 567 173-0 | ‡ RABDe 4/4 | LA GLÂNE | SIG/SWS/BBC | 16/28 | 125 | 70 | 1700 | 1983 |
| RABDe 567 181-3 | * RBDe 4/4 | | SIG/SWS/ABB | 55 | 125 | 69.7 | 1700 | 1991 |
| RABDe 567 182-1 | RBDe 4/4 | COURTEPIN | SIG/SWS/ABB | 55 | 125 | 69.7 | 1700 | 1991 |

§ Moyse Type BN24HA150 works no. 1416, delivered new to CFD Montmirail.
† Ex MThB Tm 236 648-2 in 2003. Same as SBB Class Tm 234.
‡ Ex RVT 104 in 1991.
= Ex MThB 11 (536 611) in 2006.
a Ex Deutsche Shell, Ingolstadt, no. 3 in 1983.
b Ex Tauern Scheiteltunnel (900 mm gauge) No. DL6, in 1980.
h Historic EMU.
* Named CRESSIER SUR MORAT.

# 4.41. TRANSPORTS RÉGIONAUX NEUCHÂTELOIS TRN

This company was formed in 1999 to group local rail and bus companies in the Neuchâtel area.

## CHEMINS DE FER DES MONTAGNES NEUCHÂTELOISES (214, 222) CMN

This railway comprises two completely separate lines. The Italian built cars are unusual for Switzerland although they look very similar to domestic stock of the time. The 1950 stock is used on the Les Brenets line. Units 2 and 4 were stored at the time of writing.

**Gauge:** 1000 mm.
**Electrical System:** 1500 V DC.
**Routes:**
• La Chaux-de-Fonds–Les Ponts-de-Martel (16.2 km). Maximum gradient 4%.
• Le Locle–Les Brenets (4.1 km).
**Depots:** Les Brenets, Les Ponts-de-Martel.

| Class | No. | Name | Builder | Seats | km/h | tonnes | kW | Built |
|-------|-----|------|---------|-------|------|--------|-----|-------|
| BDe 4/4 | 2 (S) | | REG/BBC/SAAS | 44 | 60 | 23.5 | 244 | 1950 |
| BDe 4/4 | 3 | | REG/BBC/SAAS | 44 | 60 | 23.5 | 244 | 1950 |
| BDe 4/4 | 4 (S) | | REG/BBC/SAAS | 44 | 60 | 23.5 | 244 | 1950 |
| BDe 4/4 | 5 | | REG/BBC/SAAS | 44 | 60 | 23.5 | 244 | 1950 |
| BDe 4/4 | 6 | La Chaux-de-Fonds | ACMV/ABB | 48 (6) | 80 | 35.5 | 752 | 1991 |
| BDe 4/4 | 7 | Les Ponts-du-Martel | ACMV/ABB | 48 (6) | 80 | 35.5 | 752 | 1991 |
| BDe 4/4 | 8 | La Sagne | ACMV/ABB | 48 (6) | 80 | 35.5 | 752 | 1996 |
| Tm 2/2 | 11 | | RACO/DZ | - | 75 | 19 | 177 | 1983 |

## RÉGIONAL DE VAL DE TRAVERS (221)                    RVT

A secondary line in the west of the country, through services running over the SBB to Neuchâtel. The Fleurier to St. Sulpice branch is freight only, but sees occasional use for steam specials. TRN bought two NINA 3-car EMUs, 527 321 and 322 in 2000 but has sold them to BLS which has similar units and has renumbered them 525 037 and 038. As a replacement TRN bought two 4-car FLIRT EMUs from Stadler. 567 316 is on long-term loan to TPF. The Val de Travers name is known in Britain thanks to the past production of asphalt in this region.

**Gauge:** 1435 mm.
**Electrical System:** 15 kV AC 16.7 Hz
**Routes:**
• Travers–Fleurier–Buttes (12.0 km).
• Fleurier–St. Sulpice (1.6 km).
**Depot:** Fleurier.

## CLASS RABe 527          FLIRT          4-CAR UNITS

Details as SBB Class 526.6 but has only one door per coach and therefore more seats, although these are arranged 2+2. These units operate the through Buttes–Neuchâtel service.

**Built:** 2007 (331); 2009 (332).
**Accommodation:** 24/23 (8) + –/38 (14) 1T + –/48 (8) + –/48 (8). 1T.

527 331-3    | 527 332-1    |

## OTHER STOCK

| No. | | Class | Old No. | Name | Builder | Seats | km/h | tonnes | kW | Built |
|-----|---|-------|---------|------|---------|-------|------|--------|-----|-------|
| Tm | 237 312-4 | Tm | 12 | | RACO/DZ | - | 75 | 19 | 177 | 1983 |
| Be | 417 301-9 | Be 4/4 | 1 | | ACMV/SAAS | - | 75 | 45 | 690 | 1951 |
| RBDe 567 315-7 | | RABDe 4/4 | 105 | FLEURIER | SIG/SWS/BBC | 43 | 125 | 70 | 1700 | 1983 |
| RBDe 567 316-5 | | RBDe 4/4 | 106 | COUVET | SWS/BBC | 54 (1) | 125 | 70 | 1700 | 1985 |
| RBDe 567 317-3 | | RBDe 4/4 | 107 | MÔTIERS (NE) | SIG/SWS/BBC | 54 (1) | 125 | 70 | 1700 | 1991 |

# 4.42. TROGENER BAHN (859)    TB

**Group:** Appenzellerbahnen

Originally an interurban tramway running from St. Gallen to Trogen, the TB has been upgraded to a light railway, mostly with roadside running, although there is still street running in St. Gallen. The line is soon to be linked to the AB Appenzell line. 21 and 24 were sold to the Rittnerbahn in Italy and 25 scrapped.

**Gauge:** 1000 mm.
**Electrical System:** 1000 V DC.
**Route:** St. Gallen–Trogen (9.8 km). Maximum gradient 7.5%.
**Depot:** Speicher.

| Class | No. | Name | Builder | Seats | km/h | tonnes | kW | Built |
|---|---|---|---|---|---|---|---|---|
| BDe 4/4 | 7 h | | SWP/MFO | 30 | 65 | 27 | 385 | 1952 |
| BDe 4/8 | 22 | | FFA/BBC/SWP | 40+34 | 65 | 39 | 405 | 1975 |
| BDe 4/8 | 23 | | FFA/BBC/SWP | 40+34 | 65 | 39 | 405 | 1975 |
| Be 4/8 | 31 | Der St. Galler | STAD/BOMB | 86 (6) | 80 | 43 | 640 | 2004 |
| Be 4/8 | 32 | Der Appenzeller | STAD/BOMB | 86 (6) | 80 | 43 | 640 | 2004 |
| Be 4/8 | 33 | Speicher | STAD/BOMB | 86 (6) | 80 | 43 | 640 | 2008 |
| Be 4/8 | 34 | Trogen | STAD/BOMB | 86 (6) | 80 | 43 | 640 | 2008 |
| Be 4/8 | 35 | Teufen | STAD/BOMB | 86 (6) | 80 | 43 | 640 | 2008 |
| Xrotm 2/2 | 72 | | RACO/BEIL/DZ | - | 30 | 15 | 150 | 1974 |

h   historic unit.

# 4.43. WALDENBURGERBAHN (502)    WB

Unique for Switzerland in being 750 mm gauge, the WB is a mainly roadside light railway with some street running, connecting with the SBB Basel–Olten line at Liestal. Power cars operate with driving trailers Bt 111–120. The company runs steam heritage trains, one Sunday a month May to September, with G 3/3 0-6-0T no. 5 "G. THOMMEN". WB was planning to buy new low floor EMUs in 2009.

**Gauge:** 750 mm.
**Electrical System:** 1500 V DC
**Route:** Liestal–Waldenburg (13.1 km)
**Depot:** Waldenburg.

| Class | No. | Name | Builder | Seats | km/h | tonnes | kW | Built |
|---|---|---|---|---|---|---|---|---|
| BDe 4/4 | 11 | Niederdorf | SWP/SIG/BBC | 33 | 75 | 24 | 446 | 1985 |
| BDe 4/4 | 12 | Oberdorf | SWP/SIG/BBC | 33 | 75 | 24 | 446 | 1986 |
| BDe 4/4 | 13 | Hölstein | SWP/SIG/BBC | 33 | 75 | 24 | 446 | 1986 |
| BDe 4/4 | 14 | Ramlinsburg | SWP/SIG/BBC | 33 | 75 | 24 | 446 | 1986 |
| BDe 4/4 | 15 | Bubendorf | SWP/SIG/ABB | 33 | 75 | 24 | 446 | 1993 |
| BDe 4/4 | 16 | Liestal | SWP/SIG/ABB | 33 | 75 | 24 | 446 | 1993 |
| BDe 4/4 | 17 | Waldenburg | SWP/SIG/ABB | 33 | 75 | 24 | 446 | 1993 |

# 4.44. WENGERNALPBAHN (311, 312) WAB

**Group:** Jungfraubahnen.

This railway operates the middle section of the route to Jungfraujoch, connecting with the BOB at Lauterbrunnen and Grindelwald and the JB at Kleine Scheidegg. The most modern stock is used from Grindelwald.

**Gauge:** 800 mm.
**Electrical System:** 1500 V DC.
**Rack System:** Riggenbach. Maximum gradient 25%.
**Routes:**
* Lauterbrunnen–Wengen–Kleine Scheidegg (11.3 km).
* Grindelwald–Kleine Scheidegg (8.6 km).
**Depots:** Lauterbrunnen (2), Grindelwald Grund (2).

## CLASS He 2/2               LOCOMOTIVES

**Built:** 1909 (1926 *, 1929 †).
**Builder:** SLM/ALIOTH (SLM/BBC*, SLM/MFO†).
**Wheel Arrangement:** B
**Traction Motors:** 2 x 110 (118*†) kW.
**Maximum Speed:** 12 km/h.
**Length over Couplers:**
**Weight:** 16 (16.5*, 17†) tonnes.

| 51 | | 52 | | 53 | | 54 | | 64 * | | 65 † |

## CLASS BDhe 4/4           SINGLE UNITS

**Built:** 1947–196.
**Builder:** SLM/BBC.
**Wheel Arrangement:** Bo-Bo.
**Traction Motors:** 2 x 220 kW.
**Accommodation:** –/40.
**Length over Couplers:**
**Weight:** 24 tonnes.
**Maximum Speed:** 25 km/h.

* Equipped with AC traction motors.

| 101 | | 106 | | 109 | | 112 | | 115 | | 117 |
| 102 | | 107 | | 110 | | 113 | | 116 | | 118 |
| 104 * | | 108 | | 111 | | 114 | | | |

## CLASS BDhe 4/4           SINGLE UNITS

**Built:** 1970.
**Builder:** SLM/SIG/BBC/SAAS.
**Wheel Arrangement:** Bo-Bo.
**Traction Motors:** 2 x 220 kW.
**Accommodation:** –/48.
**Length over Couplers:**
**Weight:** 25.7 tonnes.
**Maximum Speed:** 25 km/h.

| 119 | | 120 | | 121 | | 122 | | 123 | | 124 |

## CLASS BDhe 4/8           2-CAR UNITS

**Built:** 1988.
**Builder:** SLM/ABB.
**Wheel Arrangement:** Bo-2 + 2-Bo
**Traction Motors:** 4 x 200 kW.
**Accommodation:** 40 (6) + 48 (6)
**Length over Couplers:**
**Weight:** 43.1 tonnes.
**Maximum Speed:** 28 km/h.
All this class carry plates with a very long phrase celebrating local anniversaries.

| 131 | | 132 | | 133 | | 134 | |

## CLASS BDhe 4/8          3-SECTION UNITS

These units have low-floor entrances (350 mm) and panoramic centre cars.
**Built:** 2004.
**Builder:** Stadler/Bombardier.
**Wheel Arrangement:** 1A-1A-1A-1A.
**Traction Motors:** 4 x 220 kW.
**Accommodation:** 32 (6)+64+32 (6)
**Length over Couplers:** 41.83 m.
**Weight:** 47.5 tonnes.
**Maximum Speed:** 28 km/h.

| 141 | | 142 | | 143 | | 144 | |

## OTHER STOCK

| Class | No. | Builder | Seats | km/h | tonnes | kW | Built |
|-------|-----|---------|-------|------|--------|-----|-------|
| Xrote | 11 | SLM/MFO/BEIL | - | 11 | 13.5 | 138 | 1928 |
| Xrote | 12 | SLM/MFO | - | 11 | 15 | 290 | 1945 |
| Xrote | 21 | - | - | 17.5 | 16 | 400 | 2008 |
| He 2/2 | 31 | STAD/SLM/ABB | - | 22 | 16 | 460 | 1995 |
| He 2/2 | 32 | STAD/SLM/ABB | - | 22 | 16 | 460 | 1995 |

As cars are banned from Wengen, goods are moved from Lauterbrunnen by train. Tractors 31 and 32 and EMU power cars work these.

# 4.45. WYNENTAL- UND SUHRENTAL-BAHN (643, 644) WSB

**Group:** AAR Bus+Bahn.

Once separate lines, the two routes were linked in the station south of the SBB platforms at Aarau in 1967. Trains now usually run through Schöftland–Aarau–Menziken and return. Both lines are mainly a mixture of roadside and street running and both traverse the Lenzburg–Zofigen SBB line on the level! In 2002 the line to Menziken-Burg was relaid on the trackbed of the former SBB line from Beinwil and the section from Aarau to Suhr will soon be diverted onto another former SBB trackbed. This will involve the modern depot at Aarau being demolished. Units 10–14 are being withdrawn. 15–27 are being modernised (during which they gain two seats) by WSB and mated with new Stadler driving trailers Bt 51–61. Class Be 4/8 are very similar to, units with BDWM and RBS. The lines did carry some freight and have transfer facilities at Suhr and Unterentfelden. Locos De 4/4 43 and 45 can usually be found at Suhr. 49 and 116 carry no numbers.

**Gauge:** 1000 mm.
**Electrical System:** 750 V DC.
**Routes:**
• Aarau–Schöftland (9.6 km).
• Aarau–Menziken-Burg (22.0 km).
**Depots:** Aarau, Menziken, Schöftland.

| Class | No. | Builder | Seats | km/h | tonnes | kW | Built |
|-------|-----|---------|-------|------|--------|-----|-------|
| De 4/4 | 6 | | SWS/BBC | – | 65 | 32 | 285 | 1945 |
| Be 4/4 | 10 Holziken | | SWS/BBC | 50 | 80 | 33 | 448 | 1966 |
| Be 4/4 | 13 Leimbach | | SWS/BBC | 50 | 80 | 33 | 448 | 1966 |
| Be 4/4 | 15 Aarau | | SWS/BBC | 52 | 80 | 31 | 448 | 1979 |
| Be 4/4 | 16 Suhr | | SWS/BBC | 50 | 80 | 31 | 448 | 1979 |
| Be 4/4 | 17 Gränichen | | SWS/BBC | 50 | 80 | 31 | 448 | 1979 |
| Be 4/4 | 19 Unterkulm | | SWS/BBC | 50 | 80 | 31 | 448 | 1979 |
| Be 4/4 | 20 Oberkulm | | SWS/BBC | 50 | 80 | 31 | 448 | 1979 |
| Be 4/4 | 21 Gontenschwil | | SWS/BBC | 50 | 80 | 31 | 448 | 1979 |
| Be 4/4 | 22 Reinach | | SWS/BBC | 50 | 80 | 31 | 448 | 1979 |
| Be 4/4 | 23 Menziken | | SWS/BBC | 50 | 80 | 31 | 448 | 1979 |
| Be 4/4 | 24 Unterentfelden | | SWS/BBC | 50 | 80 | 31 | 448 | 1979 |
| Be 4/4 | 25 Oberentfelden | | SWS/BBC | 50 | 80 | 31 | 448 | 1979 |
| Be 4/4 | 26 Muhen | | SWS/BBC | 50 | 80 | 31 | 448 | 1979 |
| Be 4/4 | 27 Schöftland | | SWS/BBC | 50 | 80 | 31 | 448 | 1979 |
| Be 4/8 | 28 Kanton Aargau | | SWA/SIG/ABB | 126 | 80 | 57 | 600 | 1993 |
| Be 4/8 | 29 Bezirk Aarau | | SWA/SIG/ABB | 126 | 80 | 57 | 600 | 1993 |
| Be 4/8 | 30 Bezirk Kulm | | SWA/SIG/ABB | 126 | 80 | 57 | 600 | 1993 |
| Be 4/8 | 31 Schloss Liebegg | | SWA/SIG/ABB | 126 | 80 | 57 | 600 | 1993 |
| Be 4/8 | 32 Schloss Schöftland | | SWA/SIG/ABB | 126 | 80 | 57 | 600 | 1993 |
| Be 4/8 | 33 Schneggen Reinach | | SWA/SIG/ABB | 126 | 80 | 57 | 600 | 1993 |
| Be 4/8 | 34 Teufenthal | | SWA/SIG/ABB | 126 | 80 | 57 | 600 | 1993 |
| De 4/4 | 43 | | SWS/SE/BBC | – | 60 | 46 | 522 | 1974 |
| De 4/4 | 45 | | SWS/SE/BBC | – | 60 | 46 | 522 | 1974 |
| Te 2/2 | 49 h S'FARBIG BÄHNLI | | SWS/MFO/WSB | – | 55 | 14 | 107 | 1957 |
| BSe 4/4 | 116 h SALON WAGEN | | SWS/BBC | 33 | 65 | 28.3 | 285 | 1901 |

h  historic stock.

# 4.46. YVERDON–STE. CROIX (212) YSteC

**Group:** Travys

A light railway running from the SBB station at Yverdon into the mountains near the French border. The two Stadler units work most services. Ge 4/4 21 is a centre-cab "crocodile" and has a double-headed "croc" painted on its sides.

**Gauge:** 1000 mm.
**Electrical system:** 15 kV AC 16.7 Hz.
**Route:** Yverdon-les-Bains–Sainte Croix (24.2 km). Maximum gradient 4.4%.
**Depots: Yverdon**, Ste. Croix.

| Class | No. | Name | Builder | Seats | km/h | tonnes | kW | Built |
|---|---|---|---|---|---|---|---|---|
| Be 4/4ᴵᴵ | 1 | YVERDON-LES-BAINS | ACMV/HESS/BBC | 40 (4) | 75 | 45 | 780 | 1981 |
| Be 4/4ᴵᴵ | 2 | BAULMES | ACMV/HESS/BBC | 40 (4) | 75 | 45 | 780 | 1981 |
| Be 4/4ᴵ | 5 h | | SIG/BBC | 46 | 65 | 39 | 440 | 1945 |
| Ge 4/4 | 21 | | SIG/YStC/BBC | - | 55 | 41 | 700 | 1950 |
| Tm 2/2 | 22 | | Schöma | - | 55 | 6.5 | 78 | 1971 |
| Tm 2/2 | 23 | | Schöma | - | 50 | 21 | 300 | 1988 |
| Be 2/6 | 2000 | L'ARNON | Stadler | 88 (9) | 80 | 46.5 | 640 | 2001 |
| Be 2/6 | 2001 | La Thiéle | Stadler | 88 (9) | 80 | 46.5 | 640 | 2001 |

h  Historic railcar.

152

# 5. OPEN ACCESS OPERATORS
## 5.1. CROSSRAIL

When Regionalverkehr Mittelland's (the merger of EBT, SMB and VHB) passenger operations were merged with those of BLS, RM's freight operations, which had been using the branding Crossrail since 2004, were put up for sale. The company was taken over by Australian company Babcock and Brown (B&B) in 2006. In 2007 Belgian company DLC merged with Crossrail and is now Crossrail Benelux. In 2009, Jeroen Lejeune, a founder of DLC, bought B&B's shares.

Only locomotives which can be seen in Switzerland are included here. Crossrail has its headquarters and a terminal in Wiler. Subsidiary Crossrail Italia has a terminal in Domodossola.

Most of the Crossrail fleet is hired. In mid 2009, the locos on hire were:

### TRAXX CLASS 185.1 version DACH
185 535-2  A  Christine | 185 536-0  A

### TRAXX Class 185.2 version DACH
185 578-2  C  Christine | 185 595-6  B
185 579-0  C  Adriana | 185 596-4  B
185 580-8  C  Jana | 185 597-2  B
185 581-6  C  Celine Alia | 185 598-0  B
185 590-7  B | 185 599-8  B
185 592-3  B | 185 600-4  B
185 593-1  B | 185 601-2  B
185 594-9  B | 185 602-0  B

### TRAXX Class 186 version DACHI
186 901-5  C | 186 904-9  C
186 902-3  C | 186 905-6  C
186 903-1  C | 186 907-2  C

### TRAXX Class E.484 version CHI
E.484.901  M | E.484.902  M

A  Leased from Angel Trains Cargo
B  Leased from Beacon Rail
C  Leased from CB Rail
B  Leased from MRCE

## CLASS Re 436                                        Bo-Bo

436 111 to 113 are ex EBT Re 4/4 111 to 113, 436 114 is ex VHB 141 and 436 115 is ex SMB 181. All are equipped with ETCS Level 2. Details the same as SBB Class Re 4/4III (430) except:

**Built:** 1969 (111, 112); 1983 (113 to 115).          **Power Rating:** 4656 kW.

436 111-9 | 436 114-3  Natalie
436 112-7 | 436 115-0
436 113-5  Marianne |

### Other stock
Te 236 305-9, ex RM. Stored at Wiler.
Em 846 350-7 MaK Type G1202BB works No. 100781, 1978. ex RM, ex NIAG no. 5. Stored at Wiler.

# 5.2. MAKIE

A small quarrying firm based in Gettnau on the Huttwil–Wolhusen line between Bern and Luzern. Makies uses former SOB electric railcars to haul trains of sand from Briseck (between Zell and Gettnau) to Stalden Industrie (between Gettnau and Willisau), a distance of 3.6 km. Trains of gravel also run from Gettnau to Luzern. Trains are operated under SRT's licence.

| | | | | | | | | | |
|---|---|---|---|---|---|---|---|---|---|
| Em | Em 3/3 | 1 | | Henschel | - | - | - | - | 1964 |
| Em | Em 3/3 | 2 | | Henschel | - | - | - | - | 1965 |
| BDe 576 049-1 | BDe 4/4 | WÄDENSWIL | SIG/BBC | 32 | 110 | 71.5 | 1595 | 1959 |
| BDe 576 055-8* | BDe4/4 | STEINERBERG | SIG/BBC | 32 | 110 | 72 | 2135 | 1978 |
| BDe 576 056-6 | BDe4/4 | SATTEL SZ | SIG/BBC | 32 | 110 | 72 | 2135 | 1979 |
| BDe 576 057-4 | BDe4/4 | FEUSISBERG | SIG/BBC | 32 | 110 | 72 | 2135 | 1979 |

* For spares only. Units 576 049, 055057 are originally SOB 81 and 83–85.

1 Henschel DH 500 works no. 30590 ex GSW no. 10, ex ESW, TEW, WBB and Monteforno.
2 Henschel DHG 500 works no. 30858 ex Rheinstahl no. 56, ex WLH.

# 5.3. PANLOG

Serves a steelworks near Emmenbrücke (Luzern) plus local trips. To receive two Voith Gravita diesels in autumn 2009.

| | | | | | | |
|---|---|---|---|---|---|---|
| 1 | 847 852-1 | Vossloh G1206 | 1001019 | 1999 | B-B |
| 3 | 837 804-4 | Vossloh DE 502 | 700081 | 1986 | Co |

# *SWISS RAIL TRAFFIC*          *SRT*

This company started operations on 1 May 2008 with a freight service between Basel and a paper plant at Biberist, near Solothurn. Initially the company has hired traction and has no locos of its own. The company is allied to Rail-event, Bahn-Support and Bermane Logistics & Rail. In the first month of operation, SRT used two railcars owned by German operator Hohenzollerischen Landesbahn, ex MThB Re 4/4 I 416 628 and ex RM Be 4/4 171.

# PLATFORM 5 MAIL ORDER

## EISENBAHNATLAS DEUTSCHLAND 2009/2010

### Schweers & Wall

Fully revised and updated edition of this definitive colour atlas of Germany's railways in 1:300 000 scale. Shows all lines with identification of double track, single track, narrow gauge lines, freight only, not in use, former line now removed, rack lines and lines under construction. Colours are used to show lines of different electrification voltages and German timetable numbers are shown beside passenger lines. Also shows all stations, halts, junctions, yards, freight facilities, preservation centres, museum lines, tramways and funiculars, plus many general geographical features including rivers, motorways and canals. Includes enlargements of major centres, index maps and a full index to stations and other significant places. Key is in German, English, French and Dutch. 256 pages. Large format hardback. **£39.95** *TR Subscriber Price* **£35.95**

## EISENBAHNATLAS SCHWEIZ 2ND EDITION

### Schweers & Wall

A new updated edition of this definitive atlas of Switzerland's railways. Shows the same extensive detail as the Eisenbahnatlas Deutschland above. Also includes tramway maps and a full list of railway companies. Key is in German, English and French. Large format hardback.

**Special Note:**
Eisenbahnatlas Schweiz 2nd edition is due for publication in Spring 2010. At the time of publication of this book, we do not have any information about the price. If you would like to be notified when Eisenbahnatlas Schweiz 2nd edition is available, please contact our mail order department using the details on page 4. Note: Old edition illustrated.

**To place an order see details on page 4.**

# PLATFORM 5 MAIL ORDER

## THE ELECTRONIC TIMETABLE CD-ROM

### Cedion GmbH

The electronic timetable contains full railway timetable information* for most European countries including Great Britain, France, Germany, Belgium, The Netherlands, Luxembourg, Italy, Switzerland, Austria etc. It can produce complete travel itineraries for both international and domestic journeys, plus diagrammatic journey maps and full arrival/departure listings for any station in any country. Capable of running in English, French, German or Italian languages. Minimum system requirements: Windows 98 or later, 486/33 MHz, 8MB RAM.

The electronic timetable is issued in December every year, andcovers the 12 months from mid-December. Regular updates can be downloaded over the internet throughout the year, free of charge by selecting 'file', 'update' and following the instructions given.

**£12.95** *Today's Railways subscriber price* **£10.95** (post free) to UK and Europe. Please add £1.00 p&p to addresses outside Europe.

*In some countries where a timetable change occurs during the period of validity, information is only included up to the date of timetable change.

**Special Note:** We can accept advance orders for new versions from the beginning of November each year. Alternatively, if you would like to be notified when new editions become available, please contact our mail order department.

**To place an order see details on page 4.**

# 6. TRACK MAINTENANCE COMPANIES

## 6.1. SCHEUCHZER

This is a track maintenance with a small number of interesting locos, all with names of animals rather than numbers. Livery is blue with white cabs – very similar to Angel Trains Cargo.

| Number | Name | Type | Builder | kW | Notes | Built |
|---|---|---|---|---|---|---|
| - | BISON | DH 1500 BB | CFD | - | EVN 80 85 97 70 001-8 | - |
| - | GAZELLE | Bo-Bo | B&L | - | Ex HBNPC, France | - |
| - | HUSKY | | | | | |

## 6.2. SERSA

This is mainly a company carrying out track maintenance but ran its first test open access freight train in summer 2008.

| No. | Name | Type | Builder | kW | Notes | Built |
|---|---|---|---|---|---|---|
| Tm 237 914-7 | ERICH | - | SIG/BBC | - | ex WM 101 | 1961 |
| Tm 237 950-1 | CHRISTIAN | 54.22 | Robel | - | - | 1994 |
| Tm 237 952-7 | ERWIN | DH240B | Henschel | 200 | ex MFO, Oerlikon | 1962 |
| Tm 237 953-5 | FRITZ | - | SIG/BBC/SAU | - | ex ABB | - |
| Tm 237 970-9 | MAX | - | Robel | - | Crane trolley | 2006 |
| Tm 237 971-7 | PETER | - | Robel | - | Crane trolley | 2006 |
| Tm - | ANTONIO | - | SIG/BBC/SAU | 243 | ex BT no. 10 | 1960 |
| Em 837 901-8 | MONICA | DH500Ca | Henschel | 400 | ex H Stutz no. 1 | 1963 |
| Em - | | DH440Ca | Henschel | 400 | ex Dolomitwerke Hagen no. 1 | 1965 |
| Em 837 950-5 | | DH440 | Henschel | 350 | ex Steinkohlenbergwerk | 1960 |
| Em 837 951-3 | KARIN | DH500Ca | Henschel | 400 | ex Paperfabrik Perlen no. 7 | 1966 |
| Em 837 952-1 | SVENJA | DH 700 | Henschel | 500 | ex Werke Huls | 1962 |
| Am 843 151-2 | TRUDY | G1700 | Vossloh | 1700 | wks no. 5001492 | 2004 |
| Am 843 152-0 | BARBARA | G1700 | Vossloh | 1700 | wks no. 5001493 | 2004 |
| Am 843 153-8 | CINDERELLA | G1700 | Vossloh | 1700 | wks no. 500494 | 2004 |
| Am 843 154-6 | | G1700 | Vossloh | 1700 | wks no. 1001210* | 2003 |
| Am 847 950-3 | GRETLI I | V100 | KM | 810 | ex DB 211 320 | 1962 |
| Am 847 951-1 | GRETLI II | V100 | Krupp | 810 | ex DB 211 249 | 1962 |
| Bm 847 954-5 | FANNY | 800D | MaK | 600 | ex HFHJ M9 | 1958 |
| Am 847 957-1 | LOTTI | V100 | Henschel | 810 | ex DB 211 215 | 1962 |
| Am 847 958-6 | NICOLE | V100 | Deutz | 810 | ex DB 211 118 | 1961 |
| Am 847 959-4 | FRIEDA | 1200D | MaK | 1000 | ex WBHE V15 | 1964 |
| - | | CFL80DBR | Schöma | 80 | ex Escher & Wyss | 1964 |

\* EVN 92 80 1277 401 D-DISPO, hired from MRCE Dispolok

## 6.3. VANOLI

A track contractor based in Thalwil.

| No. | Name | Type | Builder | kW | Notes | Built |
|---|---|---|---|---|---|---|
| Bm 847 853-9 | Lok Goldau | DHG1200 | Henschel | - | Ex VNJ, Denmark DL14 | 1977 |

# OTHER COMPANIES' TRAINS

## Cisalpino

This joint venture involving SBB and Italian Railways operated international trains on the routes from Basel, Zürich and Genève to Milano and beyond. Services were intially provided by loco-hauled rakes and ETR.470 Cisalpino tilting sets, based on the ETR.460 Pendolino. In 2009 ETR.610 Cisalpino (which can work in multiple) started to enter service. Cisalpino was due to be wound up in December 2009 due to disagreements between the two companies over unreliability and late delivery. The Cisalpino fleet will now be divided between SBB and Trenitalia. With no exact details available as we completed this book, we decided to leave the trains out. Cisalpino sets are described in our companion book ITALIAN RAILWAYS.

## DB (German Railways)

Class 101 electric locomotives work IC services and Class 111 electric locomotoves work local services into Basel SBB.
A larger number of DB types work into Basel Bad Bf, including Class 143 electric locomotoves plus Class 612 and 648 DMUs.
ICE 1 (Class 401 power cars) work into Basel SBB and several trains a day continue to Bern and Interlaken Ost.

A variety of DB Schenker freight locomotive types, particularly Classes 145, 151 and 185, work as far as Basel Muttenz yard. Class 185 electric locos work throughout from Basel to Chiasso over the Gotthard route and to Domodossola over the Lötschberg route. Class 185 also operate over the Stuttgart–Singen route and into north-east Switzerland. DB Schenker Italia uses G2000 diesels from Chiasso into Italy.

## HUPAC

HUPAC is a Swiss company operating intermodal trains – both containers, piggyback and RoLa, the latter carryingh complete lorries, in Switzerland, as well as into Italy and Germany. The company owns three Taurus electric locos - ES64U2-100, 101 and 102, also known as 182 600–602 in Germany) but now contracts in traction. The HUPAC locos may be seen in Switzerland but are on hire to other operators. HUPAC also has a subsidiary in Italy whose locos do not reach Switzerland. These are included in companion book ITALIAN RAILWAYS.

## ÖBB (Austrian State Railways)

ÖBB Class 1016 and 1116 Taurus electric locomotoves operate into Buchs station on both passenger and freight trains. Class 4024 Talent EMUs work into St. Margrethen station on local services.

# SEEN IN SWITZERLAND

## Rail4Chem

When this book is first published, a few locos in Rail4Chem livery might still be seen in Switzerland. However, Veolia Cargo took over Rail4Chem in 2007 and Fret SNCF was due to take over Veolia Cargo's operations outside France in late 2009.

## SNCF (French Railways)

A variety of SNCF trains work into Basel SBB station, particularly Class BB 15000 and BB 26000 electric locos.

A variety of train types operate into Genève Cornavin from the Lyon direction, particularly Class BB 7200 electric locos and X 82500 DMUs.

TGV Sud-Est dual-voltage and TGV Duplex sets operate the Paris–Genève service.

TGV Sud-Est tri-voltage sets 110–118 operate the Paris–Lausanne service which extends to Brig in winter. These also operate the Paris–Bern service. Sets 112 and 114 are owned by SBB but maintained by SNCF.

TGV POS sets 4401–4419 operate the Paris Est–Basel–Zürich service. Set 4406 is owned by SBB but maintained by SNCF.

Z 9500 and Z 9600 EMUs work into Genève Eaux-Vives.

X 73500 diesel railcars reach La Chaux-de-Fonds from Besançon.

Fret SNCF Class BB 37000 tri-voltage locomotives operate frequently into Basel Muttenz yard but also less frequently to Zürich Limmattal and through to Buchs SG.

## Trenitalia (Italian Railways)

Trenitalia Class E.444 and E.656 electric locomotives reach Chiasso station with IC/EC services. Class E.464 head TILO suburban trains from Milano.

Class E.656 and other classes also operate freight services into Chiasso yard but this is not visible from the passenger station.

## TX Logistik (TXL)

This is a German open access company, now 51% owned by Trenitalia, with some operations through Switzerland. All of TXL's fleet is hired. The company may use Class 185, ES64U2 (Taurus) or ES64F4 (Class 189) in Switzerland.

# 7. SWISS TRAMWAY SYSTEMS

## INTRODUCTION

Switzerland had numerous urban tramways, almost all being built to metre gauge. In general, those in the smaller and medium sized towns closed down, many being replaced by trolleybuses. The larger systems have survived and been modernised, but in Neuchâtel, only a small part of a much larger system remains in use. Several systems have recently built or planned extensions, and there is one completely new standard gauge system at Lausanne. It is often difficult to differentiate between tramways and light railways; the systems detailed in this section are those that are legally classified as tramways. In spite of this some have no street running, despite this being a feature of several of the railways.

Most of the systems have museum cars that are used for specials or tourist operations. These are are not included in this publication and neither are works cars.

Note: In this section under "Accommodation" are shown the number of seats and an estimate of the amount of standing capacity (when known), e.g. 47/61 = 47 seats and room for 61 standees.

## TRAMS

In the past most systems used the "Swiss Standard Tram" a unidirectional bogie vehicle with four traction motors. Matching trailers were also built. In the 1970s and 1980s articulated vehicles from Schindler or Düwag were bought but Zürich went its own way with its "Tram 2000 design. Many trams have had low-floor centre sections added.

Recently, standard commercial products such as the Siemens "Combino" (Basel and Bern) and the Bombardier Cityrunner (Genève – now known as "Flexity Outlook") have been ordered, but as usual Zürich decided to go its own way and specified the unique "Cobra" design. Unfortunately the Siemens Combino design ran into trouble with fatigue cracking in the body and all earlier examples had to be recalled by Siemens for rebuilding. Similarly the Cobra had a fairly disastrous introduction and the six prototypes have been effectively replaced by new vehicles, although classed as rebuilds.

The Swiss firm of Stadler has now entered the fray with its new "Tango" design for Basel and four pre-production examples have been delivered to BLT for assessment.

All cars are unidirectional unless otherwise stated.

# 7.1. BASEL

The city of Basel is north-west Switzerland, hard on the borders of France and Germany, is served by two tramway operators, both publicly owned. The green trams of the BVB mostly serve the urban routes in accordance with the requirements of canton Basel Stadt. The yellow trams of the BLT serve the city and canton Basel Land on interurban routes that had their origin in separate light railways. Route 10 crosses the border to serve Leymen in France. A BVB line is being extended across the border to serve Weil-am-Rhein in Germany. Fares are integrated through the *Tarifverbund Nordwestschweiz*. New Swiss-built Tango trams are being delivered to both systems.

## 7.1.1. BASELLAND TRANSPORT BLT

The BLT was created in 1974 to operate or co-ordinate transport in the Canton of Basel Land which excludes the city itself. Of the four tram routes that extend beyond the city boundary, two (to Aesch and Pratteln) were operated by the BVB, one (the Birseckbahn to Dornach) was an independant operation, and the other (the Birsigtalbahn to Rodersdorf) was a light railway. The latter line is unusual in that it passes through French territory at Leymen. The Pratteln route continues to be operated by the BVB in compensation for BTB trams carrying passengers within the city on the other routes. The BLT is also reponsible for the Waldenburgerbahn; this is detailed separately as a railway.

**Gauge:** 1000 mm.
**Electrical System:** 600 V DC.
**Depots:** Hüslimatt, Ruchfeld, Rodersdorf, Aesch.
**Livery:** Yellow with orange stripes.

### CLASS Be 4/6          2-SECTION CARS

These cars were built for the Birseckbahn, and passed to the BLT on its formation in 1974.

**Built:** 1971–76.
**Builder–Mechanical Parts:** SWP.
**Builder–Electrical Parts:** BBC/Siemens.
**Wheel Arrangement:** Bo-2-Bo.
**Traction Motors:** 4 x 75 kW.      **Length over Couplers:** 19.20 m.
**Weight:** 25 tonnes.      **Width:** 2.20 m.
**Accommodation:** 47/61.      **Maximum Speed:** 60 km/h.
**Multiple Working:** Within class and with 200 series.

| | | | | | |
|---|---|---|---|---|---|
| 101 | 104 | 107 | 110 | 112 | 114 |
| 102 | 105 | 108 | 111 | 113 | 115 |
| 103 | 106 | 109 | | | |

### CLASS Be 4/6          2-SECTION CARS

These cars are ex-BVB. For details see BVB section. Former numbers in brackets.

| | | | | | | | |
|---|---|---|---|---|---|---|---|
| 123 | (BVB 623) | 136 | (BVB 636) | 143 | (BVB 643) | 158 | (BVB 658) |
| 135 | (BVB 635) | 141 | (BVB 641) | | | | |

### CLASS Be 6/10    TANGO    6-SECTION LOW-FLOOR CARS

These new cars feature 75% low-floor and air-conditioning. Four prototypes have been delivered and more are on order.

**Built:** 2009 onwards.
**Builder:** Stadler.
**Wheel Arrangement:** Bo-2-Bo-2-Bo.
**Traction Motors:** 6 x 125 kW.      **Length over Couplers:** 45.00 m.
**Weight:** 57 tonnes.      **Width:** 2.30 m.
**Accommodation:** 93 (1)/182.      **Maximum Speed:** 80 km/h.

| | | | | | |
|---|---|---|---|---|---|
| 151 | 158 | 165 | 172 | 178 | 184 |
| 152 | 159 | 166 | 173 | 179 | 185 |
| 153 | 160 | 167 | 174 | 180 | 186 |
| 154 | 161 | 168 | 175 | 181 | 187 |
| 155 | 162 | 169 | 176 | 182 | 188 |
| 156 | 163 | 170 | 177 | 183 | 189 |
| 157 | 164 | 171 | | | |

# CLASS Be 4/6 (Be 4/8*)　　　　2(3)-SECTION CARS

These cars operate most BLT services. The cars indicated * have been lengthened with new low-floor centre sections. They can operate in multiple (often with the 100 series) and can also haul trailers.

**Built:** 1978–81 (rebuilt 1987–95 by SWP *). Some cars did not enter service until 1984).
**Builder–Mechanical Parts:** SWP.
**Builder–Electrical Parts:** Siemens.
**Wheel Arrangement:** Bo-2-Bo (Bo-2-2-Bo*).
**Traction Motors:** 4 x 75 kW.　　　　　　　**Length over Couplers:** 19.80 m (25.40 m*).
**Weight:** 25 (31*) tonnes.　　　　　　　　　**Width:** 2.20 m.
**Accommodation:** 46/61 (58 (8)/86*).　　　**Maximum Speed:** 65 km/h.
**Multiple Working:** Within class and with 100 series.

| | | | | | | | | | | | | | |
|---|---|---|---|---|---|---|---|---|---|---|---|---|---|
| 201 | * | 212 | * | 223 | | 234 | | 245 | * | 256 | * |
| 202 | * | 213 | * | 224 | | 235 | | 246 | * | 257 | |
| 203 | * | 214 | * | 225 | | 236 | * | 247 | * | 258 | |
| 204 | * | 215 | * | 226 | | 237 | * | 248 | * | 259 | |
| 205 | * | 216 | * | 227 | | 238 | * | 249 | * | 260 | * |
| 206 | * | 217 | * | 228 | | 239 | | 250 | * | 261 | |
| 207 | * | 218 | * | 229 | | 240 | * | 251 | * | 262 | * |
| 208 | * | 219 | * | 230 | | 241 | | 252 | * | 263 | * |
| 209 | * | 220 | * | 231 | * | 242 | * | 253 | * | 264 | * |
| 210 | * | 221 | * | 232 | * | 243 | | 254 | * | 265 | * |
| 211 | * | 222 | * | 233 | * | 244 | * | 255 | * | 266 | * |

# CLASS B4　　　　　　　　　　　　　BOGIE TRAILER

Ex VBZ, BVB and SVB.
**Built:** 1961–72.
**Builder:** FFA.
**Weight:** 10.2 tonnes.　　　　　　　　　**Length over Couplers:** 13.8 m.
**Accommodation:** 26.　　　　　　　　　　**Maximum Speed:** 60 km/h.

| | | | | | | | |
|---|---|---|---|---|---|---|---|
| 1301 | (VBZ 801) | 1304 | (BVB 1404) | 1317 | (BVB 1417) | 1320 | (BVB 1420) |
| 1302 | (VBZ 799) | 1305 | (BVB 1408) | 1318 | (BVB 1418) | 1321 | (BVB 1421) |
| 1303 | (VBZ 800) | 1316 | (BVB 1416) | 1319 | (BVB 1419) | 1322 | (BVB 1422) |

# 7.1.2. BASLER VERKEHRSBETRIEBE    BVB

Today this is the second largest tram system in Switzerland, and apart from some short sections across the borders into France and Germany, very little has been closed. The operation is complicated in that Baselland Transport operate over the BVB tracks into the city.

**Gauge:** 1000 mm.
**Electrical System:** 600 V DC.
**Depots:** Allschwilerstrasse, Dreispitz, Klybeck (workshops), Wiesenplatz.
**Livery:** Green.

## CLASS Be 6/8        COMBINO          7-SECTION CARS

**Built:** 2001–02.
**Builder:** Siemens, Krefeld.
**Wheel Arrangement:** Bo-2-Bo-Bo
**Traction Motors:** 6 S-E ITB 1422-0GA03 2 of 100 kW.
**Length over Couplers:** 42.860 m.
**Weight:** 47.87 tonnes.                    **Width:** 2.30 m.
**Accommodation:** 90/163.                   **Maximum Speed:** 65 km/h.

| | | | | | |
|---|---|---|---|---|---|
| 301 | 306 | 311 | 316 | 321 | 325 |
| 302 | 307 | 312 | 317 | 322 | 326 |
| 303 | 308 | 313 | 318 | 323 | 327 |
| 304 | 309 | 314 | 319 | 324 | 328 |
| 305 | 310 | 315 | 320 | | |

## CLASS Be 6/10   TANGO   6-SECTION LOW-FLOOR CARS

These new cars feature 75% low-floor and air-conditioning. A possible order for 40 has not yet been placed. numbering not yet known.

**Built:**
**Builder:** Stadler.
**Wheel Arrangement:** Bo-2-Bo-2-Bo.
**Traction Motors:** 6 x 125 kW.
**Weight:** 57 tonnes.                        **Length over Couplers:** 45.00 m.
**Accommodation:** 93 (1)/182.               **Width:** 2.30 m.
                                             **Maximum Speed:** 80 km/h.

| | | | | | |
|---|---|---|---|---|---|
| ... | ... | ... | ... | ... | ... |
| ... | ... | ... | ... | ... | ... |
| ... | ... | ... | ... | ... | ... |
| ... | ... | | | | |

## CLASS Be 4/4                                 SINGLE CARS

These are 'Swiss Standard' bogie cars. They normally operate with bogie trailers.

**Built:** 1967–68.
**Builder–Mechanical Parts:** SWP.
**Builder–Electrical Parts:** Siemens.
**Wheel Arrangement:** Bo-Bo.
**Traction Motors:** 4 BBC 0300a of 67 kW.
**Weight:** 19.02 tonnes.                     **Length over Couplers:** 13.745 m.
**Accommodation:** 28/67.                     **Width:** 2.20 m.
                                              **Maximum Speed:** 60 km/h.

| | | | | | |
|---|---|---|---|---|---|
| 457 | 461 | 465 | 468 | 471 | 474 |
| 458 | 462 | 466 | 469 | 472 | 475 |
| 459 | 463 | 467 | 470 | 473 | 476 |
| 460 | 464 | | | | |

## CLASS Be 4/4                    SINGLE CARS

These modern bogie cars are unusual in being asymmetric; the nearside taper is less severe than that on the offside to accommodate the wide doorways. The usually operate in multiple with the 659–686 series.

**Built:** 1986–7.
**Builder–Mechanical Parts:** SWP/SIG.
**Builder–Electrical Parts:** BBC/Siemens.
**Wheel Arrangement:** B-B.
**Traction Motors:** 2 Type 4 ELO 2052T of 150 kW.    **Length over Couplers:** 13.97 m.
**Weight:** 19.50 tonnes.                              **Width:** 2.20 m.
**Accommodation:** 28/70.                              **Maximum Speed:** 60 km/h.

| | | | | | |
|---|---|---|---|---|---|
| 477 | 482 | 487 | 491 | 495 | 499 |
| 478 | 483 | 488 | 492 | 496 | 500 |
| 479 | 484 | 489 | 493 | 497 | 501 |
| 480 | 485 | 490 | 494 | 498 | 502 |
| 481 | 486 | | | | |

## CLASS Be 4/6                   2-SECTION CARS

Thes cars are the standard Düwag design of articulated car was adopted by Basel for financial reasons. All the Basel articulated cars normally operate with bogie trailers.

**Built:** 1967 (1972–3*).
**Builder–Mechanical Parts:** Düwag.
**Builder–Electrical Parts:** Siemens.
**Wheel Arrangement:** B-2-B.
**Traction Motors:** 2 Type 4 ELO 2057of 150 kW.    **Length over Couplers:** 19.735 m.
**Weight:** 23.5 tonnes.                             **Width:** 2.20 m.
**Accommodation:** 40/113.                           **Maximum Speed:** 60 km/h.

| | | | | | |
|---|---|---|---|---|---|
| 624 | 629 | 642 | 646 | 651 | 654 |
| 626 | 637 | 644 | 647 | 652 | 655 |
| 627 | 638 | 645 | 650 | 653 | 656 |
| 628 | 639 | | | | |

## CLASS Be 4/6                   3-SECTION CARS

Modern articulated cars, usually operated in multiple with the 477–502 series. New low-floor centre sections from SWG-P are have been added to these cars. They are of lightweight fibreglass construction and have single axles at each end replacing the centre bogie.

**Built:** 1990/1.
**Builder–Mechanical Parts:** SWP/SIG.
**Builder–Electrical Parts:** BBC/Siemens.
**Wheel Arrangement:** B-1-1-B.
**Traction Motors:** 2 Type 4 ELO 2052T of 150 kW.    **Length over Couplers:** 29.030 m.
**Weight:** 31.57 tonnes.                              **Width:** 2.20 m.
**Accommodation:** 59/160.                             **Maximum Speed:** 80 km/h.

| | | | | | |
|---|---|---|---|---|---|
| 659 | 664 | 669 | 674 | 679 | 683 |
| 660 | 665 | 670 | 675 | 680 | 684 |
| 661 | 666 | 671 | 676 | 681 | 685 |
| 662 | 667 | 672 | 677 | 682 | 686 |
| 663 | 668 | 673 | 678 | | |

# CLASS B4

# BOGIE TRAILER

**Built:** 1961–72.
**Builder:** FFA.
**Weight:** 10.2 tonnes.
**Accommodation:** 26.

**Length over Couplers:** 13.8 m.
**Maximum Speed:** 60 km/h.

\* Fitted with low floor section.

| | | | | | |
|---|---|---|---|---|---|
| 1427 | 1441 | 1454 | 1468 * | 1481 * | 1494 |
| 1428 | 1442 | 1455 | 1469 * | 1482 * | 1495 |
| 1429 | 1443 | 1456 * | 1470 | 1483 | 1496 |
| 1430 | 1444 * | 1457 | 1471 | 1484 * | 1497 * |
| 1431 | 1445 | 1458 | 1472 * | 1485 * | 1498 |
| 1432 | 1446 | 1459 | 1473 * | 1486 * | 1499 |
| 1433 | 1447 | 1460 | 1474 | 1487 * | 1500 |
| 1434 | 1448 | 1461 | 1475 * | 1488 * | 1501 * |
| 1435 | 1449 * | 1463 | 1476 * | 1489 * | 1502 * |
| 1436 | 1450 | 1464 | 1477 | 1490 * | 1503 * |
| 1437 | 1451 | 1465 | 1478 * | 1491 * | 1504 |
| 1438 | 1452 | 1466 * | 1479 * | 1492 * | 1505 * |
| 1439 | 1453 | 1467 | 1480 * | 1493 * | 1506 |
| 1440 | | | | | |

# 7.2. STÄDTISCHE VERKEHRSBETRIEBE BERN SVB

The Swiss capital always operated a very traditional metre-gauge urban tramway, but in recent years there has been considerable rolling stock modernisation and a bold new red livery. Now it is set to expand with the *Tram Bern West* replacing two trolleybus routes, and an integration project with the RBS interurban tramway to Worb planned. This expansion requires 21 more Siemens *Combino* trams, that started arriving in October 2008. All tram services meet at the modern interchange station outside HB.

**Gauge:** 1000 mm.
**Electrical System:** 600 V DC.
**Depots:** Eigerplatz, Burgernziel, Weissenbühl.
**Livery:** Red.

## CLASS Be 4/8        3-SECTION CARS

These double articulated cars have two Jacobs bogies under the articulations.

**Built:** 1973.
**Builder–Mechanical Parts:** SWS.
**Builder–Electrical Parts:** BBC/SAAS.
**Wheel Arrangement:** Bo-2-2-Bo.
**Traction Motors:** 4 ELG 4 2030 of 121 kW.
**Weight:** 35.00 tonnes.
**Accommodation:** 52/168.

**Length over Couplers:** 26.20 m.
**Width:** 2.20 m.
**Maximum Speed:** 60 km/h.

| | | | | | |
|---|---|---|---|---|---|
| 715 | 718 | 720 | 722 | 724 | 726 |
| 716 | 719 | 721 | 723 | 725 | |

## CLASS Be 4/8        3-SECTION CARS

These modern low-floor cars consist of a central two-bogie section and end sections with one bogie at the outer ends.

**Built:** 1989–90.
**Builder–Mechanical Parts:** ACMV/Duewag.
**Builder–Electrical Parts:** ABB.
**Wheel Arrangement:** Bo-2-2-Bo.
**Traction Motors:** 4 ELO Type 1860 B of 153 kW.
**Weight:** 34.00 tonnes.
**Accommodation:** 62 (2)/179.

**Floor Height at Doors:** 350 mm.
**Length over Couplers:** 31.03 m.
**Width:** 2.20 m.
**Maximum Speed:** 60 km/h.

| | | | | | |
|---|---|---|---|---|---|
| 731 | 733 | 735 | 737 | 739 | 741 |
| 732 | 734 | 736 | 738 | 740 | 742 |

## CLASS Be 4/6 (Be 6/8*) COMBINO ADVANCED 5 (7*)-SECTION CARS

New standard Siemens low-floor cars.

**Built:** 2002–2004.
**Builder–Mechanical Parts:** Siemens.
**Wheel Arrangement:** Bo-2-Bo (Bo-2-Bo-Bo*).
**Traction Motors:** 4 (6*) of 100 kW.
**Weight:** 36 (49*) tonnes.
**Accommodation:** 59/116.

**Floor Height at Doors:** 300 mm.
**Length over Couplers:** 31.46 m (42.9 m*).
**Width:** 2.30 m.
**Maximum Speed:** 60 km/h.

Extended to 7-section cars 2009.

| | | | | | | | | | | | |
|---|---|---|---|---|---|---|---|---|---|---|---|
| 751 | * | 754 | | 757 | | 760 | * | 762 | * | 764 | * |
| 752 | * | 755 | | 758 | | 761 | * | 763 | * | 765 | * |
| 753 | | 756 | | 759 | | | | | | | |

# CLASS Be 6/8 COMBINO CLASSIC 7-SECTION CARS

New low-floor cars.

**Built:** On order for 2009–2010.
**Builder–Mechanical Parts:** Siemens.
**Wheel Arrangement:** Bo-2-Bo-Bo.
**Traction Motors:** 6 x 100 kW.
**Weight:** 49.80 tonnes.
**Accommodation:** 59/116.

**Floor Height at Doors:** 300 mm.
**Length over Couplers:** 41.45 m.
**Width:** 2.30 m.
**Maximum Speed:** 70 km/h. (60 km/h for SVB).

| | | | | | |
|---|---|---|---|---|---|
| 771 | 775 | 779 | 783 | 787 | 790 |
| 772 | 776 | 780 | 784 | 788 | 791 |
| 773 | 777 | 781 | 785 | 789 | 792 |
| 774 | 778 | 782 | 786 | | |

651— 671

# 7.3. TRAMWAYS DE NEUCHÂTEL    TN

Although the last urban tram route closed in 1976, the lakeside metre-gauge interurban tramway to Boudry was retained and modernised, with reserved track and automatic block signalling. The yellow bogie trams run solo, coupled or with a driving trailer.

**Gauge:** 1000 mm.
**Electrical System:** 630 V DC.
**Depots:** Neuchâtel Evole, Boudry.
clow with green stripes.

## CLASS Be 4/4                    SINGLE UNITS

These are bidirectional light rail cars, and operate in various formations with driving trailers.

**Built:** 1981 (1988*).
**Builder–Mechanical Parts:** SWS (SWP/SIG*).
**Builder–Electrical Parts:** BBC.
**Wheel Arrangement:** Bo-Bo.
**Traction Motors:** 4 x 69 kW.       **Length over Couplers:** 17.5 m.
**Weight:** .                          **Width:** 2.40 m.
**Accommodation:** 42/65.              **Maximum Speed:** 75 km/h.

| | | | | | |
|---|---|---|---|---|---|
| 501 | Boudry | | 504 | | Cortaillod |
| 502 | Auvernier | | 505 | * | Ville de Neuchâtel |
| 503 | Colombier | | 506 | * | Ville de Neuchâtel |

## CLASS Bt                  BOGIE DRIVING TRAILER

**Built:** 1981.
**Builder–Mechanical Parts:** SWS.
**Builder–Electrical Parts:** BBC.
**Weight:** 17.3 tonnes.               **Length over Couplers:** 17.5 m.
**Maximum Speed:** km/h.               **Width:** 2.40 m.
**Accommodation:** 46.

551      | 552      | 553      | 554      |

# 7.4. TRANSPORTS PUBLICS GENÈVOIS TPG

After a period of closures reduced the metre-gauge tramway to one route, Genève is in expansion mode again, with new lines opened and more under construction (partly replacing trolleybuses). The whole fleet has been renewed, though the Duewag/Vevey articulated trams were the first low-floor cars to enter service anywhere, and feature a step entrance that current designs do not need. The main railway station, Gare Cornavin, now has trams waiting outside again, while inside one can find the 1500 V dc tram-trains on the SBB suburban service to La Plaine (which runs over SNCF tracks).

**Gauge:** 1000 mm.
**Electrical System:** 600 V DC.
**Depot:** Bachet de Pesay
**Liveries:**
Classes Be 4/6 and Be 4/8 were painted orange and white when delivered. Many have been reliveried in the new blue and white livery (**B**) or carry advertising livery (**A**).

## CLASS Be 4/6 — 3-SECTION CARS

The entire fleet of 'Swiss Standard' cars was replaced by these modern articulated cars.

**Built:** 1987–89 (1984†).
**Builder–Mechanical Parts:** ACMV/Duewag.
**Builder–Electrical Parts:** BBC.
**Wheel Arrangement:** B-2-B.
**Traction Motors:** 2 x 150 kW.
**Weight:** 27.9 tonnes.
**Accommodation:** 45/130.
**Length over Couplers:** 21 m.
**Width:** 2.30 m.
**Maximum Speed:** 60 km/h.

| | | | | | | | |
|---|---|---|---|---|---|---|---|
| 801 | B | † | Galliard | 813 | B | | Avucy |
| 802 | B | | Lancy | 814 | B | | Bardonnex |
| 803 | B | | Carouge | 815 | B | | Bellevue |
| 804 | B | | Chûne-Bougeries | 816 | B | | Vernier |
| 805 | A | | Thônex | 817 | B | | Dardagny |
| 806 | A | | Chûne-Bourg | 818 | B | | Satigny |
| 807 | B | | Céligny | 819 | B | | Anières |
| 808 | A | | Onex | 820 | B | | Cartigny |
| 809 | B | | Aire-la-Ville | 821 | B | | Bernex |
| 810 | B | | Ville de Genève | 822 | B | | Chancy |
| 811 | B | | Collonge Bellerive | 825 | B | | Choulex |
| 812 | B | | Avully | 826 | B | | Confignon |

## CLASS Be4/8 — 4-SECTION CARS

Class Be 4/6 lengthened with new centre sections.

**Built:** 1989. Rebuilt 1995–97, 2001.
**Builder–Mechanical Parts:** ACMV/Duewag.
**Builder–Electrical Parts:** BBC.
**Wheel Arrangement:** B-2-2-B.
**Traction Motors:** 2 x 150 kW.
**Weight:** 34.1 tonnes.
**Accommodation:** 70/200.
**Length over Couplers:** 30.9 m.
**Width:** 2.30 m.
**Maximum Speed:** 60 km/h.

| | | | | | | | |
|---|---|---|---|---|---|---|---|
| 831 | B | | Gy | 842 | | B | Pregny-Chambésy |
| 832 | B | | Hermance | 843 | | | Presinge |
| 833 | B | | Perly-Certoux | 844 | | B | Meinier |
| 834 | | | Jussy | 845 | | B | Soral |
| 835 | A | | Grand-Saconnex | 846 | | A | Vandoeuvre |
| 836 | | | Puplinge | 847 | (829) | | Genthod |
| 837 | | | Meyrin | 848 | (830) | B | Corsier |
| 838 | | | Troinex | 849 | (828) | | Veyrier |
| 839 | | | Russin | 850 | (827) | | Colongy |
| 840 | | | Laconnex | 851 | (824) | B | Versoix |
| 841 | B | | Plan-les-Ouates | 852 | (823) | | Colley-Bossy |

# CLASS Be 6/8 FLEXITY OUTLOOK     7-SECTION CARS

These are new standard Bombardier low-floor cars, formerly known as "CityRunners". 861–882 have been delivered and the first of a further 18 on order has just arrived.

**Built:** 2004–05, 2009–.
**Builder:** Bombardier.
**Wheel Arrangement:** Bo-2-Bo-Bo.
**Traction Motors:** 6 x 85 kW.
**Weight:** 50.10 tonnes.
**Accommodation:** 66/171.

**Length over Couplers:** 42.00 m.
**Width:** 2.30 m.
**Maximum Speed:** 70 km/h.

| | | | | | | | | | | | |
|---|---|---|---|---|---|---|---|---|---|---|---|
| 861 | B | 868 | A | 875 | B | 882 | B | 888 | | 894 | |
| 862 | A | 869 | B | 876 | A | 883 | | 889 | | 895 | |
| 863 | B | 870 | A | 877 | B | 884 | | 890 | | 896 | |
| 864 | A | 871 | B | 878 | B | 885 | | 891 | | 897 | |
| 865 | B | 872 | B | 879 | A | 886 | | 892 | | 898 | |
| 866 | B | 873 | B | 880 | B | 887 | | 893 | | 899 | |
| 867 | B | 874 | B | 881 | A | | | | | | |

# 7.5. TRANSPORTS PUBLICS DE LA REGION LAUSANNOISE TL

TL operates bus and trolleybus services in the Lausanne area plus a light rail line (TSOL in the Second Edition of this book) and an automatic metro line which took over the trackbed of the former LG and LO rack lines. Line **m1** Métro Ouest is the only standard-gauge tramway in Switzerland, built in 1990/91 to link a subway terminus at Flon (interchange with Line M2 and the LEB) with the south-east suburbs and the SBB at Renens. Much of the line is single-track with passing loops mostly with roadside running, but with a lengthy subway section at the Flon end. The university is a major traffic objective.

In October 2008 a French-style rubber-tyred metro **m2** was opened, partly replacing the Lausanne-Ouchy rack line, but with new construction to the north-east suburbs.

## LINE M1

**Gauge:** 1435 mm.
**Electrical System:** 750 V DC.

**Depot:** EPFL Dorigny.
**Livery:** White with blue highlights.

### CLASS Bem 4/6 B–2–B

These bi-directional articulated light rail vehicles incorporate an 88 kW diesel engine since the depot area is not electrified. They are numbered in the national computerised system for railway stock, although operation is self-contained. They often operate in pairs. Units are very similar to SBB Class 550. These are to be replaced and TL may buy them to strengthen the fleet.

**Built:** 1990/1 (1995*).
**Builder–Mechanical Parts:** ACMV/Duewag.
**Builder–Electrical Parts:** ABB.
**Traction Motors:** 2 x 188 kW
**Weight:** 42.6 tonnes.
**Accommodation:** –/28 (4) + –/28 (4).

**Length over Couplers:** 31.00 m.
**Width:**
**Maximum Speed:** 80 km/h.

| | | | |
|---|---|---|---|
| 558 201-0 | 558 206-9 | 558 210-1 | 558 214-3 * |
| 558 202-8 | 558 207-7 | 558 211-9 | 558 215-0 * |
| 558 203-6 | 558 208-5 | 558 212-7 | 558 216-8 * |
| 558 204-4 | 558 209-3 | 558 213-5 * | 558 217-6 * |
| 558 205-1 | | | |

## WORKS VEHICLES

| Class | No. | Builder | Date | Details |
|---|---|---|---|---|
| Tm2/2 | 6101 | CFD/Baudouin | 1977 | Tractor |
| Xm1/2 | 6102 | Robel/Deutz | 1957 | Ex DB Köf |

## LINE M2

**Gauge:** 1435 mm.
**Length:** 5.9 km.

**System:** 750 V DC third rail side contact.
**Depot:** Vennes.

This is a fully-automatic standard gauge metro line, modelled on Paris Line 14 but with the steepest gradients of any adhesion-worked metro in the world – an average of 6% with sections at 12%. The line runs from Ouchy to Lausanne SBB station over the former LO single-track rack line (now doubled) then from Lausanne SBB to Lausanne Flon over the former LG rack kine. Both of the latter were originally funiculars. From Flon northwards to Croisette the rest of the line was built new. The normal peak service runs every six minutes from Ouchy to Croisettes doubled over the central section between Lausanne SBB and Sarraz. To cope with the gradients, bogies are all powered and have rubber tyres as well as steel guide wheels. There are four types of brakes – regenerative, rheostatic, pneumatic tread brakes and magnetic shoes. Trains are worked by 15 2-car sets with two bogies each.

**Built:** 2005/6.
**Builder:** Alstom.
**Weight:** tonnes.
**Maximum Speed:** 60 km/h.

**Power rating:** 1200 kW.
**Length over Couplers:** 30.68 metres.
**Accommodation:** –/18 (8) + –/18 (6).

| | | | | | | | |
|---|---|---|---|---|---|---|---|
| 241 | 243 | 245 | 247 | 249 | 251 | 253 | 255 |
| 242 | 244 | 246 | 248 | 250 | 252 | 254 | |

# 7.6. VERKEHRSBETRIEBE DER STADT ZÜRICH (ZÜRI-LINIE)           VBZ

Switzerland's largest city is served by a large and efficient metre-gauge tramway that has always been modernised in a restrained way. The last high-floor *Mirage* trams are being replaced by *Cobra* low-floor cars, a design unique to Zürich that has not been without its teething troubles. Some of these are in the reversed livery (white with blue stripe) of the Glattalbahn system, a nominally independent but integrated tramway that has built new lines in the northern suburbs, including from Oerlikon to the airport. The blue and white VBZ trams of the city system are expanding as well to reach western suburbs hitherto served only by bus or trolleybus. Fares are integrated under the Zürcher Verkehrsverbund.

**Gauge:** 1000 mm.
**System:** 600 V DC.
**Depots:** Altstetten (workshops), Burgwies, Elisabethenstrasse, Hard, Kalkbreite, Irchel, Oerlikon, Wollishofen.
**Livery:** Blue & White (**G** Glattalbahn white with blue stripes).

## CLASS Be 4/6          MIRAGE          3-SECTION CARS

These cars are of an unusual 3-section design, but with only three bogies. They normally operate in pairs. These cars are being withdrawn as new Cobras are delivered.

**Built:** 1966–69.
**Builder–Mechanical Parts:** SIG (SWS†).
**Builder–Electrical Parts:** BBC/MFO/SAAS.
**Wheel Arrangement:** Bo-2-Bo
**Traction Motors:** 4 x 75 kW.
**Weight:** 25.8 tonnes .
**Accommodation:** 47/60.
**Length over Couplers:** 20.90 m.
**Width:** 2.20 m.
**Maximum Speed:** 60 km/h.

| | | | | | |
|---|---|---|---|---|---|
| 1626 † | 1649 | 1657 † | 1665 † | 1673 † | 1680 |
| 1629 † | 1650 | 1658 † | 1666 † | 1674 † | 1681 |
| 1638 † | 1651 † | 1659 † | 1667 † | 1675 † | 1684 |
| 1640 † | 1652 † | 1660 † | 1668 † | 1676 † | 1685 |
| 1646 † | 1653 † | 1662 † | 1669 † | 1677 | 1686 |
| 1647 | 1655 † | 1663 † | 1671 † | 1678 | 1688 |
| 1648 | 1656 † | 1664 † | 1672 † | 1679 | |

## CLASS Be 6/6          Bo-Bo-Bo

This was a prototype now used as a restaurant tram.

**Built:** 1961.
**Builder–Mechanical Parts:** SIG.
**Builder–Electrical Parts:** BBC.
**Wheel Arrangement:** Bo-Bo-Bo
**Traction Motors:** 400 kW.
**Weight:** 28.5 tonnes.
**Accommodation:** 40.
**Length over Couplers:**
**Width:** 2.20 m.
**Maximum Speed:** 60 km/h.

1802

# CLASS Be 4/6    TRAM 2000    3-SECTION CARS

These trams, known as "Tram 2000" normally operate in pairs, or with the non-driving 2300 and 2400 series cars.

**Built:** 1976–8.
**Builder–Mechanical Parts:** SWS/SWP.
**Builder–Electrical Parts:** BBC.
**Wheel Arrangement:** B-2-B
**Traction Motors:** 2 of 139 kW.    **Length over Couplers:** 21.4 m.
**Weight:** 26.5 tonnes.    **Width:** 2.20 m
**Accommodation:** 50/54.    **Maximum Speed:** 65 km/h.

| | | | | | |
|---|---|---|---|---|---|
| 2001 | Höngg | 2016 | | 2031 | |
| 2002 | Seebach | 2017 | | 2032 | |
| 2003 | Unterstrass | 2018 | | 2033 | |
| 2004 | | 2019 | | 2034 | |
| 2005 | Industriequartier | 2020 | | 2035 | |
| 2006 | Fluntern | 2021 | Albisrieden | 2036 | |
| 2007 | Enge | 2022 | | 2037 | Oberstrass |
| 2008 | Friesenberg | 2023 | | 2038 | Witikon |
| 2009 | Triemli | 2024 | | 2039 | Rennweg |
| 2010 | Wipkingen | 2025 | | 2040 | Rechts der Limmat |
| 2011 | Oerlikon | 2026 | | 2041 | Hottingen |
| 2012 | Wipkingen | 2027 | | 2042 | Altstetten |
| 2013 | | 2028 | | 2043 | |
| 2014 | | 2029 | | 2044 | Wollishofen |
| 2015 | | 2030 | Hirslanden | 2045 | Riesbach |

# CLASS Be 4/6    TRAM 2000    3-SECTION CARS

Development of 2000 series with higher-powered motors. 2060 was withdrawn after an accident.

**Built:** 1985–87.
**Builder–Mechanical Parts:** SIG/SWS/SWP .
**Builder–Electrical Parts:** BBC.
**Wheel Arrangement:** B-2-B
**Traction Motors:** 2 of 154 kW    **Length over Couplers:** 21.4 m.
**Weight:** 26.5 tonnes.    **Width:** 2.20 m
**Accommodation:** 50/54.    **Maximum Speed:** 65 km/h.

| | | | | | | |
|---|---|---|---|---|---|---|
| 2046 | 2055 | 2065 | 2074 | 2083 | 2091 |
| 2047 | 2056 | 2066 | 2075 | 2084 | 2092 |
| 2048 | 2057 | 2067 | 2076 | 2085 | 2093 |
| 2049 | 2058 | 2068 | 2077 | 2086 | 2094 |
| 2050 | 2059 | 2069 | 2078 | 2087 | 2095 |
| 2051 | 2061 | 2070 | 2079 | 2088 | 2096 |
| 2052 | 2062 | 2071 | 2080 | 2089 | 2097 |
| 2053 | 2063 | 2072 | 2081 | 2090 | 2098 |
| 2054 | 2064 | 2073 | 2082 | | |

# CLASS Be 4/8    TRAM 2000    4-SECTION CARS

Built as Be 4/6. Development of 2046 series with 3-phase AC drive. Rebuilt 2001–2005 as Be 4/8. Known as "Sänfte" (Sedan Chairs).

**Built:** 1991–2.
**Builder–Mechanical Parts:** SWS/SWP.
**Builder–Electrical Parts:** BBC.
**Wheel Arrangement:** B-2-2-B
**Traction Motors:** 2 of 157 kW.    **Length over Couplers:** 28.0 m.
**Weight:** 31.0 tonnes.    **Width:** 2.20 m
**Accommodation:** 68/75.    **Maximum Speed:** 65 km/h.

| | | | | | |
|---|---|---|---|---|---|
| 2099 | 2103 | 2107 | 2111 | 2115 | 2119 |
| 2100 | 2104 | 2108 | 2112 | 2116 | 2120 |
| 2101 | 2105 | 2109 | 2113 | 2117 | 2121 |
| 2102 | 2106 | 2110 | 2114 | 2118 | |

## CLASS Be 4/6     TRAM 2000     3-SECTION CARS

These cars are similar to the 2000 series, but have no driving cabs, and are used as trailing units in multiple formations.

**Built:** 1978.
**Builder–Mechanical Parts:** SWS/SWP.
**Builder–Electrical Parts:** BBC.
**Wheel Arrangement:** B-2-B
**Traction Motors:** 2 of 139 kW.     **Length over Couplers:** 21.4 m.
**Weight:** 26 tonnes.     **Width:** 2.20 m
**Accommodation:** 50/57.     **Maximum Speed:** 65 km/h.

| | | | | | |
|---|---|---|---|---|---|
| 2301 | 2304 | 2307 | 2310 | 2312 | 2314 |
| 2302 | 2305 | 2308 | 2311 | 2313 | 2315 |
| 2303 | 2306 | 2309 | | | |

## CLASS Be 2/4     TRAM 2000     SINGLE CARS

These bogie cars also have no driving cabs, and are used as trailing units in multiple formations with 2000 series cars. They are known as "ponies".

**Built:** 1985–7 (1992*).
**Builder–Mechanical Parts:** SWS/SWP.
**Builder–Electrical Parts:** BBC.
**Wheel Arrangement:** 2-B
**Traction Motor:** 154 (157*) kW.     **Length over Couplers:** 15.4 m.
**Weight:** 18.5 (16.5*) tonnes.     **Width:** 2.20 m
**Accommodation:** 35/41.     **Maximum Speed:** 65 km/h.

| | | | | | |
|---|---|---|---|---|---|
| 2401 | 2407 | 2413 | 2419 | 2425 * | 2431 * |
| 2402 | 2408 | 2414 | 2420 | 2426 * | 2432 * |
| 2403 | 2409 | 2415 | 2421 * | 2427 * | 2433 * |
| 2404 | 2410 | 2416 | 2422 * | 2428 * | 2434 * |
| 2405 | 2411 | 2417 | 2423 * | 2429 * | 2435 * |
| 2406 | 2412 | 2418 | 2424 * | 2430 * | |

## CLASS Be 5/6     COBRA     5-SECTION CARS

These new trams were specially designed for Zürich and were originally ordered from SWS/SIG/ Fiat/ADtranz. The original batch of six had many faults and have been completely "rebuilt" (renewed).

**Built:** 1999, 2002–2010.
**Builder:** Bombardier.
**Wheel Arrangement:** The Cobra has seperate stub axles on each side of the vehicle. Each has a motor drive, except that the centre two on the door side are unmotored.
**Traction Motors:** 10 of 62.5 kW.     **Length over Couplers:** 36.00 m.
**Weight:** 39.2 tonnes.     **Width:** 2.40 m
**Accommodation:** 90/113.     **Maximum Speed:** 70 km/h.

**G**   Glattalbahn livery (white with blue stripes).

| | | | | | |
|---|---|---|---|---|---|
| 3001 | 3016 | 3031 | 3046 | 3061 | 3075 |
| 3002 | 3017 | 3032 | 3047 | 3062 G | 3076 |
| 3003 | 3018 | 3033 | 3048 | 3063 G | 3077 |
| 3004 | 3019 | 3034 | 3049 | 3064 G | 3078 |
| 3005 | 3020 | 3035 | 3050 | 3065 G | 3079 |
| 3006 | 3021 | 3036 | 3051 | 3066 | 3080 |
| 3007 | 3022 | 3037 | 3052 | 3067 | 3081 |
| 3008 | 3023 | 3038 | 3053 | 3068 | 3082 |
| 3009 | 3024 | 3039 | 3054 | 3069 | 3083 |
| 3010 | 3025 | 3040 | 3055 | 3070 | 3084 |
| 3011 | 3026 | 3041 | 3056 | 3071 G | 3085 |
| 3012 | 3027 | 3042 | 3057 | 3072 G | 3086 |
| 3013 | 3028 | 3043 | 3058 | 3073 G | 3087 |
| 3014 | 3029 | 3044 | 3059 | 3074 G | 3088 |
| 3015 | 3030 | 3045 | 3060 | | |

# 8. PRESERVED LOCOMOTIVES & RAILCARS

In this section, all preserved locomotives and railcars from Swiss public railways are shown, except for those shown previously in this book, such as the SBB Historic fleet. In the case of steam locomotives, all known surviving locomotives from these railways are shown, since many of those not actually preserved will no doubt be the subject of future preservation attempts. Not detailed are industrial locomotives, trams, and items imported for preservation from countries outside Switzerland. The current status of the motive power is indicated as follows:

IA     Industrial use, still active.
M      Museum, on display (not active).
MA    Museum, active.
MR    Museum, under repair.
MS    Museum, stored.
P      Plinthed.
S      Stored.

## Additional Abbreviations used in this section

| | |
|---|---|
| AG | Altstätten - Gais |
| BDZ | Balgarski Darzhavni Zehleznitsi (Bulgarian State railways) |
| BSB | Bern Schwarzenburg Bahn |
| BTB | Burgdorf Thun Bahn |
| BTB | Birsigtalbahn |
| CP | Caminhos de Ferro Portugueses (Portuguese Railways) |
| CR | Classic Rail (locos stored at various locations) |
| DB | Deutsche Bundesbahn |
| DR | Deutsche Reichsbahn |
| EB | Emmental Bahn |
| ESZ | Elektrische Strassenbahn Zug |
| EZB | Erlenbach Zweisimmen Bahn |
| FKE | Frankfurt – Königstein Eisenbahn |
| GB | Gotthard Bahn |
| HWB | Huttwil Wolhusen Bahn |
| LHB | Langenthal Huttwil Bahn |
| LJB | Langenthal Jura Bahn |
| LLB | Leuk Leukerbad Bahn |
| MCM | Monthey Champéry Morgins |
| NOB | Nordostbahn |
| ÖBB | Österreichische Bundesbahnen |
| PKP | Polskie Koleje Padstwowe |
| RdB | Regional des Brenets |
| RhV | Rheintalische Verkehrsbetriebe |
| RSG | Regional Saignelégier Glovelier |
| RSR | Royal State Railway (Siam) |
| SAR | South African Railways |
| SCB | Schweizerischen Central Bahn |
| SeTB | Sernftalbahn |
| SGA | St Gallen Gais Appenzell |
| SiTB | Sihltalbahn |
| SNCF | Société Nationale des Chemins de Français |
| SSB | Städtische Strassenbahn Bern |
| STB | Seetalbahn (not Sensetalbahn, which is now the STB) |
| StEB | Stansstad Engelberg Bahn |
| SW | Seebach Wettingen |
| UeBB | Uerikon Bauma Bahn |
| VHS | Verkehrshaus der Schweiz (Swiss Transport Museum) |
| VHX | Vietnam Hoa Xa |
| VZ | Visp Zermatt |
| WPI | Wetzikon Meilen |

# 8.1. STEAM LOCOMOTIVES & RAILCARS

The system for describing steam locomotives used here is the one which is in general use in Germany. Firstly, letters and numbers are used to describe the wheel arrangement as follows: This is then followed by 'h' for superheated locos (from the German 'Heizdampf'), or 'n' for saturated locos (from the German 'Nassdampf'). The number of cylinders follow, then codes for various features, i.e.

v  compound.
z  rack locomotive with 1 pinion.
zz  rack locomotive with 2 pinions.
t  tank locomotive. e.g.: 1C1h2t is a superheated 2–6–2 tank locomotive with 2 cylinders.

| Rly. | Gauge | Class | No. | Details | Status | Date | Location |
|------|-------|-------|-----|---------|--------|------|----------|
| SBB | 1000 | G 3/3 | 109 (BAM 6) | Cn2t | MA | 1901 | Chaulin |
| SBB | 1000 | G 3/4 | 203 | 1Ch2t | S | 1912 | Volos (Greece) |
| SBB | 1000 | G3/4 | 208 | 1Ch2t | MA | 1913 | Interlaken |
| SBB | 1000 | HG3/3 | 1058 | Czn4vt | P | 1908 | Lárissa (Greece) |
| SBB | 1000 | HG3/3 | 1063 | Czn4vt | M | 1909 | VHS |
| SBB | 1000 | HG3/3 | 1067 | Czn4vt | MA | 1910 | Interlaken |
| SBB | 1000 | HG3/3 | 1068 | Czn4vt | MR | 1926 | Interlaken |
| SBB | 1435 | C5/6 | 2958 | 1Eh4v | MR | 1915 | Sulgen |
| SBB | 1435 | C5/6 | 2965 | 1Eh4v | M | 1916 | VHS |
| SBB | 1435 | C5/6 | 2969 | 1Eh4v | MS | 1916 | Sulgen |
| SBB | 1435 | Eb3/5 | 5810 | 1C1h2t | MR | 1911 | Burgdorf |
| SBB | 1435 | Eb3/5 | 5811 | 1C1h2t | S | 1911 | Glarus |
| SBB | 1435 | Eb3/5 | 5886 (BT 6) | 1C1h2t | MR | 1910 | Mendrisio |
| SBB | 1435 | Eb3/5 | 5889 (BT 9) | 1C1h2t | MA | 1910 | Herisau |
| SBB | 1435 | E3/3 | 8410 | Cn2t | S | 1901 | Zürich Altstetten |
| SBB | 1435 | E3/3 | 8463 | Cn2t | MA | 1904 | Mendrisio |
| SBB | 1435 | E3/3 | 8474 | Cn2t | M | 1907 | Romanshorn |
| SBB | 1435 | E3/3 | 8476 | Cn2t | MA | 1907 | Uster |
| SBB | 1435 | E3/3 | 8479 (ST 5) | Cn2t | MA | 1907 | Triengen |
| SBB | 1435 | E3/3 | 8481 | Cn2t | IA | 1907 | Rheinfelden |
| SBB | 1435 | E3/3 | 8483 | Cn2t | S | 1907 | Klus |
| SBB | 1435 | E3/3 | 8485 | Cn2t | MR | 1907 | Delémont |
| SBB | 1435 | E3/3 | 8487 | Cn2t | P | 1909 | Buchs |
| SBB | 1435 | E3/3 | 8501 | Cn2t | MA | 1910 | Mendrisio |
| SBB | 1435 | E3/3 | 8507 | Cn2t | P | 1910 | Sierre |
| SBB | 1435 | E3/3 | 8511 | Cn2t | MA | 1911 | St. Sulpice |
| SBB | 1435 | E3/3 | 8512 | Cn2t | S | 1911 | St. Maurice |
| SBB | 1435 | E3/3 | 8516 | Cn2t | MR | 1911 | Zürich |
| SBB | 1435 | E3/3 | 8518 | Cn2t | MA | 1913 | Uster |
| SBB | 1435 | E3/3 | 8522 (ST 8522) | Cn2t | MA | 1913 | Triengen |
| SBB | 1435 | E3/3 | 8523 | Cn2t | MA | 1915 | Le Pont |
| SBB | 1435 | E3/3 | 8527 | Cn2t | P | 1915 | Chur |
| SBB | 1435 | E3/3 | 8532 | Cn2t | MA | 1915 | Kandern (Germany) |
| SBB | 1435 | E3/3 | 8551 | Cn2t | P | 1894 | Kleinhüningen (Basel) |
| SBB | 1435 | E3/3 | 8554 | Cn2t | P | 1894 | Dietikon (To move to Balsthal for overhaul) |
| SBB | 1435 | E3/3 | 8573 | Cn2t | MA | 1890 | Burgdorf |
| SBB | 1435 | E3/3 | 8575 | Cn2t | M | 1890 | Kerzers |
| SBB | 1435 | E3/3 | 8651 (KLB 1) | Cn2t | MA | 1909 | Balsthal |
| SBB | 1435 | Xrot | 100 | rotary | M | 1896 | VHS |
| BLS | 1435 | E2/2 | 72 (Bodelibahn 3) | Bn2t | MA | 1874 | Delémont |
| BLS | 1435 | E3/3 | 77 (GTB 3) | Cn2t | MA | 1901 | Spiez |
| RhB | 1000 | G3/4 | 1 | 1Cn2t | MA | 1889 | Landquart |
| RhB | 1000 | G3/4 | 11 | 1Cn2t | MR | 1902 | Samedan |
| RhB | 1000 | G3/4 | 14 | 1Cn2t | MA | 1902 | Herisau |
| RhB | 1000 | G4/5 | 107 | 1Dh2 | MA | 1906 | Landquart |
| RhB | 1000 | G4/5 | 108 | 1Dh2 | MA | 1906 | Landquart |
| RhB | 1000 | G4/5 | 118 (RSR 340) | 1Dh2 | S | 1912 | Makkasan (Thailand) |
| RhB | 1000 | G4/5 | 122 (RSR 338) | 1Dh2 | S | 1913 | Chiang Mai (Thailand) (Mr. Lim) |

| Rly. | Gauge | Class | No. | Details | Status | Date | Location |
|------|-------|-------|-----|---------|--------|------|----------|
| RhB | 1000 | G4/5 | 123 (RES 336) | 1Dh2 | P | 1913 | Chiang Mai (Thailand) |
| RhB | 1000 | Xrotd | R12 | rotary | MR | 1913 | Realp |
| RhB | 1000 | Xrotd6/6 | 9214 | rotary | MA | 1912 | Chaulin |
| BSB | 1435 | Ed3/4 | 51 | 1Cn2t | MA | 1906 | Burgdorf |
| EB | 1435 | Ed3/3 | 3 | Cn2t | M | 1881 | VHS |
| EBT | 1435 | Ed4/5 | 8 | 1Dh2t | MA | 1914 | Burgdorf |
| FO | 1000 | HG3/4 | 1 (DFB 1) | 1Czzh4vt | MA | 1913 | Realp |
| FO | 1000 | HG3/4 | 3 | 1Czzh4vt | MA | 1913 | Chaulin |
| FO | 1000 | HG3/4 | 4 | 1Czzh4vt | MS | 1913 | Realp |
| FO | 1000 | HG3/4 | 9 (DFB 9) | 1Czzh4vt | MA | 1914 | Realp |
| FW | 1000 | G3/3 | 2 | Cn2t | P | 1887 | Wil |
| GB | 1435 | E2/2 | 11 | Bn2t | M | 1881 | VHS |
| GGB | 800 | HII/3 | 8 | B1zzh2t | M | 1892 | Ribes de Freser (Spain) |
| HWB | 1435 | E3/3 | 8 | Cn2t | MR | 1898 | St. Sulpice |
| LEB | 1000 | 03/3 | 5 | Cn2t | MA | 1890 | Chaulin |
| LEB | 1000 | G3/3 | 8 | Cn2t | MA | 1910 | Echallens |
| LHB | 1435 | Ed3/4 | 11 | 1Ch2t | MA | 1908 | Huttwil |
| MG | 800 | HII/3 | 2 | B1zzn2t | MA | 1890 | Capolago |
| MThB | 1435 | Ed3/5 | 3 | 1C1h2t | MA | 1912 | Romanshorn |
| NOB | 1435 | DI | 1 | 2An2 | MA | 1947 | VHS (Replica of 1847 loco) |
| OeBB | 1435 | E3/3 | 2 | Cn2t | MA | 1899 | Balsthal |
| PB | 800 | Bhm | 9 | railcar | | M | 1889 | VHS |
| PB | 800 | Bhm | 10 | railcar | | M | 1900 | München (Germany) |
| RdB | 1000 | G3/3 | 1 | Cn2t | MA | 1890 | Chaulin |
| RdB | 1000 | G3/3 | 2 | Cn2t | P | 1890 | Les Brenets |
| RdB | 1000 | G3/3 | 3 | Cn2t | M | 1892 | Le Locle (incomplete) |
| RSG | 1435 | Ed3/4 | 2 | 1Ch2t | MA | 1903 | Uster |
| SiTB | 1435 | E3/3 | 2 | Cn2t | MA | 1893 | Sihlwald |
| SiTB | 1435 | E3/3 | 4 | Cn2t | P | 1897 | Adliswil |
| SiTB | 1435 | E3/3 | 5 | Cn2t | MA | 1899 | Sihlwald |
| SMB | 1435 | Ed3/4 | 1 | 1Cn2t | MS | 1907 | Wald |
| SMB | 1435 | Ed3/4 | 2 | 1Cn2t | MA | 1907 | Huttwil |
| SMB | 1435 | Ec4/5 | 11 | 1Dh2t | MA | 1911 | Burgdorf |
| SOB | 1435 | E3/3 | 4 | Cn2t | MA | 1887 | Uster |
| SPB | 800 | HII/3 | 5 | B1zzh2t | MA | 1894 | Wilderswil |
| STB | 1435 | Ed3/3 | 3 | Cn2t | MA | 1884 | Bremgarten |
| UeBB | 1435 | E3/3 | 401 | Ch2t | MA | 1901 | Uster |
| VRB | 1435 | HI/2 | 7 | 1Azn2t | MA | 1873 | Vitznau (VHS) |
| VRB | 1435 | HII/S | 16 | B1zzh2t | MA | 1923 | Vitznau |
| VRB | 1435 | HII/S | 17 | B1zzh2t | MA | 1925 | Vitznau |
| VZ | 1000 | HG2/3 | 6 | B1zzh4vt | MA | 1902 | Realp |
| VZ | 1000 | HG2/3 | 7 | B1zzh4vt | MA | 1906 | Visp |
| WB | 750 | G3/3 | 5 | Cn2t | MA | 1902 | Waldenburg |
| WB | 750 | G3/3 | 6 | Cn2t | M | 1912 | VHS |
| YSC | 1000 | G4/4 | 4 | Dh2t | P | 1911 | Lárissa (Greece) |

# 8.2. DIESEL & ELECTRIC LOCOMOTIVES & RAILCARS

| Rly. | Gauge | Class | No. | Status | Date | Location |
|------|-------|-------|-----|--------|------|----------|
| SBB | 1000 | HG4/4 | 1992 | MS | 1953 | Luzern |
| SBB | 1435 | Re4/4<sup>I</sup> | 10034 | MA | 1950 | Koblenz |
| SBB | 1435 | Re4/4<sup>I</sup> | 10042 | S | 1951 | Basel Dreispitz  CR |
| SBB | 1435 | Ae3/6<sup>II</sup> | 10448 | MS | 1925 | Payerne (Swisstrain) |
| SBB | 1435 | Ae3/6<sup>I</sup> | 10601 | MS | 1921 | Le Locle (Swisstrain) |
| SBB | 1435 | Ae3/6<sup>I</sup> | 10639 | M | 1925 | Payerne (Swisstrain) |
| SBB | 1435 | Ae3/6<sup>I</sup> | 10693 | M | 1927 | Payerne (Swisstrain) |
| SBB | 1435 | Ae4/7 | 10902 | MA | 1927 | Payerne (Swisstrain) |
| SBB | 1435 | Ae4/7 | 10908 | S | 1928 | Romanshorn (CR) |
| SBB | 1435 | Ae4/7 | 10914 | S | 1928 | Le Locle (CR) |
| SBB | 1435 | Ae4/7 | 10922 | S | 1928 | Le Locle (CR) |
| SBB | 1435 | Ae4/7 | 10943 | S | 1931 | Le Locle (CR) |
| SBB | 1435 | Ae4/7 | 10948 | MS | 1931 | Payerne (Swisstrain) |
| SBB | 1435 | Ae4/7 | 10949 | M | 1931 | Bahnpark Augsburg (Germany) |
| SBB | 1435 | Ae4/7 | 10950 | S | 1931 | Dreispitz (CR – was Rail4Chem) |
| SBB | 1435 | Ae4/7 | 10951 | S | 1931 | Sulgen (CR) |
| SBB | 1435 | Ae4/7 | 10961 | S | 1931 | Romanshorn (CR) |
| SBB | 1435 | Ae4/7 | 10987 | S | 1932 | Le Locle (CR) |
| SBB | 1435 | Ae4/7 | 10997 | MA | 1933 | Mendrisio |
| SBB | 1435 | Ae4/7 | 10999 | S | 1933 | Glarus (CR) |
| SBB | 1435 | Ae4/7 | 11000 | S | 1934 | Le Locle (CR) |
| SBB | 1435 | Ae4/7 | 11001 | S | 1934 | Münchenstein (CR) |
| SBB | 1435 | Ae4/7 | 11002 | S | 1934 | Winterthur (CR) |
| SBB | 1435 | Ae4/7 | 11010 | S | 1932 | Dreispitz (CR – was Rail4Chem) |
| SBB | 1435 | Ae4/7 | 11015 | S | 1933 | Sulgen (CR) |
| SBB | 1435 | Ae4/7 | 11022 | S | 1933 | Münchenstein (CR) |
| SBB | 1435 | Ae4/7 | 11026 | MA | 1934 | Brugg |
| SBB | 1435 | Ae6/6 | 11401 | S | 1951 | Bellinzona |
| SBB | 1435 | Ae6/6 | 11406 | P | 1955 | Alpnach (Body shell) |
| SBB | 1435 | Ae6/6 | 11407 | MR | 1955 | Brugg |
| SBB | 1435 | Ae6/6 | 11411 | MA | 1955 | Erstfeld |
| SBB | 1435 | Ae6/6 | 11413 | M | 1955 | VHS (SBB Historic) |
| SBB | 1435 | Ae6/6 | 11416 | S | 1957 | Olten (SBB Historic) |
| SBB | 1435 | Ae6/6 | 11418 | P | 1957 | Altishofen |
| SBB | 1435 | Ae6/6 | 11425 | MA | 1957 | Olten (SBB Historic) |
| SBB | 1435 | Ae8/12 | 11852 | MS | 1940 | Erstfeld |
| SBB | 1435 | Be4/6 | 12332 | M | 1922 | VHS (SBB Historic) |
| SBB | 1435 | Be4/6 | 12339 | M | 1923 | Luino (Italy) |
| SBB | 1435 | Be6/8<sup>II</sup> | 13254 | M | 1920 | VHS (SBB Historic) |
| SBB | 1435 | Be6/8<sup>II</sup> | 13257 | M | 1920 | Mürzzuschlag (Austria) |
| SBB | 1435 | Be6/8<sup>III</sup> | 13302 | MA | 1925 | Rapperswil |
| SBB | 1435 | Ce4/4 | 13501 (SW 1) | M | 1904 | VHS |
| SBB | 1435 | Ce4/4 | 13502 (SW 2) | MS | 1904 | VHS (stored elsewhere – Erstfeld?) |
| SBB | 1435 | Ce6/8<sup>I</sup> | 14201 | MS | 1920 | Erstfeld (SBB Historic) |
| SBB | 1435 | Ce6/8<sup>II</sup> | 14267 | M | 1921 | Speyer (Germany) |
| SBB | 1435 | Ce6/8<sup>II</sup> | 14270 | P | 1921 | Erstfeld |
| SBB | 1435 | Ce6/8<sup>II</sup> | 14276 | MR | 1922 | Mendrisio |
| SBB | 1435 | Ce6/8<sup>II</sup> | 14282 | M | 1922 | Sinsheim (Germany) |
| SBB | 1435 | Ee3/3 | 16311 | M | 1926 | Payerne |
| SBB | 1435 | Ee3/3 | 16315 | S | 1926 | Holderbank |
| SBB | 1435 | Ee3/3 | 16316 | S | 1926 | Holderbank |
| SBB | 1435 | Ee3/3 | 16326 | S | 1928 | Holderbank |
| SBB | 1435 | Ee3/3 | 16332 | S | 1930 | Holderbank |
| SBB | 1435 | Te<sup>I</sup> | 47 | MA | 1941 | Mendrisio |
| SBB | 1435 | Te<sup>III</sup> | 130 | MR | 1946 | Koblenz |
| SBB | 1435 | Te<sup>III</sup> | 177 | MS | 1965 | Olten |
| SBB | 1000 | Te | 198 | MS | 1941 | Luzern |
| SBB | 1000 | Te | 199 | MS | 1941 | Luzern |

| Rly. | Gauge | Class | No. | Status | Date | Location |
|------|-------|-------|-----|--------|------|----------|
| SBB | 1435 | TeIII | 221 | M | 1927 | Payerne, Swisstrain. |
| SBB | 1435 | Tem<sup>I</sup> | 263 | MS | 1955 | Winterthur (SBB Historic) |
| SBB | 1435 | Tem<sup>I</sup> | 273 | MR | 1957 | Sulgen |
| SBB | 1435 | Tem<sup>I</sup> | 275 | MR | 1957 | Koblenz |
| SBB | 1435 | Tem<sup>II</sup> | 277 | MS | 1967 | Olten (SBB Historic) |
| SBB | 1435 | Tem<sup>II</sup> | 285 | M | 1967 | Romanshorn (SBB Historic) |
| SBB | 1435 | Tem<sup>II</sup> | 288 | MA | 1967 | Le Pont |
| SBB | 1435 | Tem<sup>II</sup> | 292 | MA | 1967 | Travers |
| SBB | 1435 | Tem<sup>III</sup> | 334 | MA | 1957 | Schaffhausen |
| SBB | 1435 | Tem<sup>III</sup> | 340 | MA | 1957 | Winterthur |
| SBB | 1435 | Tem<sup>III</sup> | 351 | MA | 1962 | Winterthur |
| SBB | 1435 | Tem<sup>III</sup> | 354 | MA | 1958 | Uster, DVZO |
| SBB | 1435 | Tm<sup>I</sup> | 413 | S | 1960 | Le Locle, Swisstrain |
| SBB | 1435 | Tm<sup>I</sup> | 425 | M | 1961 | Mendrisio |
| SBB | 1435 | Tm<sup>I</sup> | 438 | MA | 1928 | St. Sulpice |
| SBB | 1435 | Tm<sup>I</sup> | 453 | S | 1962 | Vallorbe (SBB Historic) |
| SBB | 1435 | Tm<sup>I</sup> | 464 | M | 1931 | VHS |
| SBB | 1435 | Tm<sup>I</sup> | 465 | MA | 1962 | Bremgarten West |
| SBB | 1435 | Tm<sup>I</sup> | 475 | MA | 1964 | Delémont |
| SBB | 1435 | Tm<sup>I</sup> | 485 | MR | 1964 | Zürich |
| SBB | 1435 | Tm<sup>I</sup> | 511 | MS | 1935 | Laufenburg |
| SBB | 1435 | Tm<sup>I</sup> | 534 | MS | 1937 | Laufenburg |
| SBB | 1435 | Tm<sup>II</sup> | 617 | MA | 1956 | Koblenz |
| SBB | 1435 | Tm<sup>II</sup> | 620 | M | 1956 | Delémont |
| SBB | 1435 | Tm<sup>II</sup> | 631 | P | 1957 | Sargans |
| SBB | 1435 | Tm<sup>II</sup> | 656 | S | 1958 | Rivera-Bironico (Private) |
| SBB | 1435 | Tm<sup>II</sup> | 662 | S | 1959 | Bodio (Private) |
| SBB | 1435 | Tm<sup>II</sup> | 685 | S | 1959 | Brittnau Wikon |
| SBB | 1435 | Tm<sup>II</sup> | 706 | MA | 1961 | Uster DVZO (as "93") |
| SBB | 1435 | Tm<sup>II</sup> | 717 | MA | 1961 | Full |
| SBB | 1435 | Tm<sup>II</sup> | 725 | MA | 1963 | Mendrisio |
| SBB | 1435 | Tm<sup>II</sup> | 749 | MS | 1951 | Location unknown in Aargau. |
| SBB | 1435 | Tm<sup>II</sup> | 758 | MA | 1952 | Brugg |
| SBB | 1435 | Tm<sup>II</sup> | 769 | MA | 1953 | Mendrisio |
| SBB | 1435 | Tm<sup>II</sup> | 777 | MS | 1953 | Le Locle |
| SBB | 1435 | Tm<sup>II</sup> | 784 | MA | 1955 | Koblenz/Laufenburg |
| SBB | 1435 | Tm<sup>II</sup> | 785 | MA | 1955 | Mendrisio |
| SBB | 1435 | Tm<sup>II</sup> | 787 or 797 | M | 1955 | Romanshorn |
| SBB | 1435 | Tm<sup>II</sup> | 801 | MR | 1964 | Ramsen |
| SBB | 1435 | Tm<sup>II</sup> | 813 | MA | 1965 | Brugg |
| SBB | 1435 | Tm | 873 | S | 1925 | Langenthal |
| SBB | 1435 | Tm | 899 | MA | 1930 | St. Sulpice |
| SBB | 1435 | Ta | 971 | M | 1927 | VHS |
| SBB | 1000 | Tmh | 985 | MA | 1965 | Realp |
| SBB | 1000 | Tmh | 986 | MA | 1962 | Realp |
| SBB | 1435 | Tm<sup>III</sup> | 9501 | MA | 1982 | Uster |
| SBB | 1435 | Tm<sup>III</sup> | 9526 | MA | 1986 | Payerne |
| SBB | 1435 | Tm<sup>III</sup> | 9527 | MA | 1986 | Konolfingen |
| SBB | 1435 | Tm<sup>III</sup> | 9529 | MA | 1986 | Uster |
| SBB | 1435 | RCe2/4 | 203 (1003) | M | 1936 | VHS |
| SBB | 1435 | RAe4/8 | 1021 | MA | 1939 | Samstagern |
| SBB | 1435 | Fe4/4 | 18518 (1678) | M | 1928 | VHS |
| SBB | 1000 | Deh 120 | 120 009 | MS | 1941 | Alpnachstad |
| SBB | 1000 | Deh 120 | 120 012 | MR | 1942 | Meiringen |
| BLS | 1435 | Te2/3 | 31 | MA | 1925 | Konolfingen |
| BLS | 1435 | Tm2/2 | 75 | MA | 1955 | Burgdorf |
| BLS | 1435 | Be5/7 | 151 | M | 1912 | VHS |
| BLS | 1435 | Ae6/8 | 206 | S | 1939 | Winterthur |
| BLS | 1435 | Ae6/8 | 208 | MA | 1943 | Payerne |
| BLS | 1435 | Ce4/6 | 307 | MA | 1919 | Spiez |
| BLS | 1435 | Ce4/4 | 311 | MS | 1919 | Le Locle |
| GBS | 1435 | Ce4/4 | 312 (SZU 49) | MS | 1920 | Mendrisio |

| Rly. | Gauge | Class | No. | Status | Date | Location |
|------|-------|-------|-----|--------|------|----------|
| BLS | 1435 | Ce4/4 | 315 | S | 1924 | Le Locle |
| BLS | 1435 | De4/5 | 796 | MS | 1929 | St. Sulpice |
| | | | | | | |
| RhB | 1000 | Tm2/2 | 68 | MA | 1948 | Realp |
| RhB | 1000 | Tm2/2 | 91 | MA | 1959 | Realp |
| RhB | 1000 | Tm2/2 | 92 | MA | 1959 | Realp |
| RhB | 1000 | Ge4/4 | 181 | MA | 1916 | Chaulin |
| RhB | 1000 | Ge4/4 | 182 | MR | 1928 | Poschiavo |
| RhB | 1000 | Ge2/4 | 205 | R | 1913 | Goldau |
| RhB | 1000 | Ge2/4 | 207 | M | 1913 | VHS |
| RhB | 1000 | Ge4/6 | 391 | M | 1913 | Berlin (Germany) |
| RhB | 1000 | Ge6/6 | 402 | M | 1921 | VHS |
| RhB | 1000 | Ge6/6 | 406 | M | 1921 | Kerzers |
| RhB | 1000 | Ge6/6 | 407 | P | 1922 | Bergün |
| RhB | 1000 | Ge6/6 | 411 | M | 1925 | München (Germany) |
| RhB | 1000 | ABDe4/4 | 453 | S | 1907 | Castione |
| RhB | 1000 | ABDe4/4 | 454 | MR | 1909 | Mendrisio |
| RhB | 1000 | ABe4/4 | 484 | MS | 1958 | La Mure (France) |
| RhB | 1000 | ABe4/4 | 486 | MR | 1958 | La Mure (France) |
| RhB | 1000 | Be4/4 | 491 | MA | 1958 | Castione |
| | | | | | | |
| AB | 1000 | ABe4/4 | 41 | MA | 1933 | Castione |
| AB | 1000 | ABe4/4 | 42 | MA | 1933 | Castione |
| AB | 1000 | Xeh4/4 | 91 | MS | 1931 | Pré Petitjean |
| AG | 1000 | CFeh3/3 | 1 (SGA 16) | M | 1911 | VHS |
| ASD | 1000 | ABDe4/4 | 3 | MS | 1913 | La Mure (France) |
| ASD | 1000 | ABDe4/4 | 12 | MS | 1913 | La Mure (France) |
| ASm(BTI) | 1000 | Be4/4 | 521 | MS | 1963 | Castione |
| BN | 1435 | Ce4/4 | 315 | S | 1924 | CR |
| BN | 1435 | Ce2/4 | 727 | M | 1935 | VHS |
| BOB | 1000 | HGe3/3 | 26 | M | 1915 | Kerzers |
| BT | 1435 | Be4/4 | 12 | MS | 1931 | Le Locle |
| BT | 1435 | Be4/4 | 13 | M | 1932 | Romanshorn |
| BT | 1435 | Be4/4 | 14 | MR | 1932 | Sulgen |
| BT | 1435 | Be4/4 | 15 | MA | 1932 | Uster |
| BT | 1435 | Be3/4 | 43 | MA | 1938 | Herisau |
| BTB | 1435 | De2/2 | 1 | M | 1899 | München (Germany) |
| BTB | 1435 | De2/2 | 2 | M | 1899 | VHS |
| BTB | 1435 | Be4/4 | 7 | S | 1923 | Oberwil |
| BTI | 1000 | BDe4/4 | 6 | M | 1947 | Täuffelen |
| CEV | 1000 | BDe4/4 | 105 | MR | 1913 | Vevey |
| CJ | 1000 | Tm | 506 | MA | 1953 | Realp |
| EBT | 1435 | Be4/4 | 101 | MS | 1932 | Le Locle |
| EBT | 1435 | Be4/4 | 104 | MS | 1932 | Le Locle |
| EBT | 1435 | Be4/4 | 105 | MS | 1930 | Le Locle |
| EBT | 1435 | Te2/2 | 155 | MA | 1946 | Burgdorf |
| EBT | 1435 | Te2/2 | 157 | MA | 1946 | Burgdorf |
| EBT | 1435 | De4/4 | 102 | MA | 1932 | Konolfingen |
| EBT | 1435 | BDe2/4 | 240 | MA | 1932 | Konolfingen |
| EZB | 1435 | Ce4/6 | 307 | MA | 1920 | Spiez |
| FART | 1000 | ABDe4/4 | 1 | MS | 1907 | Uster |
| FLP | 1000 | Ce4/4 | 3 | MA | 1912 | Grono |
| FO | 1000 | CFm2/2 | 21 | MA | 1927 | Realp (VHS) |
| FO | 1000 | Te2/2 | 4926 | MA | 1946 | Realp |
| FO | 1000 | Te2/2 | 4930 | MA | 194. | Realp |
| FO | 1000 | XRote | 4931 | MA | 1958 | Realp |
| FO | 1000 | Dmh1/2 | 4961 | MA | 1945 | Realp |
| FW | 1000 | Ce4/4 | 1 | MS | 1921 | Roggwil-Wynau |
| GFM | 1435 | Tm2/2 | 81 | MS | 1943 | Le Locle |
| GFM | 1000 | Be4/4 | 111 | MA | 1904 | Chaulin |
| JB | 1000 | He2/2 | 1 | M | 1898 | VHS |
| JB | 1000 | He2/2 | 6 | M | 1904 | Kallnach |
| LEB | 1000 | Te2/2 | 2 | MA | 1896 | Chaulin |

| Rly. | Gauge | Class | No. | Status | Date | Location |
|------|-------|-------|-----|--------|------|----------|
| LJB | 1000 | Ce2/2 | 12 | MA | 1907 | Chaulin |
| LLB | 1000 | BCFeh4/4 | 10 | MA | 1914 | Chaulin |
| LMB | 1000 | Ce2/4 | 14 | MR | 1917 | Langenthal or Melchnau? |
| LSE | 1000 | Tm | 100 | MS | 1931 | Alpnachstad |
| MC | 1000 | BCFeh4/4 | 14 | M | 1908 | Vernayaz |
| MC | 1000 | ABDeh4/4 | 15 | MA | 1909 | Martigny |
| MC | 1000 | ABDeh4/4 | 31 | MA | 1921 | Martigny |
| MC | 1000 | ABDeh4/4 | 32 | MA | 1921 | Martigny |
| MCM | 1000 | BCFeh4/4 | 6 | MA | 1909 | Chaulin |
| MIB | 1000 | Ta2/2 | 3 | MA | 1931 | Bruchhausen Vilsen (Germany) |
| MIB | 1000 | CFa2/2 | 4 | M | 1939 | VHS |
| MIB | 1000 | CFa2/2 | 5 | P | 1949 | Innertkirchen |
| MO | 1435 | ABDe4/4 | 5 | M | 1955 | Kallnach |
| MO | 1435 | ABDe4/4 | 8 | MR | 1965 | Koblenz |
| MO | 1435 | Tm2/2 | 511 | MS | 1937 | Le Locle |
| MOB | 1000 | BCFe4/4 | 6 | M | 1905 | Bern |
| MOB | 1000 | ABDe4/4 | 11 | MR | 1904 | Chaulin |
| MOB | 1000 | BDe4/4 | 16 | S | 1905 | Niederscherli |
| MOB | 1000 | BCFe4/4 | 20 | MA | 1905 | Chaulin |
| MOB | 1000 | De4/4 | 26 | MR | 1912 | Saanen |
| MOB | 1000 | DZe6/6 | 2001 | M | 1932 | Chernex |
| MOB | 1000 | DZe6/6 | 2002 | MA | 1932 | Chaulin |
| MThB | 1435 | ABDe4/4 | 12 | MA | 1965 | Romanshorn |
| NStCM | 1000 | ABDe4/4 | 1 | MS | 1916 | La Mure (France) |
| NStCM | 1000 | ABDe4/4 | 5 | MS | 1916 | La Mure (France) |
| NStCM | 1000 | ABDe4/4 | 10 | MS | 1918 | La Mure (France) |
| NStCM | 1000 | ABDe4/4 | 11 | MS | 1918 | La Mure (France) |
| OC | 1435 | CFe2/2 | 11 | MS | 1894 | VHS (stored elsewhere) |
| OeBB | 1435 | Be2/4 | 201 | MS | 1935 | Klus |
| OeBB | 1435 | ABDe2/8 | 203 | P | 1937 | Balsthal (ex GBS 704) |
| OeBB | 1435 | BDe4/12 | 204 | S | 1935 | Stuttgart (Germany) |
| OeBB | 1435 | ABDe4/8 | 742 | M | 1931 | Kallnach (ex BLS) |
| PTT | 1435 | Tm | 1 | S | 1930 | Le Locle |
| RBS | 1000 | BDe4/4 | 6 | M | 1950 | Solothurn |
| RBS | 1000 | Gem4/4 | 122 | MA | 1916 | Pré Petitjean |
| RVO | 1000 | De4/4 | 122 | S | 1917 | Niederscherli |
| RVO | 1000 | Xe4/4 | 131 | MR | 1913 | Zug |
| RVT | 1435 | BCm2/5 | 9 | M | 1914 | VHS |
| RVT | 1435 | ABDe2/4 | 102 | MA | 1945 | Fleurier |
| RVT | 1435 | ABDe4/4 | 313 | S | 1929 | St. Sulpice |
| SeTB | 1000 | BDe2/2 | 4 | MA | 1928 | Chaulin |
| SGA | 1000 | BCFeh4/4 | 5 | MA | 1931 | Gais |
| SGA | 1000 | CFeh2/3 | 2 (17) | MA | 1911 | Wasserauen |
| SihlTB | 1435 | FCe2/4 | 84 | MR | 1924 | Sihlwald |
| SMB | 1435 | Be4/4 | 171 | MA | 1932 | Payerne |
| SOB | 1435 | ABe4/4 | 5 | MS | 1939 | Arth Goldau |
| SOB | 1435 | De4/4 | 21 | MR | 1936 | Payerne (SBB 603) |
| SOB | 1435 | Tm2/2 | 32 | MA | 1958 | Full |
| SOB | 1435 | BDe | 576 060 | MA | 1966 | Mendrisio |
| SOB | 1435 | BDe4/4 | 82 | MA | 1966 | Zell |
| STB | 1435 | BDe4/6 | 103 | MA | 1938 | Huttwil |
| StEB | 1000 | HGe2/2 | 1 | M | 1898 | VHS |
| SZU | 1435 | Tm | 8 | MA | 1975 | Uster |
| SZU | 1435 | Tm2/2 | 10 | MA | 1949 | Sihlwald (SBB 536) |
| SZU | 1435 | Ce4/4 | 42 | MA | 1920 | Mendrisio (BLS 312) |
| SZU | 1435 | Em836 | 506 | MA | 1959 | Mendrisio |
| TB | 1000 | CFe4/4 | 1 | P | 1903 | Grüningen |
| TBN | 1000 | BCe2/4 | 70 | M | 1913 | Saignelégier |
| UeB | 1435 | Ce2/2 | 2 | M | 1923 | Zürich |
| VBW | 1000 | Be4/4 | 30 | MS | 1910 | Ungersheim (France) |
| VBW | 1000 | BDe4/4 | 38 | MS | 1913 | Ungersheim (France) |
| VHB | 1435 | BDe2/4 | 240 | MA | 1932 | Huttwil |

| Rly. | Gauge | Class | No. | Status | Date | Location |
|------|-------|-------|-----|--------|------|----------|
| VHB | 1435 | De4/4 | 257 | MA | 1933 | Interlaken West |
| VHB | 1435 | De4/4 | 258 | MS | 1933 | Konolfingen |
| VHB | 1435 | De4/4 | 259 | MA | 1933 | Konolfingen |
| WAB | 800 | HGe2/2 | 55 | P | 1910 | Münchenstein |
| WB | 750 | BDe4/4 | 1 | MS | 1953 | Prora (Germany) (Existence now doubted) |
| WB | 750 | BDe4/4 | 3 | MS | 1953 | Prora (Germany) (Existence now doubted) |
| WM | 1435 | BDe4/4 | 2 | MA | 1966 | Koblenz |
| WM | 1435 | BDe2/4 | 3 | MA | 1938 | Sihlwald |
| WM | 1435 | Ta2/2 | 31? | MA | 1915 | Kallnach |

# 8.3. FOREIGN LOCOMOTIVES PRESERVED IN SWITZERLAND (from state railways)

| Rly. | Gauge | Class | No. | Details | Status | Date | Location |
|------|-------|-------|-----|---------|--------|------|----------|
| SBB | 1000 | G3/3 | 109 (BAM 6) | Cn2t | MA | 1901 | Chaulin |
| BDZ | 1435 | 01 | 01.22 | 1D1h | MR | 1935 | St. Sulpice |
| CP | 1000 | | E164 | BBn4vt | MA | 1905 | Pré Petitjean |
| CP | 1000 | | E206 | 1BCn4vt | MA | 1913 | Pré Petitjean |
| DB | 1435 | 01 | 01 180 | 2C1h2 | P | 1936 | Bowil |
| DB | 1435 | 01 | 01 202 | 2C1h2 | MA | 1936 | Lyss |
| DB | 1435 | 18 | 18 508 | 2C1h2v | M | 1924 | Romanshorn |
| DR | 1435 | 52.80 | 52 8055 | 1Eh2 | MA | 1943 | Schaffhausen |
| DB | 1435 | 64 | 64 518 | 1C1h2t | MA | 1940 | Huttwil |
| DB | 1000 | 99 | 99 193 | Eht | MR | 1927 | Chaulin |
| DR | 600 | 99 | 99 3311 | Dn2t | MA | 1917 | Schinznach |
| DB | 1435 | Köf II | 323 235 | Bdh | MA | 1960 | Full |
| DB | 1435 | Köf II | 323 782 | Bdh | MA | 1950 | St. Sulpice |
| DB | 1435 | Köf | 333 902 | Bdh | MA | 1958 | Realp |
| FKE | 1435 | | 262 | 1D1h2t | MA | 1954 | Huttwil |
| ÖBB | 1435 | 152 | 152.221 | 1Eh2 | MA | 1943 | St. Sulpice |
| PKP | 1435 | TKt48 | TKt48-188 | 141h2t | MA | 1956 | St. Sulpice |
| PKP | 600 | Ty3 | Ty3-194 | Cn2t | MA | 1944 | Schinznach |
| SAR | 600 | NGG13 | 60 | 1C1+1C1n2 | MA | 1927 | Schinznach |
| SNCF | 1435 | 141R | 141R73 | 1D1h2 | MR | 1945 | Winterthur |
| SNCF | 1435 | 141R | 141R568 | 1D1h2 | MA | 1945 | Schaffhausen |
| SNCF | 1435 | 141R | 141R1207 | 1D1h2 | MR | 1947 | Winterthur |
| SNCF | 1435 | 141R | 141R1244 | 1D1h2 | MA | 1947 | Brugg |
| SNCF | 1435 | 241A | 241A65 | 241h4v | MA | 1931 | Full |
| SNCF | 1435 | 241P | 241P30 | 241h4v | MR | 1951 | St. Sulpice |
| Vietnam | 1000 | HG4/4 | 40-304 | Dzh4t | MR | 1924 | Chur |
| Vietnam | 1000 | HG4/4 | 40-308 | Dzh4t | MR | 1930 | Chur |

# 9. MUSEUMS AND MUSEUM LINES

There are few museum lines as such in Switzerland, due to the fact that very few lines have been closed by either the SBB or the various private railways. As detailed in the SBB section a number of old electric locomotives have been retained as official museum locomotives that are used on specials, and appear at open days etc. Several of the private railways have retained steam locomotives, or older examples of more modern traction, and these either operate at weekends, or are available for private hire.

The Swiss Transport Museum is located at Luzern, and is well worth a visit. It covers all aspects of communications, not just railways. The best known museum line operated by enthusiasts is perhaps the Blonay-Chamby line near Montreux, but there are a number of other operations, often over the lines of private railways.

The Verband Öffentliche Verkehr publishes each year on its website details of steam specials and public excursions. (www/voev.ch). Many of these trains also appear in the public timetable.
Also of interest are the paddle steamers operating on the Brienzersee, Lac Léman (Lake Geneva), Thunersee, Vierwaldstättersee (Lake Lucerne) and Zürichsee. These are also detailed in the SBB timetable.

It should be noted that all the above operations are summer only, usually from May to September.

The list below of museum operations is arranged into alphabetical order of Cantons.

# AARGAU

## Bremgarten West

**Website:** www.historische-seethalbahn.ch

Historische Seethalbahn operates excursions over the Seethalbahn line from its temporary base at Bremgarten West once or twice a year. It is possible the operating base will move in the near future.

## Brugg

**Website:** www.mikado1244.ch

The 'Mikado 1244' Club operate ex SNCF 141R 1244 on occasional public excursions over SBB main lines. It has been out of use for some years but is expected to return to use by the end of 2009. Meanwhile a new acquisition is an Ae4/7 which is in full working order. The group also has a few Tms.

## Brugg

SBB now keeps its Zürich area steam locomotives at Brugg in the old roundhouse there. These premises were until recently the home to departmental shunting locos.

1 steam, 1 electric and 2 diesels.

## Koblenz

**Website:** www.draisine.ch

Draisine Sammlung Fricktal has set up home in the old depot at Koblenz and restored the building to some order for its collection of locomotives and railcars. Most of its draisines are kept in its workshops in Laufenburg.

3 EMUs, 2 diesels.

## Rheinfelden

Not really a museum operation, but the Feldschlösschen Brewery near the station still owns an active steam loco, nowadays mainly for publicity. A diesel normally carries out the regular shunting. A set of coaches is available to take parties from the SBB station to the brewery.

1 steam (and another on a plinth!)

## Schinznach Bad
**Website:** www.schbb.ch

A 600 mm gauge line operating at weekends around a garden centre. Operating days are usually Saturdays and Sundays from mid-April until mid-October

9 steam, 5 diesel.

# APPENZELL

## Herisau
The Appenzellerbahnen have one steam locomotive available for charter also two historic EMUs.

## Herisau
Former Bodensee Toggenburg Bahn No. 9 (2-6-2T) steam locomotive is available for charter. Route available quoted as Romanshorn–St. Gallen–Rapperswil.

# BASEL

## Eurovapor
**Website:** www.nostalgie-rhein-express.ch

Eurovapor run public excursions from Basel several times a year using a mixture of steam and electric traction. Destinations outside Switzerland are also featured.

# BASEL LAND

## Waldenburg
**Website:** www.waldenburgerbahn.ch

The Waldenburgerbahn has one steam locomotive used on public excursions on the last Sunday of the month (June to September) between Liestal and Waldenburg.

# BERN

## Bern
**Website:** www.dampftram.ch

The Berner Tramway Gesellschaft operates a steam tram around the city once a month May to October but not in July.

## Brienz
**Website:** www.brienz-rothorn-bahn.ch

As detailed under the Brienz Rothorn Bahn, this railway still uses steam in regular service.

## Burgdorf
**Website:** www.dbb.ch

The Verein Dampfbahn Bern is based in the old depot here and runs various public excursion trains May to October.

6 steam, 2 electric, 2 diesel.

## Huttwil

**Website:** www.historische-eisenbahn-emmental.ch

Verein Historische Eisenbahn Emmental is based in the old depot and runs public excursions May–October.

4 steam, 2 EMUs.

## Interlaken

**Website:** www.dampfbahnen.ch

The Ballenberg Dampfbahn has two steam locomotives based at Interlaken Ost and used on occasional excursions on the metre gauge line to Meiringen and also over the rack to Giswil. There are occasional trips on the BOB as well.

## Lyss

**Website:** www.dampflok.ch

The Verein Pacific 01 202 has former DB 01 202 is based here and works several public excursions each year.

## Spiez

**Website:** www.bls.ch

BLS Lötschbergbahn has its historic collection based here. As most are in working order they could be anywhere on the BLS system.

## Wilderswil

**Website:** www.jungfraubahn.ch

The Schynige Platte Bahn has one steam locomotive available for charter and in the summer period June to August it sees regular use on alternate Sundays.

# FRIBOURG

## Kerzers/Kallnach

**Website:** www.bahnmuseum-kerzers.ch

Bahn Museum Kerzers is in the process of moving up the line to Kallnach so stock may be at both locations. It is not yet officially open to the public.

1 steam, 6 electric, 15 diesel, 4 EMUs.

# GRAUBÜNDEN

## Landquart/Samedan

**Website:** www.rhb.ch

The Rhätische Bahn continues to operate historic/nostalgic trains using steam or electric locomotives. Watch out in winter for the operation of the steam rotary snow plough

3 steam, 4 electric, 3 EMUs

# JURA

## Delémont

**Website:** www.volldampf.ch

The old roundhouse here is now a listed monument. SBB Historic keeps some stock here but also based here is the Historische Eisenbahn Gesellschaft.

5 steam 3 diesel

## Pré Petitjean

**Website:** www.les.cj.ch

La Traction have two steam locomotives, plus other stock, used on occasional public excursions over the CF de Jura metre gauge system July–September.

2 steam, 3 electric, 1 EMUs

# LUZERN

## Luzern

**Website:** www.verkehrshaus.ch

The National Transport Museum (Verkehrshaus) is located on the north side of the Vierwaldstättersee, about 2 km from the station (take a No. 2 trolleybus). The lake steamers also call at a pier adjacent to the museum. Some of the exhibits are changed from time to time, so not all are on display.

9 steam, 11 electrics, 9 EMUs

## Triengen

**Website:** www.dampfzug.ch

The Sursee Triengen Bahn has 2 steam locomotives available for charter but public excursions are operated two or three times a year.

2 steam.

## Vitznau

**Website:** www.rigi.ch

The Rigibahnen runs regular steam trips often running Arth Goldau–Rigi Kulm–Vitznau and v.v.

# NEUCHÂTEL

## St. Sulpice

**Website:** www.vvt.ch

The "Vapeur Val de Travers" Society operate steam services on certain weekends over the Régional Val de Travers. Including the normally freight only St. Sulpice–Fleurier section.  However in 2009 no trains operated as the society decided to concentrate all their activities on repairs and restoration. The collection includes a large number of Swiss and foreign locomotives

13 steam, 6 diesels.

# ST. GALLEN

## Rorschach

**Website:** www.appenzellerbahnen.ch; www.eurovapor-sulgen.ch

Eurovapor uses a former Swiss industrial steam rack 0-4-0T locomotive for excursions on the Rorschach to Heiden line usually on the first Sunday of the month May–October.

# SCHAFFHAUSEN

## Schaffhausen

**Website**: www.dlm.ag.ch

Two organisations are based in the old SBB depot near the station.

Dampflokomotiv und Maschinenfabrik DLM AG operates excursions form Schaffhausen several times a year using modernised former DR 52 8055 which is also available for hire.

Former SNCF 141R568 is also based here now owned by William Cook Rail which intends to offer excursion trains around Switzerland in suitably restored Swiss rolling stock. Operations with this train should start in 2010.

## Stein am Rhein

**Website**: www.etzwilen-singen.ch

A relatively new society Verein zur Erhaltung der Bahnlinie Etzwilen–Singen is now operating excursion trains over the former SBB non-electrified line from Etzwilen as far as Ramsen. They usually start from Stein am Rhein.

1 steam, 3 diesels.

# SOLOTHURN

## Balsthal

**Website**: www.oebb.ch

The Oensingen Balsthal Bahn has 3 steam locomotives used on public excursions over its own line several times a year. The depot at Balsthal is home to various museum locomotives.

5 steam, 2 diesels, 1 electric, 1 EMU.

## Olten

**Website**:www.sbbhistoric.ch

The old SBB depot in Olten is now one of the main holding points for the SBB Historic collection. However it is not a museum but a storage point and SBB day to day operations still take place at the facility.

7 electrics, 1 diesel, 2 EMUs.

# THURGAU

## Romanshorn

**Website**: www.lokorama.ch; www.lokorama.org

The old SBB depot at Romanshorn is being transformed into a museum. In 2009 opening days were Saturdays and Sundays 26 April to 18 October, 14.00–17.00.

3 steam, 4 electric, 2 diesel, 1 EMU

## Sulgen

**Website**: www.eurovapor-sulgen.ch

Eurovapor have ex DB 23.058 based here for use on occasional excursions over main lines. The 0-4-0RT that operates from Rorschach is also based here.

3 steam, 3 electrics, 2 diesels.

# TICINO

## Capolago

**Website:** www.montegeneroso.ch

The Ferrovia Monte Generoso has one steam locomotive used on occasional public excursions.

## Castione

**Website:** www.seft-fm.ch

The Società Esercizio Ferroviario Turistico (SEFT) runs tourist trains over part of the old Bellinzona to Mesocco line; Castione–Grono–Cama.

5 railcars.

## Mendrisio

**Website:** www.clubsangottardo.ch

The Club San Gottardo operate regular excursions on the closed Mendrisio–Stabio–Valmorea (Italy) line. However, this line is scheduled to be reopened to regular passenger services so the future of this operation may be in some doubt. Operational Ae4/7 10997 is also based here but privately owned.

3 steam, 4 electrics, 5 diesels, 1 railcar.

# URI

## Realp

**Website:** www.dfb.ch

The Dampfbahn Furka Bergstrecke Society has restored part of the Furka Oberalp Bahn over the Furka Pass, abandoned when the Furka Base Tunnel was opened. Three steam locomotives have been restored, including two repatriated from Vietnam! The terminus at Realp is close to the FO station.

7 steam, 11 diesel, 1 railcar.

# VALAIS/WALLIS

## Brig/Visp

**Website:** www.mgbahn.ch.

The Matterhorn Gotthard Bahn has one steam locomotive available for charter which also operates two or three public excursions during the year. In 2009 some regular excursions on Sundays were operated from Brig to Oberwald.

## Château d'Eau

**Website:** www.emosson.ch

The S.A. des Transports Emosson Barbarine (SATEB) is a most unusual line, originally built to provide access to a hydroelectric scheme. It connects with the MC at Le Châtelard–Giétroz. There is a funicular to Château d'Eau and a 600 mm gauge line from here to Emosson. From Emosson a second funicular continues to Barrage.

5 diesel.

## Le Châtelard

**Website:** www.chatelard.net

The Train Touristique d'Emosson is a tourist operation over a former industrial railway which was used for the construction of a dam and later maintenance of the installations.

2 diesels, 5 battery electrics.

# VAUD

## Chaulin

**Website:** www.blonay-chamby.ch.

The Blonay Chamby metre gauge line is undoubtedly Switzerland's premier enthusiast-operated line, with excellent views over Lake Geneva. Operates at weekends using both steam and electric traction. Some of the stock is stored at other locations.

In 2009 it operated Blonay–Chamby Saturdays and Sundays 2 May to 25 October and also operated on selected weekends Vevey to Blonay.

11 steam, 3 electrics, 1 diesel, 7 railcars, 9 trams.

## Echallens

**Website:** www.leb.ch

The Lausanne–Echallens–Bercher railway has one steam loco and uses it between Cheseaux and Bercher on public excursions.

## Le Pont

**Website:** www.ctvj.ch

The Compagnie du Trains à Vapeur de la Vallée de Joux has two steam locomotives used between Le Pont and Le Sentier on public excursions over the Pont Brassus Bahn. Usually operates on two Sundays a month late June to early October.

2 steam, 1 diesel, 1 electro-diesel

# ZÜRICH

## Bauma/Uster

**Website:** www.dvzo.ch

The Dampfverein Zürcher Oberland (DVZO) run steam trains over the normally freight-only SBB line between Bauma and Hinwil on the first and third Sunday of the month May to October.. The DVZO depot is at Uster; locos are based at Bauma as required.

7 steam, 1 electrics, 1 electro-diesel, 3 diesels.

## Sihlwald

**Website:** www.museumsbahn.ch

The Sihltal Zürich Uetliberg Bahn has one steam locomotive available for charter plus other vintage stock which is now under the Zürcher Museums Bahn. Operates on the last Sunday of the month April to October.

2 steam, 1 electric, 2 EMUs, 2 diesels

# 10. PADDLE STEAMERS

The details of these steam operations are covered since most are included witihin the availability of the Swiss Pass, and can be easily combined with other railway visits. Generally, the steamers only operate from June to September; full details of the steam services are shown in the SBB Timetable. The services below operate daily unless noted otherwise. There are numerous diesel ships also operating on these lakes, and diesel substitutions do occasionally take place.

## BRIENZERSEE

Two return trips operate from Interlaken Ost to Brienz (connection the the Brienz-Rothorn and Brünig lines).

**Ship:** LÖTSCHBERG   Escher Wyss 1914

## LAC LEMAN (Lake Geneva)

Four paddle steamers operate one return trip for the full length of the lake from Geneve to Bouveret, two circular trips from Lausanne covering the east end of the lake (one clockwise, one anticlockwise), and additional sailings operating from Lausanne to Thonon and Evian. Calls are made at numerous piers, several of which are in France. Round trips can be made in conjunction with the Train de Rive Bleu operation between Evian and Bouveret. Note there are a further four paddle steamers here that have been converted to diesel operation; in appearance they look very similar to their steam operated sisters.

**Ships:**

| | | |
|---|---|---|
| LA SUISSE | Sulzer | 1910 |
| SAVOIE | Sulzer | 1914 |
| SIMPLON | Sulzer | 1920 |
| RHÔNE | Sulzer | 1927 |

The diesel conversions are MONTREUX (1904), VEVEY (1907), ITALIE (1908) and HELVETIE (1926).

## THUNERSEE

One return sailing operates from Thun to Interlaken West via Spiez.

**Ship:** BLÜMLISALP   Escher Wyss   1906

## VIERWALDSTÄTTERSEE (Lake Lucerne)

Five paddle steamers operate on this lake. The principal route is from Luzern to Fluelen (on the Gotthard main line), a 3 hour trip each way with up to four sailings per day. En route calls are made at the pier adjacent to the Swiss Transport Museum, and at Vitznau (terminus of the Rigibahnen). Numerous other calls are made. There are also up to two sailings per day to Alpnachstad (connection with the Zentralbahn and Pilatus Bahn) calling at Stansstad (connection with the line to Engelberg).

**Ships:**

| | | |
|---|---|---|
| URI | Sulzer | 1901 |
| UNTERWALDEN | Escher Wyss | 1902 |
| SCHILLER | Sulzer | 1906 |
| GALLIA | Escher Wyss | 1913 |
| STADT LUZERN | Sachsenberg | 1928 |

## ZÜRICHSEE

The two paddle steamers cover two return trips from Zürich to Rapperswil, with a third on Wednesdays and Saturdays operating the full length of the lake from Zürich to Schmerikan.

**Ships:**

STADT ZÜRICH   Escher Wyss 1909
STADT RAPPERSWIL  Escher Wyss 1914

In additional to the above, there are paddle steamers on the Bodensee (HOHENTWIEL) based in Austria, but operting to Germany and Switzerland, Lago Maggiore (PIEMONTE) based in Italy, but operating to Lugano, plus a small steam screw ship (GREIF) on the Greifensee at Uster. These ships operate various public excursions, but are not shown in the timetable.

# APPENDIX I. BUILDERS

The following builder codes are used in this publication (all are in Switzerland, unless stated):

| | |
|---|---|
| ABB | ASEA Brown Boveri, Baden & Zürich Oerlikon (now Bombardier). |
| ACEC | Ateliers de Constructions Électriques de Charleroi, Belgium. |
| ACMV | Ateliers de Constructions Mécaniques de Vevey SA, Villeneuve (now Bombardier). |
| AD | ADtranz (ABB Daimler-Benz Transportation Systems), Oerlikon & Pratteln (now Bombardier) |
| AEG | Allgemeine Elektrizitätsgesellschaft, Berlin, Germany (now Bombardier). |
| ALIOTH | Elektrizitätsgesellschaft Alioth, Münchenstein. |
| ALSTOM | Alstom, several plants. |
| ASPER | Viktor Asper AG Maschinenbau, Küsnacht. |
| BBC | AG Brown Boveri & Cie, Baden, Münchenstein, Oerlikon (now Bombardier). |
| BBC (M) | AG Brown Boveri & Cie, Mannheim, Germany (now Bombardier). |
| BEIL | Martin Beilhack Maschinenfabrik, Rosenheim, Germany. |
| BIBUS | Bibus Hydraulik AG, Zumikon. |
| BL | Anciens Établissements Brissonneau & Lotz, Creil, France. |
| BOMB | Bombardier (numerous plants). |
| BREDA | SA Ernesto Breda, Milano, Italy. |
| BüH | Bühler SA, Taverne. |
| BüS | Büssing Fahrzeug und Motorenbau, Braunschweig, Germany. |
| CAT | Caterpillar, Peoria, Illinois, USA. |
| CEG | Chemins de Fer Électriques de la Gruyère (predecessor of GFM). |
| CEM | Compagnie Électro-Mécanique, France. |
| CET | Carminati e Toselli, Milano, Italy. |
| CFD | Chemins de Fer Départementaux, Montmirail, France. |
| CGV | Compagnie Générale de Villefranche sur Saône, France. |
| CMR | Constructions Mécaniques SA, Renens. |
| CUM | Cummins Engine Corporation, Columbus, Indiana, USA. |
| DBZ | Daimler Benz AG, Stuttgart, Germany. |
| DIEMA | Diepholzer Maschinenfabrik (Fr. Schöttler GmbH), Diepholz, Germany. |
| DMG | Daimler Motoren Gesellschaft, Stuttgart, Germany. |
| DUEWAG | Düsseldorfer Waggonfabrik (now Siemens). |
| DZ | Klöckner Humboldt Deutz AG, Köln, Germany. |
| DWA | Deutsche Waggonbau AG, Ammendorf, Bautzen, Görlitz, Germany (now Bombardier). |
| FFA | Flug- und Fahrzeugwerke AG, Altenrhein (later SWA). |
| FIAT-SIG | Fiat-SIG Schienenfahrzeuge, Neuhausen am Rheinfall (now Alstom). |
| FORD | Ford Motor Company, Detroit, Michigan, USA. |
| FUCHS | H. Fuchs Waggonfabrik AG, Heidelberg, Germany. |
| GANG | Carrosserie Gangloff AG, Bern. |
| GEC-A | GEC-Alsthom, several plants (now Alstom). |
| Gm | Gmeinder & Co GmbH, Maschinenfabrik Mosbach, Germany. |
| GM | General Motors AG, Biel. |
| GSEG | Gewerkschaft Schalker-Eisenhütte, Gelsenkirchen, Germany. |
| HEN | Henschel Werke AG, Kassel, Germany (now part of Bombardier). |
| HESS | Hess AG, Carrosserien, Bellach SO. |
| HÜR | H. Hürlimann Tractorenwerke, Wil SG. |
| IEG | Compagnie de l'Industrie Électrique, Genève. |
| JMR | J. Meyer AG, Rheinfelden. |
| JUNG | A. Jung Lokomotivfabrik GmbH, Jungenthal bei Kirchberg an der Sieg, Germany. |
| Kaeble | Kaeble-Gmeinder, Mosbach, Germany. |
| KM | Krauss Maffei AG, München, Germany (now Siemens). |
| KRON | L. Kronenberger & Söhne, Luzern. |
| KRUPP | Fried. Krupp Maschinenfabriken, Essen, Germany. |
| LEW | Lokomotivbau-Elektrotechnische Werke, Hennigsdorf, Germany (now Bombardier). |
| LISTER | R & A Lister & Co Ltd., Dursley, Glos., UK. |
| LMG | Lübecker Maschinenbau AG, Werk Dorstfeld, Germany. |
| LÜTHI | Eduard Lüthi, Worb. |
| MaK | Maschinenbau Kiel GmbH, Kiel, Germany (now Vossloh). |
| MAN | Maschinenfabrik Augsburg-Nürnberg AG, Germany. |
| MAYBACH | Maybach Motorenbau, Friedrichshafen, Germany. |
| MB | Mercedes Benz, Berlin Marienfeld, Germany. |
| MFO | Maschinenfabrik Oerlikon, Zürich Oerlikon (now part of Bombardier). |

| MOY | Établissement Gaston Moyse, La Courneuve, France. |
| MTU | Motoren- und Turbinen-Union GmbH, Friedrichshafen, Germany. |
| MWM | Motorenwerke Mannheim, Germany. |
| NEN | Martin Nencki AG, Fahrzeugbau und Hydraulik, Langenthal. |
| OK | Orenstein & Koppel AG, Dortmund, Germany. |
| PER | Perkins Engines Ltd., Peterborough, UK. |
| PETER | Konrad Peter, Maschinenfabrik, Liestal. |
| PFING | Pfingstweid AG, Zürich. |
| PLEI | Paul Pleiger Maschinenfabrik, Blankenstein, Germany. |
| POY | Moteurs Poyaud, Surgères, France. |
| Puch | Puch Werke. |
| RACO | Robert Aebi & Co AG, Regensdorf (later SLM). |
| RC | Regazzoni Costruzioni, Lugano. |
| REG | Officine Meccaniche Italiane Reggiane, Reggio Emilia, Italy. |
| REN | Régie Nationale des Usines Renault, Billancourt, France. |
| RIET | AG vormals J. J. Rieter, Winterthur. |
| RING | F. Ringhoffer Werke AG, Waggon & Tenderfabrik, Smichow, Czech Republic (later CKD, then Siemens). |
| ROBEL | Robel Maschinenfabrik, München, Germany. |
| RUHR | Ruhrthaler Maschinenfabrik, Mülheim, Germany. |
| SAAS | SA des Ateliers de Sécheron, Genève (later BBC, now part of Bombardier) |
| SAU | AG Adolf Saurer, Arbon. |
| SCH | Christoph Schöttler Maschinenfabrik GmbH, Diepholz, Germany (trade name Schöma). |
| SCIN | Scintilla AG, Zuchwil. |
| SE | Siemens AG, Werk Erlangen, Germany. |
| SIG | Schweizerische Industrie-Gesellschaft, Neuhausen am Rheinfall (now Alstom). |
| SLM | Schweizerische Lokomotiv- und Maschinenfabrik, Winterthur (now Bombardier and Stadler). |
| SSW | Siemens Schuckert Werke, Berlin, Germany. |
| STAD | Ernst Stadler AG, Fahrzeugbau, Bussnang. |
| STECK | Ferdinand Steck, Maschinenfabrik, Bowil. |
| SWA | Schindler Waggon, Altenrhein (now Stadler). |
| SWP | Schindler Waggon AG, Pratteln (now Bombardier). |
| SWS | Schweizerische Wagons- und Aufzügefabrik AG, Schlieren. |
| SZ | Gebrüder Sulzer AG, Winterthur. |
| TIBB | Tecnomasio Italiano Brown Boveri, Milano, Italy (now Bombardier). |
| TUCH | Gebrüder Tuchschmid AG, Frauenfeld. |
| U23A | Uzinele 23 August, Bucuresti, Romania. |
| VBZ | Verkehrsbetriebe der Stadt Zürich (Zürich Tramways). |
| VM | Stabilimenti Meccanici VM SpA, Cento Ferrara, Italy. |
| VOITH | J. M. Voith GmbH, Heidenheim, Germany. |
| VOSS | Vossloh Locomotives GmbH, Kiel, Germany |
| VR | von Rollsche Eisenwerke, Gerlafingen. |
| VW | Volkswagenwerke, Wolfsburg, Germany. |
| WIND | Rheiner Maschinenfabrik Windhoff AG, Rheine, Germany. |
| WINPRO | Winpro AG, Winterthur (formerly SLM, now Stadler). |
| ZÜR | Zürcher & Cie SA, St. Aubin. |

Other initials used for builders are the railway companies which built or rebuilt stock.

# APPENDIX II. COMMON TERMS IN ENGLISH, FRENCH and GERMAN

| English | French | German |
|---|---|---|
| railway | le chemin de fer | Die Eisenbahn |
| train | le train | Der Zug |
| locomotive | la locomotive | Die Lokomotive (Lok) |
| electric loco | la locomotive électrique | Die Elllok |
| steam loco | la locomotive à vapeur | Die Dampflok |
| shunter | la locomotive de manoeuvre | Die Kleinlok |
| passenger coach | la voiture | Der Reisezugwagen |
| couchette | la couchette | Der Liegewagen |
| restaurant car | la voiture-restaurant | Der Speisewagen |
| electric multiple unit | l'automotrice éléctrique | Der Elektrotriebwagen |
| trailer car | la remorque | Der Beiwagen |
| freight train | le train de marchandises | Der Güterzug |
| sleeping car | la voiture-lits | Der Schlafwagen |
| class (of vehicles) | la série | Baureihe |
| wheel | la roue | Das Rad |
| station | la gare | Der Bahnhof (Bhf) |
| main station | la gare principale | Der Hauptbahnhof (HB) |
| platform | le quai | Der Bahnsteig |
| rail | le rail | Die Schiene |
| track | la ligne/la voie | Der Gleis |
| (narrow) gauge | voie (étroite) | Das Spurweite (schmalspur) |
| goods depot | la gare de marchandiises | Der GuterbahnhoF |
| marshalling yard | (la gare de) triage | Der Rangierbahnhof (abbreviated to Rbf) |
| loco depot | le dépôt | Der Bahnbetriebswerke (abbreviated to Bw) |
| stabling point | la remise | |
| works | le dépôt | Ausbesserungswerke (abbreviated to AW) |
| passenger | le voyageur | Der Reisender (m), Die Reisende (f) |
| ticket | le billet | Die Fahrkarte |
| single | aller simple | einfache Fahrt |
| return | aller-retour | hin-und-rück Fahrt |
| first class | la première classe | Erste Klasse |
| second class | la deuxième classe | Zweite Klasse |
| to change (trains) | changer (de train) | umsteigen |
| late | en retard | haben Verspätung |
| driver | le conducteur | Der Lokführer |
| guard, conductor | le chef de train/controleur | Der Zugführer (m)/Die Zugführerin (f) |
| strike | la grève | Das Streik |
| timetable | les horaires | Der Fahrplan, das Kursbuch |
| | l'indicateur (on paper) | |